⚓ NATIONAL MARITIME MUSEUM

Guide to
MARITIME
BRITAIN

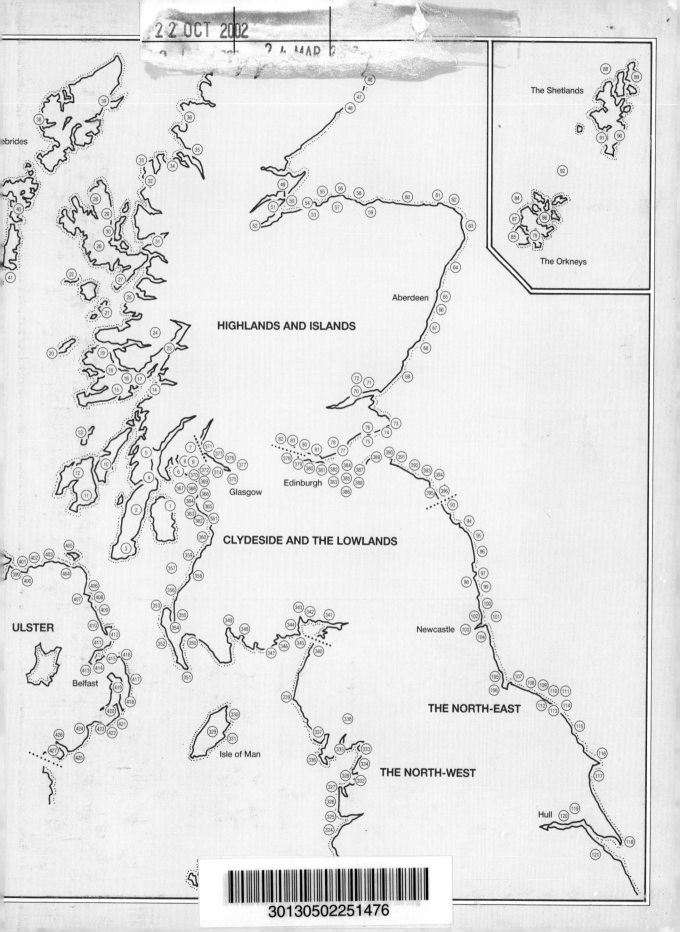

HIGHLANDS AND ISLANDS

The Shetlands

The Orkneys

Aberdeen

CLYDESIDE AND THE LOWLANDS

Glasgow

Edinburgh

Newcastle

THE NORTH-EAST

ULSTER

Belfast

Isle of Man

THE NORTH-WEST

Hull

NATIONAL MARITIME MUSEUM

Guide to
MARITIME
BRITAIN

Keith Wheatley

FOREWORD BY
HRH THE DUKE OF EDINBURGH KG, KT

PREFACE BY RICHARD ORMOND,
DIRECTOR OF THE NATIONAL MARITIME MUSEUM

CAXTON EDITIONS

MONTAGUE, DAWSON,

For my father, who first showed me the sea and ships

Specially commissioned photographs by Simon McBride
on pages 14/15, 34/5, 54/5, 74/5, 92/3, 114/15,
138/9, 158/9, 174/5 and 192/3

First published in Great Britain 1990 by
Webb & Bower (Publishers) Limited
5 Cathedral Close, Exeter, Devon EX1 1EZ
in association with the National Maritime Museum, Greenwich, London

This Edition published in 2000 by
Caxton Editions
20 Bloomsbury Street,
London WC1B 3QA
an Imprint of the Caxton Publishing Group

Designed by Ron Pickless

Introduction Copyright © 1990 The National Maritime Museum
Text Copyright © 1990 Keith Wheatley
Additional research by Kelly Polanski

Picture research by Shirley Seaton

British Library Cataloguing in Publication Data
Wheatley, Keith
National Maritime Museum guide to maritime Britain.
1. Great Britain coastal regions – visitors guide
I. Title II. National Maritime Museum
914.1′04858

ISBN : 1 84067 2323

Text is set in Plantin Light
Typeset in Great Britain by Bookworm Typesetting
Colour and mono reproduction by Mandarin Offset, Hong Kong
Printed and bound in Indonesia

CONTENTS

Location Maps
The regions of the British Isles, and specific locations within each region in the Gazetteer sections, are listed as they occur in a clockwise direction around the coast. The endpaper maps refer to the Gazetteer entries.

H. M. YACHT BRITANNIA

There have been many communities around the world which have had access to the sea, but that does not mean that they have ventured out of the sight of land. The British have every reason to be thankful to their ancestors for their courage and sense of adventure. Trade, empire and prosperity followed in the wake of seamen who set out from these shores into the unknown.

I hope that this 'Guide to Maritime Britain' will serve as a reminder of the momentous part which the sea has played in the life and history of this country, and that it will also make people reflect about the future of our maritime industries.

The Guide is produced under the auspices of the National Maritime Museum at Greenwich, of which I am a Trustee. The Museum has the responsibility of preserving and displaying our maritime heritage, but that is too big a subject to be contained within the walls of any single building. Every coastal town, castle and estuary has its part of the story to tell, and I am sure that this book will help those who are interested in our maritime history to get a better feel for the many strands and the events, great and small, that have had such an important influence on our national destiny.

1989

PREFACE
THE MARITIME HERITAGE

Britain grew to power and influence as a seaborne Empire. Separated and protected from Europe by the English Channel and the North Sea, she was ideally situated to take advantage of the Atlantic routes that opened up the prospect of world trade from the sixteenth century. From trade grew the web of Empire guarded, supplied and exploited by continuing control of the sea lanes. To our forebears the sea was a dominant principle, and one which helped to frame national policies and attitudes. Britain only tried the experiment of a standing army on one occasion, the Commonwealth, and it was never repeated. Instead we have maintained a formidable fleet for over 450 years, and that has been at the heart of much British success in the sphere of war and diplomacy. From modest beginnings, Britain's merchant fleet grew eventually to outnumber the tonnage of the rest of the world. For generations, the dockyards and ports supporting British shipping were the largest industrial complexes of their time.

In today's technological world, we are less conscious than we were of the importance of the sea in all our lives. The Channel remains a formidable defence against the threat of invasion. We have not been self-sufficient for centuries, and the vast proportion of our trade with other countries continues to be carried in ships. They are far larger than they were, they do not need elaborate port installations, and they can unload and turn round in a matter of hours rather than weeks. Britain's decline as a maritime power is a reflection of our economic decline. Though we still maintain the world's third largest fleet, it is tiny in comparison with those of the USA and USSR. Much of our merchant fleet is flagged out (there are less than 500 ships on the British register), and the shipbuilding industry is a pale shadow of what it was once. There is a danger that we shall run down our shipping industry to the point where we become wholly dependent on others. The great maritime artefacts we have inherited not only conjure up past glory but remind us that the sea is just as active and significant in our lives as it has ever been.

HERITAGE DOCKS The receding tides of maritime enterprise have left behind substantial reminders of the past in the form of old docks, buildings and ships. Much has been destroyed but a great deal remains, and it is encouraging to see the imaginative use to which old facilities are being put. Many redundant ports are being developed with a combination of new commercial use and a will towards historic preservation. The London Dockland Development Company, which has brought new life to large derelict areas bordering the Thames, is the prototype for developments taking place along the Mersey, the Clyde and the Laggan.

Local councils are proud of their maritime past and are trying to use their waterways in a creative way. So, alongside new offices and housing projects, there are museums and maritime attractions springing up, along with the old impedimenta of the docks. The superb Albert Dock in Liverpool now houses a major maritime museum, the Tate Gallery of the North, a group of historic vessels, together with flourishing shops and restaurants. Developments along the Tyne include facilities for restoring historic vessels, and plans for a centre devoted to the story of the nation's shipbuilding. Similar developments are underway at Manchester and Glasgow, Plymouth and Bristol.

At the Chatham Historic Dockyard you can still see rope being spun by machines of the industrial revolution, while in the dry docks modern ship repairers are at work. These new maritime attractions are exciting places, stressing age old traditions and methods in an active environment. The revival of waterside areas now plays an important part in urban renewal, giving those cities with a river or estuary an asset which they are gradually beginning to exploit.

SHIP PRESERVATION Historic docks cry out for historic vessels, and romantic sails silhouetted against the sky are very beautiful, but they are also expensive. Keeping a wooden vessel well preserved requires large initial capital outlays, and substantial ongoing maintenance costs. The costs are higher if the vessel is in the water, and so prone to the problems of rot and stress. HMS *Victory*, the world's most famous wooden warship, retains only about ten per cent of her 1805 timbers, and she is never out of the hands of the shipwrights. The projected cost of restoring HMS *Foudroyant*, a veteran of 1817 and until recently still afloat, is estimated in millions. It is one thing to raise funds for vessels as famous as these two, but what can be done with the middle run of historic ships?

The Cutty Sark Maritime Trust, charged with national responsibility for ship preservation, finds it increasingly difficult to maintain its small fleet. It has chartered Scott of the Antarctic's ship *Discovery* to the City of Dundee, and the armed sloop HMS *Gannet* to Chatham Historic Dockyard, and this may well be a pattern for the future. The most famous of the ships owned by the Trust is *Cutty Sark* herself, whose masts and rigging dominate the Greenwich skyline. She makes a profit and is one of the very few historic vessels able to pay her way. Situated at the gateway to a major tourist centre, she attracts over 300,000 visitors a year. At Portsmouth Historic Dockyard HMS *Victory* and *Mary Rose* have recently been joined by HMS *Warrior*, a technological wonder of 1860 that rendered conventional fleets obsolete overnight. Together with the Royal Naval Museum, these vessels constitute an attraction of the first rank, with enormous potential for growth. All that is lacking, some say, is a warship of the twentieth century. By contrast, those historic vessels without a household name or popular location stand little chance of raising significant revenue.

There have been several attempts to preserve modern warships, all fraught with problems. The most successful of these has been HMS *Belfast*, a Second World War cruiser moored in the Pool of London and already an established tourist attraction in the capital. The costs involved in saving warships of any size are frequently prohibitive, and enthusiasm and goodwill are no answer to the hard realities of the balance sheet. More success has been achieved in the United States, where a policy of leasing named warships to their namesake states has paid dividends. The ship becomes identified with the state, and its upkeep a matter of local pride. The same civic spirit can be seen at work in the case of Brunel's *Great Britain*, repatriated as a hulk from the Falklands in the 1970s, and still undergoing complete refitting in her original dock in Bristol. A scheme to bring back the schooner *County of Peebles* from Chile to Glasgow has been promoted as a symbol of the city's great maritime past. Ship preservation is booming, but it is a field where expectations are rarely fully satisfied.

UNDERWATER ARCHAEOLOGY Preservation of the maritime sites and vessels extends underwater as well as on shore, and here the situation is more serious. Only a handful of underwater sites receive protection under current legislation, and little work has been done to carry out archaeological surveys of the sea-bed. Responsibility for protecting sites rests with the Department of Transport, whose primary concern is with commercial salvage. As a result many archaeological sites are now at risk from the unscrupulous depredations of salvors and treasure seekers, and from the growing activities of dredging and extraction companies.

The hull of the *Mary Rose*, preserved at Portsmouth.

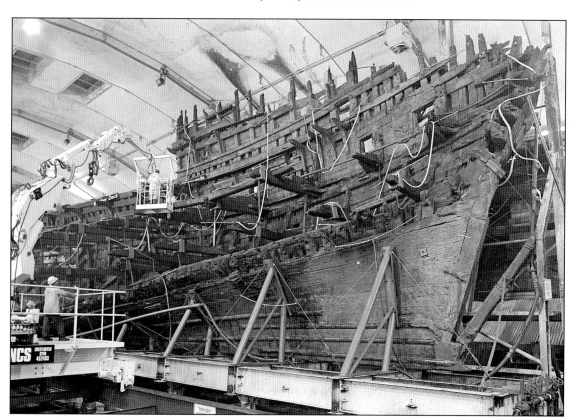

A shipwreck site represents a unique time capsule. Loot a site for its treasures, and the significance of the whole is destroyed. Only the most careful methods can reveal the evidence needed to build up a picture of the past life of the ship as a whole. It is imperative to train amateur divers in the 'dos' and 'don'ts' of nautical archaeology. Responsible divers have an important role to play in finding, recording and working on underwater sites.

The *Mary Rose* is proof that a great deal can be preserved underwater. The survival of such a large proportion of hull demonstrates the advanced nature of Tudor technology. Guns and gun carriages are evidence of the formidable new armament deployed on Henry VIII's fleet. A set of spare sails, still intact, sophisticated parrels and pulleys, lengths of rope, several compasses and navigational intruments, bring home the reality of seamanship. Before the discovery of the *Mary Rose*, no example of the English longbow was known; now there are hundreds. Most graphic of all are the items belonging to individual sailors, the barber surgeon's box and cap, a leather shoe and a folding backgammon board, a carpenter's plane and a tabor pipe. A whole world lay hidden under the silt mud of the Solent, one which has vastly increased our knowledge and understanding of Tudor shipping.

Thousands of other ships lie wrecked around the British coastline, and there are submerged shore sites as well. If care is not taken now to protect this potentialy large and vital inheritance, it could be wantonly dissipated. A joint Nautical Archaeology Policy Committee, representing many bodies and institutions, has put forward a series of proposals for improving the present unsatisfactory situation, and for co-ordinating protection and recovery work underwater. These proposals have been generally welcomed, and are currently being studied by the government.

MUSEUMS The problem of what to keep and what to discard is as pressing an issue in the field of museumology as it is in that of ship preservation and nautical archaeology. With over a million ship plans, two miles of shipping records, half a million historic photographs, three thousand ship models, and countless other collections, the National Maritime Museum is rapidly running out of space and resources. It can no longer afford to collect all and everything maritime, and yet its holdings in the modern field are slender and inadequate. No one institution can hope to cover the past and present of Britain and the sea comprehensively. Over twenty major maritime institutions in this country discussed their respective spheres of interest at a conference held at Greenwich in December 1988. It is essential that these institutions collaborate in the definition of subject and collecting policies. As worrying as the issue of overlap and competition is that of underlap, where important technologies are allowed to disappear unrecorded. No institution can afford to work in isolation, and we have much to gain from shared information and initiatives.

In a competitive world, where the customer is increasingly important, maritime museums face a challenge in attracting more visitors and exciting their interest. With expectations raised by attractions like Jorvik and the Museum of the Moving Image, many visitors are in search of more active forms of experience. The emigration gallery at the Merseyside Maritime Museum takes people from Liverpool to New York on board a nineteenth-

The National Maritime Museum at Greenwich.

century emigrant ship, in company with character actors. The *Armada Exhibition* at the National Maritime Museum in 1988 contrasted original Elizabethan treasure with a quarter-size Spanish galleon complete with sound and light effects. The ability to experience the realities of life at sea, or to see a traditional craft being practised and interpreted, has a strong public appeal. Some maritime museums emphasize this 'hands-on' approach to display and demonstration, like the National Museum of the Boat at Ellesmere Port, and the Chatham Historic Dockyard. The trend is clearly increasing, providing scope of the use of volunteers in restoration, boat-building and other skilled activities.

MARITIME RESEARCH Museums preserve the material remains of the past, but what of the study of history itself? There is no shortage of devoted and enthusiastic maritime historians, and the output of studies on every aspect of ships and the sea grows by the year, especially on the more practical aspects of how and why things were made. The Society for Nautical Research numbers over 2,000 members and publishes the best magazine on maritime history anywhere in the world, *Mariner's Mirror*.

Here learned articles on archaeology, rigging and exploration are complemented by notes and queries on the most recondite topics. In its early days, the Society was responsible for saving HMS *Victory* and for founding the National Maritime Museum, two momentous events. There are other learned bodies contributing to the continuing study of the maritime past, The Navy Records Society, the Hakluyt Society, and, further afield, the International Congress of Maritime History. In view of their importance and the vast body of surviving documentary evidence about them, maritime studies are strangely neglected at university level. There are no chairs of maritime history, and the subject tends to be an adjunct to conventional history, relying on the enthusiasm of a handful of lecturers.

It is encouraging to see that British History features strongly in the draft national curriculum, and that emphasis will be given to trade and navigation, science and technology. Knowledge of seafaring is essential for anyone who wishes to understand the life of the nation. The wonder remains how a relatively obscure island on the fringes of Europe became a world power.

THE COASTLINE Histories and artefacts represent one form of heritage, the natural world another. We take the magnificent beaches, cliffs and headlands of the British coastline for granted. We beachcomb, walk, fish, swim and explore an environment which for most of us is our closest contact with the sea.

Natural erosion, pollution, commercial exploitation, all threaten the delicate fabric and environment of the coast. Imaginative campaigns, like that of *Enterprise Neptune,* have helped to preserve long stretches of coastline from developement. Careful policies are also needed to protect the coastal environment as a whole. Maritime disasters today are of a different order and scale from those of the past. A collision at sea, or a blow-out on an oil rig, can spell ecological disaster for a whole region. Indiscriminate fishing leads to loss of stocks that can take years to replenish. Industrial effluents and waste products pollute the ocean; imported seaweeds grow out of control and destroy other forms of life; land crumbles and disappears before the relentless onslaught of the sea. The coast contains histories and marval just as much in need of preservation as buildings and ships.

LEISURE The one maritime activity that has increased rather than declined in recent years is sailing and boating. The number of privately owned boats has soared, wind-surfing has brought the excitement of sailing within everyone's reach, and the coasts of Britain are dotted with clubs and marinas. Amid the luxury yachts, sleek powerboats and fibre-glass dinghies, a growing fleet of traditional craft is emerging. The Wooden Boat Show at Greenwich attracts more and more enthusiasts each year, proving that traditional skills and materials remain very much in demand.

There is growing interest in the restoration of old boats, and hours of devoted labour and expertise are expended on bringing decayed classics back to life.

The popularity of certain types of boat, such as the Thames sailing barge and the Norfolk wherry, has led to the formation of flourishing clubs, with regattas, newsletters and regular interchanges. Without this individual enthusiasm many traditional types of craft would become extinct, to be recorded only in pictorial and documentary form. There have been many losses already, and some rare survivals, like that of *Shamrock,* the last of the

Tamar working barges, now berthed at Cotehele in Cornwall. The National Maritime Museum is hoping one day to house its considerable collection of boats in a centre with access to water where they can be worked and demonstrated. This is done very successfully at the Exeter Maritime Museum, which has a world-wide collecting policy, showing Chinese junks side by side with Arab dhows and Welsh coracles.

There has been talk of a yachting museum, to be sited somewhere on the Solent. The history of yacht-racing goes back to the time of Charles II, who was also responsible for promoting horse-racing and other forms of sport. It was the British who took the lead in establishing rules and rates for racing yachts, and there are many racing clubs with long and distinguished histories, such as the Royal Yacht Squadron at Cowes, which are themselves owners of important maritime collections. Such is the international and commercial hype that is associated with yacht-racing today that it is often forgotten that the America's Cup was exclusively an Anglo-American challenge for more than a hundred years. Britain has also had its share of famous circumnavigators, including Sir Francis Chichester, whose *Gypsy Moth IV* can be seen at Greenwich. It is popular boats like the Mirror dinghy class, however, which have brought racing within the reach of the ordinary man, and given pleasure to thousands.

The depth and range of Britain's maritime heritage is amply demonstrated in this admirable guide, which draws together all its many strands in a comprehensive and fascinating manner. It will have great practical value as a gazetteer, charting the history and survivals of each region, and cumulatively it paints an impressive picture of Britain and the sea. The maritime heritage is not simply about preserving what remains, it is also about a living and working environment. This is the message which historic sites and museums must demonstrate to those who visit them, to adults, to children, to everyone. The history of the sea has been in large part the history of this country, it informs the present and it will continue to shape the future.

Richard Ormond
Director
National Maritime Museum

HIGHLANDS AND ISLANDS

Oil rigs illuminate the Cromarty Firth

HIGHLANDS AND ISLANDS

NOWHERE more encapsulates the notion of the 'Highlands and Islands' than the Outer Hebrides. There are five islands in this 150-mile (242-kilometre) string: Lewis and Harris are actually joined like Siamese twins, then comes North and South Uist, Benbecula and Barra. The whole is sometimes known as the 'long island'. The population of the islands, which now largely subsists on a mixture of tourism, crofting and fishing, is the largest intact group of Gaelic speakers left anywhere in the British Isles.

As is so often the case in the far northern regions of Scotland, the area's maritime past is astonishing in both its scale and variety, while the present day is both low key and sparse. Commercial fishing began off Lewis in 1594 with the arrival of the Dutch herring busses. The leading citizens of Stornoway, capital of the island, debated an issue that would still be a European flashpoint four centuries later and decided to sell the Dutch visitors rights to fish twenty-eight miles (forty-five kilometres) offshore. Of course, the attractions of a virtual gold mine just off the harbour was too much for the rest of the world to ignore and by the mid-nineteenth century Stornoway was a pivot of the herring industry, landing as much fish by volume as Yarmouth or Lowestoft. Equally predictably, by the end of the First World War it had fallen into almost total decline through over-fishing.

There was a rather curious chance of a revival in the 1920s when the industrial magnate Lord Leverhulme bought all of Lewis and Harris, with the semi-philanthropic intention of reversing Stornoway's decline and transforming it into the largest and most prosperous fishing and fish-processing centre in the world. With the teeming Atlantic on the doorstep there was certainly no shortage of raw material. Indifference from the locals and a dispute with the government over the land rights of returning servicemen disillusioned Leverhulme after he

Herring fishing off the Hebrides in the eighteenth century.

had spent the equivalent of £75 million. Stornoway was given to the townspeople and the noble lord retreated forty miles (sixty-four kilometres) south to the tip of Harris, where he tried to recreate his vision on a smaller scale. The tiny fishing village of Obbe was renamed Leverburgh and attempts were begun to create an industrial complex. Like the larger vision at Stornoway, it too failed, although there is a legacy of some much-improved housing and a modernized harbour.

During the nineteenth-century herring boom Stornoway prospered in two areas connected to the larger ocean trade. Schooners were built in great numbers and so too was the occasional tea clipper, such as the famous *Lady Hood Mackenzie*. Local seamen became the backbone of the emergent British merchant marine. In their integrity, hardihood and small boat skills the men of the Outer Hebrides became an international byword for high standards.

Many clippers were almost entirely manned by Hebridean crews and the tradition continued well into the steamships of the present century, with many Cunard skippers having been Lewis men. The Cunard surname is an evolution of the Gaelic words *Cuan Ard* (meaning high seas).

Bos'un Kenneth Stewart was the model for the Merchant Navy Memorial at Tower Hill, just outside Stornoway. Born at Tong, several miles up the coast, his description meets every ideal of the Scottish seaman:

His handsome rugged Scottish face and great
powerful hands have been tanned by hot
tropical suns and salt sea breezes. His
incredibly bright light blue eyes are of the
kind only ever found in men who have spent
a lifetime gazing at a distant horizon.

One other Outer Hebridean legend deserves a mention. The small island of Eriskay off the southern tip of South Uist has achieved literary immortality through the shipwreck of a rather humdrum Second World War Liber-

ty ship. In 1941 a 12,000-ton freighter loaded with 24,000 cases of finest Scotch whisky bound for America ran aground in the Sound. The flotsam and jetsam did not even have time to reach the beach before it was gathered up by locals and hidden in caves and cellars. Fortunately for history and entertainment, author Compton Mackenzie was living at the time on the neighbouring island of Barra and his version of the story, as *Whisky Galore*, made a superb novel and film.

Fishing is once more booming in the Hebrides, but not offshore. There are now only around 120 boats in the islands' fleet, and they are small at an average of only forty feet (twelve metres). The growth is in fish-farming salmon, an industry only ten years old but already providing extraordinary amounts of income and employment.

On the mainland west coast of Scotland no marine industries other than localized fishing developed. From the Mull of Kintyre right up the west coast to Cape Wrath there are numerous scattered towns, villages and crofts, whose only trade links with the rest of the world were by sea. In transport terms the Atlantic was both a highway and a problem. Viewed practically these isolated communities might as well have been islands. On the gale-swept coast the sailing craft of earlier centuries dodged from one headland shelter to another, making all cargoes costly in terms of time. The indented, fjord-like nature of the coastline made land transport exceedingly long winded, what roads there were taking the most incredibly circuitous routes.

On the northern coastline of Caithness, the six miles from Scrabster to Castlehill were dotted with quarries, and thousands of tons of dress-stone for paving the streets of the rapidly growing Victorian cities were shipped away. Thurso and its dock was the centre of this specialized trade but in some places the schooners used to come right into the cliff-face to load stone. In Scrabster harbour, for instance, there was a place known as the Chains where trading vessels lay bows out to sea, an anchor set, and the stern made fast to

Tarbert harbour, Lewis, on the eve of the First World War.

iron rings set in the cliff-face. The flagstones weighed about two hundredweight and were a devil to load, being moved around on special wheelbarrows. In 1900 there were twenty or so schooners and ketches owned in Thurso and employed solely in the flagstone trade.

The two maritime cities of northern Scotland are Aberdeeen and Dundee. Both have strong connections with the Viking raiders and settlers of the first millennia but their recorded history begins rather later. The first significant visit to Dundee by sea was in 1040 when the small fleet of King Malcolm of Scotland anchored there while in pursuit of the renegade thane, Macbeth. By the end of the twelfth century Dundee was confirmed enough in its marine importance for the burghers to be granted a free harbour, immune from crown taxes, a status later ratified by Robert the Bruce.

Dundee had an association with textiles since the 1500s. Wool, linen and hemp were the major items and specialities and links developed with the weavers and producers across in the Baltic region. But it was jute that

was to provide the city's industrial base. Jute is the fibre from the bark of the *Corchorus capsularis* plant, found mainly in Bengal, which can be woven into coarse sacking and light cordage of very great strength. In the days of sailing ships such products were needed daily and in vast quantities just to keep the running rigging functioning. A

Kintyre fishermen, 1924.

Discharging cargo into carts from a beached ship.

clipper ship would be totally dependent upon the products of Dundee simply to get to sea.

Jute had been known and used for centuries in a limited way. What changed everything was the discovery of William Taylor, at Ruthven Mill, Dundee. He found that the jute fibres could be softened by the addition of whale oil and made pliable enough to spin and hence weave. The whale oil trade was already hugely significant in the city, as was a textile knowledge, so the factors for a boom industry were already in place.

The first complete load of 300 tons of jute landed from Bombay in 1840. By 1866 the volume had become 62,000 tons a year and by the turn of the century it had reached 300,000 tons. In the age before polythene or heavy cardboard containers, all dry goods travelled in sacks. And most of the world's sacks were made in Dundee. The appetite for oil fuelled the whaling industry and by 1870 the city was Britain's top port in the trade. However, innovation proved a fickle mistress, for in the 1890s the jute barons began to experiment with the substitution of a much cheaper mineral oil in the manufacturing process and the manufacture of jute ceased to depend upon whale oil. By the 1890s whaling was on its knees.

Building whalers for the ice-bound waters of the polar regions had become a speciality of the Dundee shipyards and made them a natural choice for exploration ships built for those regions. The most famous was *Discovery*, launched in 1901 from Stephens Yard where many whalers had been built. She left

Launch of HMS *Discovery* at Dundee, 1901.

almost immediately for the South Pole on Captain Scott's ill-fated expedition. She returned to the Antarctic in 1929 with Sir Douglas Mawson's party and thereafter passed to the Royal Naval Volunteer Reserve, becoming a familiar sight on the Thames embankment below the Inns of Court. However, after intervention and restoration by the Maritime Trust she has been returned to her home port and is now one of Dundee's leading attractions for visitors.

Aberdeen has an immensely long maritime history. Being set on the mouths of two rivers in a good natural harbour sea travel became almost a genetic tendency. The Romans knews the settlement well as Devana, and it was Apardion to the Norwegian seafarers, who effectively gave the city its modern name. In 1162 the great Norse leader Swein Asleifson visited Aberdeen for a month of feasting and alliance-planning with the boy-king Malcolm IV.

By 1200 the 'Granite City' had been granted a charter as a free port. Repeated raids from hostile Scandinavians in their 'piratical cruzers' was the impetus which led to the construction of the castle around this time. In the fifteenth century an entirely separate fishing community began to emerge in the Footdee district to the west of the original town. Several centuries later the little hamlet was professionally re-planned with the aid of the fishermen themselves and turned into a model village, with particularly good housing for the time.

Since the late 1960s Aberdeen has enjoyed an unprecedented boom and prosperity through its role as the principal support base for the offshore oil industry. The exploration stage of the North Sea fields came at a particularly opportune moment when Aberdeen's traditional deep-sea fishing industry was entering a period of terminal decline. The trawlers were quickly converted to the role of supplying services and personnel to the huge oil rigs and production platforms that began to mushroom in the waters to the north. Rigs are serviced, supplied and crewed from Aberdeen. The harbour is now home to a huge variety of rugged and specialized support vessels, crew boats and diving ships. The airport sees more helicoptor movements than anywhere else in the British Isles. The city is perhaps more vulnerable to the short-term boom-and-bust cycles of the oil industry but the prosperity that this new use of the sea has brought is no figment of the imagination.

Aberdeen harbour thrives on the oil industry.

GAZETTEER

HIGHLANDS AND ISLANDS FROM ARRAN TO THE FIRTH OF FORTH

ARRAN has a gentle southern plain and 2,000 ft (600 m) high mountains in the north. Two miles (3 km) north of Blackwater Foot to the west of the isle is King's Cave, one of a number of caverns believed to have been inhabited by Robert Bruce or perhaps Fingal, the Celtic hero.

ISLE OF ARRAN HERITAGE MUSEUM
Rosaburn, Brodick.
Local social history.
Open May – Sept, (Mon – Fri).

KINTYRE, but for a tiny isthmus, would be the innermost island of the Hebrides. From its southernmost extremity at Southend it is only 15 miles (24 km) to Ireland from where, tradition has it, St Columba arrived AD 560.

CAMPBELTOWN, a century ago, was an important whaling town with interests in the coal, distilling and herring-fishing trades. Barley for the distillery was delivered by 'puffer' from Kincardineshire.

The use of the cruiser stern in local fishing boats was started by Robert Robertson of Campbeltown in 1921, who had the *Falcon* and other boats built in this style. This stern was used on Scottish fishing boats until about 1970 and is still regarded by fishermen as being the most seaworthy hull form.

Gutting herring on Arran, 1902.

TARBERT (meaning isthmus in Gaelic) is situated in the north of Kintyre at the south of Loch Fyne and guarding the road south from Knapdale down the long promontory of Kintyre. It is still a bustling port and fishing centre. 'The Beilding', a square raised platform in the middle of the harbour, is a relic of the days of sail when a capstan used to be mounted on it and cables run out to haul in sailing boats.

ARDRISHAIG, north of Tarbert and on the mainland of Knapdale, stands at the southern end

Euphemia discharging cargo in Kilbrannan Sound.

of the Crinan Canal. It was built by John Rennie in 1794 linking over 9 miles (14 km) the north of Knapdale and Loch Fyne with the Sound of Jura and the Atlantic thereby enabling ships to bypass a journey of 130 miles (209 km). The canal was used not only by the herring fleets but also by travellers to Glasgow and the south, many of whom travelled by paddle-steamers such as the 300 ft (90 m) *Columba* which could travel at 19 knots carrying 2,000 passengers in luxurious conditions. Yachts and dinghies now outnumber the fishing boats.

ISLAND OF BUTE, situated north-east of Arran, has been described as a lowland island in a highland setting. Much of it consists of low hills. In the east Rothesay Castle has a museum.

BUTESHIRE NATURAL HISTORY SOCIETY MUSEUM
Stuart St.
Collections of natural history, archaeology, geology and history of the isle.
Open Apr – Sept, daily.

HOLY LOCH, to the north-east, an inlet off the Firth of Clyde north of Isle of Bute is named because a vessel carrying earth from the Holy Land sank here.

SANDBANK on the south shore was the place where *Sceptre* and *Sovereign*, Britain's unsuccessful 1960s challengers for the America's Cup were built.

DUNOON is a resort notable for sea fishing especially from the rocks known as the Gantocks, some 600 yd (550 m) off the end of the pier, where the wreck of a Swedish ore carrier provides a home for cod of up to 46 lb (20 kg).

ISLE OF JURA over in south-west Jura's wilderness of rock moor and peat bog was settled in Viking days when it was called Deer Island. It is now one of the largest uninhabited regions in Britain.

At its northern point lies the notorious Gulf of Corryvreckan, separating Jura from the Isle of Scarba. For centuries it was believed that Corryvreckan was a whirl pool but in fact it is a massive tide race caused by the current funnelling through a narrow channel. It is the most dangerous stretch of water in the British Isles and the white boiling surface has claimed many vessels over the centuries.

ISLE OF ISLAY is the southermost of the Inner Hebrides and famed for its distilleries. The island has 2 ports: Port Askaig in the north-east is reached from mainland Kintyre and Port Ellen in the south. West of Port Ellen is the bleak peninsula called the Oa from where, on a good day, the Giant's Causeway can be glimpsed. At the Mull of Oa is a monument to American servicemen who died when the troopships *Tuscania* and *Otranto* sank nearby in 1918.

The west wind of the island is known as The Rhinns of Islay. The neat little fishing village of **PORT CHARLOTTE** has:

MUSEUM OF ISLAY LIFE
Housed in the former kirk showing among many local displays, exhibitions of maritime interest. Open Apr – Sept, (Mon – Fri).

COLONSAY falls under the influence of the North Atlantic Drift and joins up with Oronsay at each low tide. One hundred years ago a Viking warship and the remains of a Viking warlord were dug up in Kiloran Bay. The wild goats, long haired and black fleeced, are said to be descended from goats that swam ashore from the wrecked ships of the Armada in 1588.

OBAN, in a bay on the Firth of Lorn and sheltered by the close lying island of Kerrera, has long been a major ferry point to both the Inner and Outer Hebrides and is a flourishing port.

ISLE OF MULL is only 26 miles (42 km) across at its widest point but its deep creeks and fissures give it a coastline of 300 miles (482 km) and it is the second largest island of the Inner Hebrides.

CRAIGNURE, with its sheltered deep-water bay, has become Craignure Mull's link with the mainland and principal port for cruise steamers. The pier, built in 1964, handles timber shipments from Forestry Commission plantations on the island.

DUART CASTLE, magnificently sited southeast of Craignure on Duart Point, is open to the public in the summer. A tableau in the dungeon has models of Spanish prisoners from the galleon *Florencia* which was blown up and later sunk in Tobermory Bay in 1588. Other relics on display include guns salvaged from the wreck. From the Sea Room are breath-taking views of Ben Nevis more than 30 miles (48 km) away.

GRIBUN, on the west coast, has sheer cliffs streaked with narrow waterfalls which make this one of the most dramatic parts of Mull. From here can be seen the uninhabited island of Staffa, which inspired Mendelssohn to write his Hebrides Overture. The 'Sacred Isle' steamer cruise from Oban to Iona sails past this remarkable island.

TOBERMORY, Mull's capital, was founded by the British Society for Encouraging Fisheries in 1788, to take advantage of its natural harbour. Fishing never really flourished here but it is a haven for yachting enthusiasts. It is best known locally for the wreck of the Spanish galleon, reputedly carrying 3 million gold doubloons, which lies about 300 yd (270 m) off the pier. Numerous relics have been recovered but the treasure has never been found.

The Inner Hebridean islands of Rhum, Eigg, Muck and Canna, Coll and Tiree all lie to the north-west of Mull.

TIREE is a low-lying isle with no trees because of the 120-knot gales that come off the Atlantic. To the south, at Hynish, there is a derelict collection of houses, a pier and signalling station used when Alan Stevenson, uncle of the novelist R L Stevenson, built the far out Skerryvore lighthouse in the 1840s.

EIGG, forming a group with Canna, Rhum and Muck, is known for the phenomenon of 'The Singing Sands'. At Cammas Sgiotaig there are quartzite sands which squeak when walked on, or even emit a long continuous moan if the wind is in the right direction.

CANNA in the extreme north of the group, has one of the finest deep-water harbours in the Hebrides, making it popular with yachtsmen in the summer despite the hazard of distortion to compass bearings caused by the magnetism of basalt rocks, 3 miles (5 km) away. The inhabitants live precariously by farming and lobster fishing.

Back at the mainland to the west of this group and north of Mull, Loch Linnhe stretches away to the north-east of Mull. On one of its inlets, north of Oban at Loch Creran can be found The Sea Life Centre. Here live some 2,000 specimens of

Atlantic sea creatures. There are also displays of fish-farming techniques.

CORRAN NARROWS is a point where the shores of Loch Linnhe are barely 1/4 mile (400 m) apart. The tidal water flows swiftly through here. The view northwards up the loch includes the glowering peak of Britain's highest mountain, Ben Nevis, south-east of Fort William: to the south of the Narrows is the wide seaward end of Loch Linnhe sweeping down to Lismore island and the Firth of Lorne with a glimpse of Mull in the west.

STRONTIAN at the head of Lake Sunart in the west is famous for the mineral strontianite discovered there in 1787.

MALLAIG is important as the terminus of the West Highland Railway and is a busy harbour and fishing port.

SKYE, or Isle of Mists, is the most popular and famous of the West Highlands and also the largest with 600 sq miles (1550 sq km) of varied scenery riven deeply by sea lochs which means that no place is more than 5 miles (8 km) from the sea.

ARMDALE in the south is the disembarkation point for ferry passengers from Mallaig.

UIG is sited in a magnificent horseshoe of a natural harbour. It was here, 1 mile (1.6 km) to the north-west of Uig, that Bonny Prince Charlie landed in 1746, on his flight into exile.

QUIRAING in the north-eastern corner of Skye has some of the most fantastic rock formations in Britain, thrown up by volcanic activity some 70 million years ago. Quiraing's features include a 120-ft (36-m) stack called the Needle, castellated crags, caves and chasms.

PORTREE's name means 'King's Port' and refers to a visit by James V in 1540. It overlooks a broad bay that provides a well-sheltered anchorage for fishing boats. The hills that flank the bay rise to more than 1,300 ft (400 km).

Back on the mainland north-east of Skye **PLOCKTON** is where palm trees flourish along the shore side. The warming effect of the North Atlantic Drift extends north to the coast of Wester Ross which, though on the same latitude as Siberia and Hudson Bay, has subtropical plants growing in seaside gardens.

GAIRLOCH is a busy West Highland coastal village situated at the head of Loch Cair. From here fishing boats sell their main catches of white fish and lobster, crab and prawns.

RUBHA REIDA is the headland at the end of the peninsula which projects north of Cairloch into the Minch. From the lighthouse there are fine views of the Hebrides. South of the headland at Loch Ewe, remnants of wartime defences such as pill boxes and gun emplacements are reminders that the sheltered waters of the loch were the assembly point for the North Atlantic convoys.

Beyond Greenstone Point is **GRUINARD BAY** with pink sandy coves formed of red sandstone. Gruinard Island in its middle is a danger zone – its land is still contaminated from chemical warfare experimentation during the Second World War.

ULLAPOOL is another fishing port established in 1788 by the British Fisheries Society to exploit the herring in Loch Broom. One hundred years later the area was overfished and the industry collapsed. However, inshore boats still use it as a base for going after the Minch herring: a purser with highly technical equipment can take a 100-ton herring shoal in one night. The old herring curing factory along Shore St now houses a small museum of local exhibits.

LOCHINVER is situated on the wild rocky coastal district known as the Assynt. Despite its tiny population, it is a popular tourist centre and a busy port for the landing of white fish. It was from here that many Highlanders expelled from their crofts set sail for Australia and New Zealand.

KINLOCHBERVIE is the most important fishing port in the far north-west of the Highlands. It has a double harbour – either side of a narrow isthmus between Loch Inchard and Loch Clash from where east-coast fishing boats land catches of white fish which are then transported to Aberdeen, Hull and Grimsby. From here in 1963 Frank Dye, a dinghy sailor famous among yachtsmen, made a spectacular voyage to Iceland and in 1964 he set sail from Kinlochbervie to the Norwegian coast and almost into the Arctic Circle.

OUTER HEBRIDES: Lewis and Harris form a single island that, with the Uists, Benbecula and Barra provide a 150-mile (240-km) long storm break for the Inner Hebrides and Western Isles.

STORNOWAY is the main town in the Outer Hebrides established by the Vikings because there was an excellent natural harbour here. It is now a fishing port, a market and the centre of the Harris tweed industry.

Between the seventeenth and nineteenth centuries, Stornoway was involved in hunting pilot whales: in 1629 100 whales were killed off Stornoway with swords and bows and arrows. It switched to herring during the boom and by 1912 was one of the main Scottish herring ports with 1,000 drifters mostly from the east coast coming here in the season.

BENBECULA, south of North Uist, makes its living from crofting and fishing. South of the 408 ft (124 m) Rueval is a cave in which Bonny Prince Charlie hid while waiting for Flora MacDonald to bring him maid's clothing.

ERISKAY is an attractive 3-mile (5-km) long island between South Uist and Barra whose inhabitants are dependent on prawn, herring and lobster fishing. The women are renowned for knitting gossamer shawls and fishermen's jerseys with the unique Eriskay patterns of sails, waves and harbour scenes.

Scotland's far north is one of the most sparsely inhabited areas of Britain.

To the east of **SANDSIDE BAY** lies the Dounreay Reactor Station bringing an air of science fiction to this part of the Caithness coast. Reay, the village at the head of the bay, was rebuilt when the original village was buried by sand dunes.

SCRABSTER, like many other ports in Caithness, started as a centre for exporting flagstones during the nineteenth century. It was from here that Lord Kitchener sailed in the ill-fated HMS *Hampshire* in June 1916. Scrabster now offers anchorage to trawlers and sailing boats and runs a daily ferry to Stromness in the Orkneys and is one of Britain's largest sea-angling centres. Its lifeboat station is sometimes open to visitors.

THURSO, the northern most town on the British mainland, is surrounded by quarries from which thousands of tons of street paving stones were shipped away by schooners. Below, Holborn Head lighthouse was a loading berth known as the Chains where traders lay stern on, their prows held off by their anchors and their sterns made fast to iron rings set in the cliff-face.

DUNNET HEAD nearby is the most northerly point on the British mainland. Most prominent of the islands that can be seen from the promontory is Hoy with cliffs at some points 1,000 ft (300 m) high and the famous Old Man of Hoy. It is also possible to see Cape Wrath almost 60 miles (96 km) to the west. Sand yachting is a popular sport in Dunnet Bay.

WICK was an early Viking anchorage and settlement. It depended on cod and salmon fishing until 1786 when the newly established British Fishery Society encouraged boats to go north after herring. By the 1860s Wick was a boom town during the 6-week herring season with some 1,700 boats coming here with hundreds of fishermen from all over eastern Scotland. It is now the main inshore fishing fleet base in the Highlands.

WICK HERITAGE CENTRE
Bank Row (near the harbour).
Displays of Wick history. With award-winning exhibition on fishing industry and domestic life of fishermen.
Open June – Sept, daily.

WHALIGOE, 6 miles (9.5 km) south of Wick, is a tiny cove in the cliff and once an important herring curing station. A flight of 365 steps is cut into the steep cliffs leading down to the cove. Women used to carry fully laden baskets of fish up these steps before journeying by foot with them north to Wick.

LYBSTER harbour is situated 1/4 mile (400 m) from the village and is set amid steep cliffs facing Lybster Bay and dominated by its lighthouse. A stone pier was built in 1830 to protect the entrance to this cove and to form a herring harbour. During the season, the harbour was packed with lug-rigged scaffies and the quays piled high with barrels of herring waiting to be shipped out in schooners. In 1881 there were 129 boats but by the 1960s the fleet had been cut to 5 boats. Crab and lobster are the main catches now.

INVERGORDON has a long history as the landing point for a ferry to the Black Isle, a peninsula to its south. Built around a deep water anchorage it is famous as the former Royal Naval base in both world wars. On the last day of 1915, the armoured cruiser *Natal* exploded losing half the ship's company, nearly 400 men. In 1931, the Invergordon Mutiny by naval personnel took place here.

The height of the herring season at Wick.

THE MORAY FIRTH is guarded by *Fortrose* on its northern bank, which today is a busy sailing area. **AVOCH** to its immediate west is a thriving fishing village whose inhabitants claim descent from Spaniards wrecked here after the defeat of the Armada. An interesting feature of the fishermen's cottages which cluster about the small harbour is that their gable ends face the sea so that fishing boats could be drawn up between them in rough weather.

INVERNESS, capital of the Highlands, straddles the Caledonian Canal and the River Ness. It was made a royal burgh in 1150 on the strength of its importance as a trading port. The hinterland at that time was densely wooded and the trees were used for building a ship, the *Comte de St Paul et Blois*, which accompanied Louis V11 of France to the Crusades. Because it is the northern terminus of the Caledonian Canal, it has varied shipping.

The coast sweeps east in a series of sheltered bays with huge stretches of dunes. **NAIRN**, once a busy fishing harbour is now a popular resort and used by pleasure craft.

NAIRN FISHERTOWN MUSEUM
Laing Hall, King St.
Photographs and articles connected with the Moray Firth and herring fishing industry during the steam drifter era.
Open May – Sept, (Mon – Sat).

FINDHORN BAY is a tidal bay whose original settlement was buried beneath the sand during fierce storms in the seventeenth century. The second village was destroyed by floods in 1701. The modern settlement was once an important port but is now a sailing centre with competitions throughout the summer.

Inland from Findhorn Bay is **FORRES** an ancient town with a 70-ft (21-m) Nelson Tower built in 1806 to commemorate Trafalgar. From the top of this are magnificent views of the Moray Firth.

BURGH HEAD is known to have been occupied by the Romans from which time the Well, a chamber cut into the rock, probably dates.

LOSSIEMOUTH, by 1881, had 149 herring boats. The local fishermen were the first to adopt the Danish seine-net method of fishing.

LOSSIEMOUTH FISHERIES AND COMMUNITY
MUSEUM
Pitgaveny St.
Fishing heritage of Lossiemouth, models of
fishing boats and photos.
Open May – Sept, (Mon – Sat).

ELGIN, situated inland from Lossiemouth, has
in its museum reputedly the only Scottish coracle
to survive. At **SPEY BAY** the Tugney Ice-house
can be visited. It is the largest ice-house in
Scotland built to store ice for packing salmon
caught in the Spey. There is an exhibition on this
and the life on the Spey estuary.

BUCKIE is a typical north-east fishing port
established in 1645 as a fishing station. The
harbour was started in 1843 when boats were still
open and the fishermen were resisting the fitting
of decks. Single-masted scaffies were replaced
firstly by 2-masted Zulus and then by steam
drifters. There is still an active fishing fleet here.

BUCKIE MARITIME MUSEUM
Townhouse West, Cluny Place.
Exhibits on fishing industry in Buckie. Fish
market sheds, ice works, chandlers, sailmakers
and yards still building traditional timber boats in
town. Watercolours of town and fishing villages
by Peter Anson.
Open Mon – Sat.

BANFF, originally a Hanseatic trading town of
the twelfth century, is an attractive port of grey
stone houses. Records show that in 1838, 30,000
barrels of herring were exported from here.
Although the shallow harbour has now silted up,
it is a local sailing and leisure fishing centre.

BANFF MUSEUM
High St.
Model ships and thematic photographic display
on fishing industry.
Open June – Sept, (Wed – Fri).

ROSEHEARTY is one of the oldest sea-ports in
Scotland going back to the time of the Viking
raids. It was once a fishing rival to Fraserburg 5
miles (8 km) to the west, which has now taken
over. Rosehearty's harbour is still used by inshore
fishermen, the characteristic small sailing craft
here being the salmon coble.

ROSEHEARTY HERITAGE MUSEUM
Union St.
Housed in old Seceders church built by fishermen
in 1787. Displays fishing gear, photos and records
of Rosehearty's development as a busy fishing
port in the nineteenth century.
Open July – Sept, (Mon – Sat).

FRASERBURGH stands facing the North Sea
and the Moray Firth at the end of rocky Kinnairds
Head. Its heyday was during the herring boom of
the late nineteenth century but today it is still a
flourishing port because of its proximity to the
North Sea fishing grounds.

PETERHEAD, once Scotland's most important
whaling port, today has the largest white-fish
landings in Europe. In the 1880s along with
Aberdeen, Peterhead was the main Scottish herring port. Today, although not dealing with
herring it is extremely prosperous and supplies
the North Sea oilfields.

ABUTHNOT MUSEUM
St Peter St, Peterhead.
Exhibitions showing development of fishing boat
from sail to diesel. Relics of sailing ships trading
out of Peterhead.
Displays on the whaling industry.
Open Mon – Sat.

COLLIESTON is typical of the little villages
which flourished on fishing and smuggling with
contraband being hidden in the prolific caves
nearby. In the mid-nineteenth century over 250
people were fully employed in the herring industry until the 1880s when the larger fishing boats
could no longer use the harbour. St Catherine's
Dub, a rocky cove north of the village takes its
name from the Spanish galleon *Santa Caterina*
wrecked here in 1594.

ABERDEEN: in the early nineteenth century
there was fierce competition for the London
packet trade between Aberdeen and Leith.
Aberdonians commissioned Alexander Hall to
build a sailing packet to compete against Leith.
The result was the 92-ft (28-m) clipper schooner
Scottish Maid launched in 1839. She had what
became known as the 'Aberdeen bow' and later a
'clipper bow'. She was the forerunner of the
British clippers that blossomed into their full form
in the 1850s.
  Aberdeen stayed in the forefront of the development of clipper ships. Yards such as Duthie and
Sons and Walter Hood and Co built a series of
clippers for the China tea trade for George
Thompson's White Star Line.

Planking-up at William Hall's yard, Aberdeen.

ABERDEEN MARITIME MUSEUM
Provost Ross's House, Shiprow.
Displays on local shipbuilding, fishing, North Sea oil, ship models including the steam whaler *Eclipse* and paintings, *Explorer* (smaller *Discovery*).
Open Mon – Sat.

FINDON is a small fishing village that had its prosperity dashed from it by an Act of Parliament in 1870 forbidding the smoking of fish over open cottage fires. It gave its name to the locally smoked haddock 'Finnan Haddies'.

At **STONEHAVEN**, the 2-basin picturesque harbour, is sheltered from the south by Downie Point, but has always had problems with silting. However, the old town still retains much of its maritime character with boats and quayside crowded with lobster pots and fishing gear.

TOLBOOTH MUSEUM
The Harbour.

Local history and fishing displays and information about the fishing community.
Open June – Sept, daily.

INVERBERVIE was a herring port during the eighteenth century but it no longer has a fishing fleet. Birthplace of Hercules Linton, the designer of the *Cutty Sark*.

MONTROSE MUSEUM
Has a good section on the maritime history of the port and some Napoleonic items.
Open Apr – Oct, daily.

ARBROATH is famous for its smokies of which a constant reminder hangs over the town as the smell of smouldering wood drifts from the harbour area. The first harbour was built of wood here in 1194. Arbroath and Gourock were well known in the sailing-ship age as being places where flax canvas was manufactured: one of the mills remains operative.

Overlooking the harbour is the Signal Tower Lady Loan. Now a museum and once a tower built in the nineteenth century to communicate

with the lighthouse on Bell Rock 11 miles (17 km) offshore, which warns ships off the notorious Inchcape Rock.
Open daily.

FIRTH OF TAY

BROUGHTY FERRY is a small busy harbour at the eastern extremity of Dundee at the head of the Firth of Tay. Broughty Castle is a former estuary fort with splendid views over the Tay estuary. It has displays on seashore creatures and Scotland's best collection of whaling memorabilia.
Open Mon – Thurs & Sat.

DUNDEE, is a major port on the north bank of the Firth of Tay whose name was once synonymous with whaling. In 1756 a whaling company was started and Dundee was one of the last British ports to send whalers into the Arctic. Charles Barrie had 2 well-known 4-masted barques built for the Dundee-Calcutta jute trade. These were built by Thompson at Dundee and the first was *Juteopolis* in 1891.

Later, under the name *Carthpool*, this vessel although technically registered in Montreal, became the last British square rigger in the ocean trades until she was wrecked in 1929.

BARRACK STREET MUSEUM
Barrack St.
Mainly a museum of local history with a good section on shipping including a Victorian racing skiff. Also models and navigation instruments.
Open Mon – Sat.

RRS *DISCOVERY*
Dundee Industrial Heritage, Maritime House.
26 East Dock St.
Built in 1901 by Dundee Shipping Co for the 1901 Antarctic Expedition. Ship's hull was built of massive timber construction to withstand ice-pressure. The 'National Antarctic Expedition' exhibition in the hold displays models and illustrations.
Open June – Oct, daily.

HMS *UNICORN*
Victoria Dock.
Oldest British-built ship afloat and an important example of post Industrial Revolution constructional ideas. Still undergoing renovation.
Open April – Oct, daily.

ANSTRUTHER is an old-established Fife fishing town. Until the Second World War it was a fishing port but now it is important as the home of

THE SCOTTISH FISHERIES MUSEUM
St Ayles, Anstruther Harbour.
Comprehensive displays covering the fishing industry and associated skills. Fishing and ship's gear, period fishermen's home interiors. In the courtyard are 2 small open fishing yawls and in the harbour is the 70-ft (21-m) fifie *Reaper* (1902) and also the largest wooden line fishing craft built in Britain, *Radiation* (1957). Also on view is the Zulu sailing herring drifter *Research* (1901).
Open Apr – Oct, daily.

ST MONACE's motto is 'We live by the sea', and this is borne out by the many graves of fishermen buried in the local churchyard. The church contains some maritime relics including a model of a 100-gun man-of-war donated by a local naval officer out of prize money he had gained during the Napoleonic Wars and a memorial to 37 St Monace fishermen who lost their lives in an 1875 storm. It used to have a thriving shipbuilding business (Miller & Sons) and indeed has the oldest surviving builder's yard in Scotland, established in 1714.

FIRTH OF FORTH NORTHERN SHORE

This stretch of the Fife coast is, apart from Kirkaldy, no longer engaged in earlier occupations of fishing and trading in coal and fish.

LOWER LARGO, a one-time fishing hamlet, is famous as the birthplace of Alexander Selkirk, whose adventures as a castaway were the inspiration for *Robinson Crusoe*. There is a statue of him on the site of his cottage. In the church is buried Scotland's greatest admiral, Sir Andrew Wood, who led the Scots to victory against the English in 1489 in his ship *Yellow Caravel*. When he retired, he dug a canal from his castle to the church so that he might be rowed to the service by his old shipmates each Sunday.

BURNTISLAND is where Agricola landed in AD 83 and convoys assembled in the harbour during the Second World War. Its earlier eminence as a herring port has declined.

INVERKEITHING, from where the Forth Bridge spans south, now mainly concentrates on ship breaking.

INVERKEITHING MUSEUM
Queen St.

SCAPA FLOW – LAST RESTING PLACE FOR THE GERMAN FLEET

The importance of the Orkneys in naval strategy has been apparent as far back in maritime history as the Vikings. If the English Channel is closed to traffic, which has always been easy enough for the English and French (whether or not on the same side) to achieve, then the route to open seas for the Low Countries and Scandinavia has to be north around the Orkneys.

In the early years of the twentieth century Germany was preparing for war, that much was evident to the Lords of the Admiralty. If the Channel was denied to the Berlin High Command, they would inevitably try to slip the battleships based at Kiel and the Elbe out to the Atlantic by the northern route.

The perfect base to maintain guard over the passage was Scapa Flow and the Admiralty began to create a substantial naval base. The facilities tended to be afloat on depot ships rather than in permanent shoreside developments. No dockyard, for instance, was built. When war broke out in August 1914 the Admiralty ordered the Home

and Atlantic Fleets of the Royal Navy to Scapa. Minefields and sunken block ships were strewn across the wide approaches to protect the British fleet from submarine attack.

For two years a demoralized and angry fleet swung around mooring buoys in Scapa Flow. The climate was cold and wet. Nearly all the men were a long way from their homes in southern England. There was no town to speak of ashore and the only recreation on dry land was compulsory gardening in order to raise vegetables to feed the fleet.

Lord Kitchener, the British commander-in-chief, sailed from here in 1916 aboard the cruiser HMS *Hampshire* on a mission to Russia to bolster the morale of our flagging Eastern allies. A mine sunk the *Hampshire* off Birsay and there were few survivors, Kitchener not being among them. There is a memorial to him on Marwick Head.

It is the events that came after the First World War had ended which most clearly made Scapa Flow a name that evokes more than boredom in British mariners. The Armistice document re-

quired that the German navy be interned in an allied or neutral port to await the details of the peace treaty. Scapa Flow was chosen and the first of the Kaiser's ships entered the anchorage on 23 November 1918. There were nearly eighty ships, possibly the most militarily powerful fleet in the world. The war had not been particularly damaging to the German navy, with the one major engagement with the British, the Battle of Jutland, inconclusive to the extent that both sides argued that they had won.

After a week or two, troop transports arrived to take off all but skeleton crews. Officers and ratings to perform necessary maintenance remained. They quickly became as bored as the British matelots had been before them. Morale plummeted and newspaper pictures were published of German seamen roller-skating around the decks of the battleships.

While a situation of near mutiny obtained in Scapa, the Allies could not agree on how to dispose of the ships. German officers, sensing deadlock at the Versailles peace conference, began to make plans to destroy the fleet if the outcome was not acceptable to them.

News reaching the German officers was patchy and incomplete. They lived a bizarre existence of almost total isolation, food being brought to them from Bremen. Since post-war Germany was an economy virtually on its knees the diet was an inadequate mixture of black bread and potatoes with very little meat. The German crews fished incessantly to stave off protein deficiencies in their diet, and to relieve boredom.

When the peace terms were published they were extremely punitive towards Germany, to the extent that Berlin refused to sign. The Germans were given a deadline of 21 June 1919 to sign, or hostilities would resume. The German admiral in charge at Scapa Flow read about this in a copy of *The Times* passed to him by a friendly Orcadian. He decided to scuttle the fleet before his former enemies took possession of his ships.

The afternoon of 21 June was fine and sunny and there were pleasure cruisers out looking at the German fleet – which had become a tourist attraction in the Orkneys. Suddenly there were knots of men running everywhere on the decks of the destroyers, cruisers and battleships.

Before the eyes of the startled onlookers, the ships began to sink into the clear green water. One cruiser turned turtle and sank upside down. The British fleet was away on exercises so there were very few Royal Navy personnel available to take any action.

Some destroyers were beached by the Royal Navy and the battleship *Baden* was saved after her seacocks refused to open properly, but the rest sank quickly. By teatime seventy-four warships were on the bottom, the largest and most powerful fleet of warships ever sunk and not a gun fired in anger.

Much of the German fleet was raised in later years, although for scrap rather than military use. In fact, the steel became particularly sought after because it was cast before the atomic bombs of 1945. Therefore it was the only source of high-grade steel that contained no atomic fall-out whatsoever, an important consideration in certain scientific usages.

Prison for the battleships: Scapa Flow, November 1918.

Lerwick harbour at the end of the day's fishing.

Small local history museum with a collection of material relating to Admiral Sir Samuel Grieg (native of Inverkeithing) who became 'Father of the Russian Navy' in the mid-eighteenth century.
Open Wed – Sun.

ROSYTH, west of the Forth Road Bridge, is the Royal Naval base which can be visited by the public on annual open days. Rosyth churchyard near Limekilns to the west has a 'stranger's ground' where stones commemorate the names of foreign seamen who died there.

LIMEKILNS: Breck House in Red Row is the place where David Balfour and Alan Breck in RL Stevenson's *Kidnapped* waited for a boat to cross the Forth.

A harbour started at **CHARLESTOWN** in about 1765 by the 5th Earl of Elgin as an outlet for the mines and quarries on his estate. A later earl sold out to the North British Railway in 1860 and the port was expanded so that by 1880 200,000 tons of coal was exported from here. However, when other Forth ports built wet docks, Charlestown, which dried out at low tide, steadily declined. Several stone limekilns can still be seen here on the old quays.

CULCROSS was once a well-known port trading in coal and salt with the Low Countries from where it imported the red pantiles which cover the old town's roofs giving it a distinctively Dutch air.

THE ORKNEYS AND SHETLANDS

THE ORKNEYS are made up of some 70 islands of which 18 are inhabited. **HOY** is perhaps the most famous area of the group. The island helps form the south-west shore of **SCAPA FLOW** one of the finest natural harbours in the world, giving an anchorage of 80 sq miles (207 sq km) of sheltered water. It is indicative of Orkney's strong sense of independence that whereas elsewhere in Britain the seashore belongs to the Crown, in Orkney the coastal land is owned by islanders as far as the low-tide mark.

KIRKWALL in the south-east is a busy harbour and base for a large fleet landing white fish and lobster.

STROMNESS began its existence offering shelter for French and Spanish ships sailing to the New World. It became the British base for the stocking and preparing of ships before they crossed the Atlantic. Whalers used to call here to recruit men for harpooning and dismembering whales. Login's Wellat south of the town has an inscription saying it was used by Hudson's Bay ships between 1670 – 1891.

STROMNESS MUSEUM
Orkney and the sea, fishing, whaling, boat-building. Ship models including first steamers to sail between Orkney and the mainland in 1856: schooner *Lavinia* 1859, *Great Eastern* 1858, and the yole *Edith*. Lighthouse models. Permanent feature on First World War. Hudson's Bay Co display.
Open all year Mon – Sat.

THE SHETLANDS lie 110 miles (177 km) to the north-east of Scotland's north coast and are Britain's most northerly community.

OUT SKERRIES: Until the Out Skerries Lighthouse was built in 1852, these land rocks were a graveyard for shipping, the main casualties being Dutch East Indiamen laden with treasure. Divers still recover coins and valuables from the wrecks here.

LERWICK, the capital, is the only town established in the seventeenth century by the Dutch, when it was a thriving fishing port. By the eighteenth century smuggling had added to the town's prosperity and was so well developed during the nineteenth century that contraband from abroad was carried to London. Ships leaving Lerwick bound for London would obtain customs clearance for a coastal journey only, leave British waters, load up and complete the voyage as if they had been merely held up by bad weather.

SCALLOWAY was the chief town on the mainland, and today has a busy fishing harbour. During the Second World War Scalloway was the base for the 'Shetland Bus' an operation designed for landing saboteurs by sea in German-occupied Norway and bringing out Norwegian freedom fighters.

FAIR ISLE lies about half-way between Orkney and Shetland and is the most remote permanently inhabited island in Britain. There is a weekly boat running to Grutness on the southern end of mainland Shetland. The Fair Isle skiffs were double-ended open boats very similar to Norwegian craft. A 22-ft (7-m) skiff rowed by 3 men could achieve 45 strokes a minute. At the turn of the century the men used to go a long way off the island selling fresh food and hand-knitted jerseys to passing ships. The famous Fair Isle knitwear pattern is believed to be Norse in origin.

THE NORTH-EAST

Sunset over a Hartlepool colliery

THE NORTH-EAST

TECHNOLOGY has been the great harbinger of change, growth and eventual decline for the coast of North-East England. It has accordingly come in great savage leaps and unpredictable spurts. What a contrast with its more tranquil neighbour to the south, East Anglia. There the patterns of trade and life have altered more gently, eroded or reinforced by centuries of gradual change.

From a national perspective the engine-room of the North East has been Newcastle and its immediate hinterland. Its heyday as an international focus of shipbuilding and engineering, particularly in the field of weapons manufacture, was the second half of the nineteenth century and early part of the twentieth. In 1862 William Gladstone made a visit to Newcastle in his capacity as Chancellor of the Exchequer. The overawed Victorian statesman observed:

> I do not know where to seek even in this busy country of ours, a spot or district in which we perceive so extraordinary and multifarious a combination of the various great branches of mining, manufacturing, trading and shipbuilding. I greatly doubt whether the like can be shown upon the whole surface of the globe.

What was even more singular was the way that in this hot-house atmosphere an invention could become an industry and then a

Newcastle 1889, shipbuilder to the world.

memory in the space of a single generation. A classic example came in the way the fishing industry, the non-manufacturing backbone of the North-East, responded to change at Scarborough, further down the coast. In 1877 William Purdy, a shipbuilder of North Shields, announced the first paddle-steamer boat to pull a beam trawl. By 1880 there was a fleet of Purdy's paddle-trawlers operating out of Scarborough. Yet by 1904 not a single one survived – ousted by the frantic change to propellor-driven trawlers.

Just as coal provided fuel for Britain's industrial revolution, so it is the key to understanding the maritime development of the North-East. The Romans are supposed to have begun the movement and export of coal from the region. However, the first documented example concerns the Prior of Tynemouth in the twelfth century. In an early example of monopoly abuse and trade favouritism, Edward III decided that coal won on the Durham side of the River Tyne had to go first to Newcastle for shipment, thus benefiting the monks.

Those primitive colliers of 900 years ago were but little developed from the Viking longships. They were clinker-built, sharp-sterned, carried one sail on a single mast and were steered by sweep oar. The only navigational aids on the hazardous voyage down to the markets of London were cressets, or beacons, burning in the towers of coastal monasteries such as Whitby and Blakeney. There were neither compasses nor leadline aboard. Yet by 1369 the trade had flourished sufficiently for the City of London to appoint four 'coal meters', who supervised unloading and controlled short measure. The appetite of the growing metropolis for winter fuel seemed endless. Although the coal of Wales and the Midlands was worked at this time, before the coming of railways and canals sea transport was the only option and that gave the North-East an effective stranglehold on supplies and prices.

Specialized ports or 'staithes' – coming from the Old Norse word *stoth*, meaning a

The Humber keel *Willie*, unladen.

wharf – sprang up along the Northumberland and Durham coasts at places like Blyth, Amble and Seaham. Often a local landowner with a colliery near the sea would build his own small jetty to load the coal. But the most significant port by far was Newcastle itself. The collier brigs would come as far up the Tyne as they could – and it was a shallow river dogged by sandbanks and shifting hazards – before anchoring and waiting for cargo to be brought to them in keels.

The keels were peculiar to the rivers Tyne and Wear, although there are similarities with other simple, hard-working river boats such as the trows found on the Severn and the Norfolk wherries. They were double-ended boats of forty feet (twelve metres) overall, drawing four feet six inches (1.4 metres) when loaded and exceptionally beamy. A keel of coal was a standard measure in the trade and amounted to twenty chaldrons (around seventeen tons in modern units). The exact capacity of a chaldron shifted down the years but coal was still sold by the 'keelload' until the nineteenth century.

A keel's crew would consist of the skipper, one or two shovellers and the boy. Coming down to the anchorage on the fierce Tyne ebb, with the hold full to the boards, the

Colliers off Flamborough Head.

boats were not easy to control. They would be propelled by a pair of oars and steered by a twenty-five-foot (eight-metre) 'swape' mounted over the stern. If the breeze was fair a single grubby square sail might be set.

The keelmen were a gypsy-like band of intermarried families, fierce and almost tribal in their attitudes. They kept to their own district, almost a ghetto, in Newcastle at the river's edge. Their yellow waistcoats and black silk neckerchiefs made them visually conspicuous. In 1700 there were 400 working keels on the Tyne and 1,500 crew. Such was their sense of community and self-sufficiency that in 1710 the keelmen built their own hospital, which stands to this day on the river front. They were early radicals and staged strikes at the drop of a silk 'kerchief, quickly getting their message through to the chilly Londoners.

One of their strikes provides yet another example of the speed with which innovation could grow on Tyneside. During an 1822 stoppage, one enterprising owner of a fleet of stranded colliers installed a Hedley pioneer steam engine in an old hulk and began to tow other keels down to the ships. Within eight years Marshall's yard at South Shields was building and exporting steam-powered tugs.

The colliers themselves began to evolve quite markedly from the primitive double-enders which started the trade. One constant factor was the demand from ship-owners and merchants for bigger cargoes. That in turn meant bigger and stronger ships, for the steep choppy seas of the North Sea were no place to struggle with an overladen vessel. By the late sixteenth century the traditional clinker construction, where each plank overlaps its neighbour below, had reached its technical limits. Carvel planking had to be mastered. Putting the heavy strips of oak and elm edge-to-edge in the style favoured by Mediterranean shipwrights gave the capacity to create larger and more powerful ships.

Before this technical change in construction, the Dutch had a well-recognized advantage in the building of collier brigs. Owners regarded the British-built competitors as too small, too costly and carrying too little cargo. The coal trade was nothing if not European at this stage. In 1616 for every English or Scots vessel sailing over Tyne Bar, there were seven foreigners. This frequent interaction with ideas from other nations was like a shot of adrenalin to the imagination. The growth in the complexity of a collier's rig and sail-plan during Tudor times would have astonished a sailor from 100 years earlier.

By the mid-seventeenth century there were numerous shipyards active on the Wear at Sunderland, building colliers to a pattern that was to change little over the next two centuries. They were short, dumpy little ships not more than 100 feet (thirty metres) overall and displacing at most 150 tons. Although their bow and stern were raised up well from the water the midships section tended to be low in order to load coal more easily from a keel lying alongside.

By around 1700 there were over 1,000 British colliers. The Stuart kings came to regard this fleet as the backbone of their navy. The main reason was the quality of the seamen, nowhere else in the kingdom was there a body of close to 10,000 men used to handling the largest ships afloat in all weathers. A book called *The Trades Increase*, written in 1615, noted that 'The Newcastle voyage, if not the only, yet is the especial nursery and school of seamen. For as it is the chiefest employment of sailors, so it is the gentlest and most open to landsmen.'

It was almost inevitable that Captain James Cook, the greatest navigator and seaman of his age, would spring from the nursery of the collier fleet. Cook was born at Whitby, on the Yorkshire coast. Although not on a coal-field, the collier brigs built in this town became world renowned, as did those of Whitby's neighbour to the south, Scarborough. In 1816 the Whitby fleet was 280 vessels of 46,341 aggregate tons. 'In strength, beauty and symmetry our vessels are equalled by few, and may I say, excelled by none,' puffed a contemporary writer.

Captain Cook RN.

Nevertheless, he was right. Although the son of a mendicant farm worker Cook was well-educated thanks to the generosity of the local squire. He served his apprenticeship at sea aboard the Whitby brigs before joining the Royal Navy. When the king asked him to undertake his great voyages to the South Seas, it was to Whitby that Cook turned for ships. *Endeavour*, the barque that found Australia, was from Cook's home town as were his other ships. 'I can assure you that I have never set foot on a finer ship,' testified the explorer as he boarded the *Resolution*.

The eighteenth-century boom in wooden-shipbuilding based around the collier fleet was little short of extraordinary. In 1700 these little craft, not much longer than a modern Grand Prix racing yacht, were moving slightly over half-a-million tons of coal a year past Gravesend. In 1740 South Shields was home port to four ships with a total weight of 800 tons. In 1809 that figure had become 500 ships displacing over 100,000 tons. Just as important as volume, in a world where communications were becoming easier, the North-East was acquiring a pre-eminent reputation for shipbuilding. 'They build ships here to perfection – I mean as to strength and firmness and to bear the sea,' wrote that acute traveller Daniel Defoe.

The ships needed to be tough. In the middle of the eighteenth century whaling became the economic boom industry of the era. Colliers were adapted to the trade and from May to October the ports of Whitby and Hull saw a steady stream of brigs sailing north to the wild waters of Greenland and the Arctic Circle. They did not altogether give up the coal trade. Wily owners saw that a couple of Newcastle/London voyages could be fitted in during the early spring. In the winter months the colliers never left harbour. The prevailing north-east wind makes the Northumberland coast a dangerous lee shore and the marine insurance companies – by this time Lloyds was already flourishing – refused to provide cover for vessels who wished to trade through this period.

In terms of numbers of ships, whaling never remotely rivalled the coal trade but it was a very profitable business. In 1788 there were thirty-six whalers based at Hull and twenty at Whitby. Techniques improved at an enormous speed. In the ten years from 1803, the *Resolution*, Whitby's champion boat, took 249 whales. In the previous decade she had managed only sixty-five – which at the time had been thought a huge tally. However, the whaling boom was a phenomenon not unlike the gold rushes in Australia and the United States. Too many competitors and a dwindling resource brought North-East whaling to a sudden end. Whitby gave up in the 1830s and by 1840 Hull's whaling fleet was down to two ships.

At this moment in history the real industrial dynamic was further north up the coast, on the rivers Tyne and Wear. The latter had become the major concentration of British shipbuilding, producing one-third of the nation's tonnage in the 1830s. Yet it was still essentially a craft industry, however large and

significant its aggregate production. In 1850 the Wear produced slightly over 50,000 tons of shipping, in excess of 200 individual vessels, but only eight out of the fifty or so firms involved employed more than 100 men. It was a cottage industry, essentially.

Iron ships were the key to change. In 1830 the Stephensons were galvanizing the North-East with their railway enterprises. It could only be a matter of time before the industrial processes that were revolutionizing land transport came into the maritime sphere. In the 1820s four iron barges with primitive steam engines had been built at Manchester for river use. But the first true iron ship was built in the North-East at South Shields. The *Star* was a small passenger craft built in 1839 to shuttle along the Tyne between Newcastle and North Shields.

Two years later the same innovative yard, Marshalls, built another landmark iron vessel, the 214-ton *Bedlington* propelled by twin propellors. Iron ships were received sceptically at first, not least by the shipbuilders of the Thames estuary. Their proximity to London gave them a huge advantage in securing naval contracts and their skills were the equal of those on the Tyne, Wear or Tees. But what they did not have was access to the coal of Northumberland and Durham nor the fine iron ore deposits of nearby Cleveland. The oak forests of Kent and Sussex would be of little use to the yards of Gravesend and Deptford once the new technology caught hold.

From the 1840s onward through the nineteenth century almost every stepping-stone development in shipping happened in the north-east of England. Ships were the glamour technology of the century, aerospace and computers rolled into one, and Tyne and Wear were the Silicon Valley of their day. John Coutts, originally of Aberdeen, was among the greatest challengers of the status quo. In 1844 he designed and built the 271-ton auxiliary schooner *QED*. She was the first ship in the world to have double-bottoms, a space between inner and outer hulls into which water could be pumped to act as ballast when the ship was sailing without cargo. The traditional ballast for colliers returning north had been either chalk or large rocks; both of which were expensive to load and had a tendency to damage the holds. To be able simply to pump in no-cost sea water and sail directly home transformed the economics of coal-carrying for many small shipowners. Coutts was also a proponent of bigger ships. In 1852 at Willington Quay on the Tyne he launched the *Thomas Hamlin*, at 1,350 tons easily the biggest iron ship the world had yet seen.

Yet despite its intense development into newer and bigger ships, the merchant marine of the North-East was not without problems and competition to face. As the railways came into the Midlands so the coal trade from Newcastle began to have a rival and was unable completely to dictate prices on the London market. There was a good deal for the merchants of Newcastle and Sunderland to defend. In 1844 2.5 million tons of coal were shipped down to London in 9,500 separate voyages. Over 10,000 men were employed full-time in the trade. It was at precisely this economic zenith that the proposal for a Newcastle to London railway hit the North-East like a bolt from the blue. To a few affluent and leisured folk it raised the prospect of quick and comfortable travel to the pleasures of the capital, but for the workers and the merchants it looked a black prospect.

One young man, the heir to a thriving coal business, saw that the only way to challenge the railways was by superior innovation, not blunt opposition. Charles Palmer, born of a wealthy merchant family in South Shields, was twenty-nine when, in 1851, he formed the General Iron Screw Collier Company at Jarrow on the south bank of the Tyne estuary.

John Bowes was the name of the yard's first steam collier, launched a year later in 1852. In later years it was the great liners that grabbed headlines but few ships have ever done as much to change the marine world as this little tub. She cost £10,000 to build compared with the £1,000 price tag of a similar sized sailing ship. Businessmen had a field day with that figure and the technical critics claimed that the iron would rust in months and that her compasses would fail.

On her first voyage the little ship confounded every sceptic. *John Bowes* travelled to London and back in five days, discharging 650 tons of coal. She had done as much work as a sailing ship could manage in two months. 'No single event ever had a greater effect on the progress of the Tyne than the building of the *John Bowes*,' observed one contemporary writer. In pursuit of that inexorable truth that there is no power on earth like an idea whose time has come, the heirs of the *John Bowes* claimed the North Sea as their own. By 1855 there were eight Tyne yards capable of building iron colliers but Palmer's remained consistently the most successful. One contemporary joke had it that they built the little ships by the mile and cut them off as required. Even though the railway was eventually built it was unable to compete with the little steamships in the movement of coal. Every year from 1851 to the turn of the century the volume of coal shipped from the North-East increased, an extraordinary record of growth.

The sailing colliers did not disappear all at once but their days were numbered. Each year the fleet declined and in 1904 the last collier brig, the *Remembrance*, sank in a south-westerly gale off Aldeburgh in Suffolk. She was bound for London, five days out from Hartlepool – the exact period of time for the *John Bowes*'s round trip half-a-century earlier.

The Royal Navy of the mid-nineteenth century was by this time far from relying on converted colliers for their fleet. However, the bulk of the senior service's offensive power rested in wooden walled ships of the line such as HMS *Victory*, built in the final years of the previous century. The Crimean War panicked a highly conservative Admiral-

HMS *Victoria* at the Armstrong-Mitchell yard, 1887.

ty into coming to grips with iron. Palmer's agreed to build a ship in only three months. The yard kept their word and HMS *Terror*, 2,000 tons displacement and carrying sixteen 300-pound guns, surrounded by the new invention of armour plate was launched on time. Unfortunately, as is so often the case with a radical weapons system ordered for a specific conflict, the war finished before HMS *Terror* had even fitted out.

Nevertheless the new sector of warship building had come to the North-East and in the late years of the nineteenth century the region acquired an astonishing dominance of the global trade. From the opium trade of Shanghai to the guano dug from South America, cargoes were being carried primarily in British-built ships. In the 1880s and 1890s this forty miles (sixty-four kilometres) of bleak English coast produced over forty per cent of the world's total shipbuilding.

Nor did the technical innovation pause. In 1886 the Armstrong Mitchell yard launched the 2,300-ton *Gluckauf* for a German owner. This little coaster was the world's first purpose-built oil tanker of a fundamental design that would be familiar to any contemporary oil company.

Another Tyneside innovation of possibly greater significance was the use of a steam turbine engine to power ships at undreamed of speeds. In 1893 the Hon Charles Algernon Parsons, an extraordinarily inventive astronomer and engineer born in Newcastle, built the *Turbinia* on the banks of the Tyne. Visitors who go to the ship now in the Newcastle museum still wonder at her lethal stiletto-like hull shape. *Turbinia* was 100 feet (thirty metres) at the waterline with a beam of only nine feet. A single 2,000hp radial-flow turbine drove three propellor shafts at the then unbelievably high speeds of 2,200rpm.

By 1897 the ebullient Parsons was achieving speeds of over thirty knots in *Turbinia*.

Turbinia at full power.

With typical aristocratic bravura he allowed his two children Rachel, eleven, and Algy, ten, aboard for trial runs sending them down to the stokehold to dry out if a chance wave should soak them. Here two stokers shovelled at almost fever-pitch once Turbinia was

Rule Britannia: HMS Monarch leaves Tyneside.

flat-out, shouting up to 'Master Algy' to slow down. Her most notorious display of speed was at Queen Victoria's Diamond Jubilee review at Spithead. Parsons wove his 'flying toothpick' through the anchored fleet to the delight of the spectators and the consternation of the admirals. The future of the steam turbine was assured.

From 1900 the developed world was hit by 'battleship fever'. It was the equivalent of the 1960s 'space race' but with more players than simply the USA and USSR. Some wealthy South American countries were spending over a quarter of their gross national product on warships. Turkey, Brazil, Argentina, Chile and Italy were among the principal customers for the North-East's warships but many smaller countries ordered destroyers and frigates by the handful.

Armstrongs on the Tyne was one of only six yards in the world capable of building the 'dreadnoughts' so desired by foreign governments. When the Japanese navy, largely built by Armstrong, routed the Russian navy in

Mauretania leaving all in her wake.

1905, the queue for bigger and better Tyne-built warships became nearly unmanageable.

Another field of growing pre-eminence was the passenger liner. The launch of the *Mauretania* on the Tyne during 1906 attracted awe around the world. Eighty thousand people watched 17,000 tons in motion down the slipway, a magnitude never achieved before. Everything about the liner was radical, from her steam turbine engines to a complete internal telephone system – at a time when these were still a novelty ashore.

Mauretania carried 3,260 passengers and crew on her nine decks, all served with electric lifts. She was the wonder of the early twentieth century and the legend became complete when on her return maiden voyage from Sandy Hook to the Irish coast she managed a record time of four days twenty-two hours nine minutes. For twenty-three years until 1929 she dominated the North Atlantic as the fastest liner afloat.

If this small coastal region became for a time the industrial and technological furnace of the world, it was not achieved without cost. 'It is unfortunate that Newcastle presents its least pleasing features to the casual observer,' wrote a contemporary visitor. 'Old tumbledown houses with blackened walls line a dingy river. The water is of a muddy brown and many factories on the bank are of unrelieved ugliness.' And, like all good things, infinite prosperity and bulging order books were not destined to last for ever.

The launch of the *Mauretania* was probably the grace-note for shipbuilding in the area. Throughout the early years of this century a gradual decline began in the face of foreign competition. It was unrealistic to suppose that other countries would not acquire the skills that Tyne, Wear and Tees had learnt first. When the slump of the 1930s came, the fall was savage. In the early summer of 1934 Palmer's Shipyard was sold to National Shipbuilders Security Ltd and closed. 'The death warrant of Palmer's was signed. The entire reason for Jarrow's existence had vanished,' wrote the Member of Parliament Ellen Wilkinson.

On 5 October 1936, the 200 Jarrow marchers set off on their famous march to London, against the advice of the Labour party and the TUC. Paradoxically the worst of the recession was now over but the town was still full of jobless shipbuilders. The march shocked the nation's conscience but ships would never again be launched at the yard that once 'built colliers by the mile'.

Since the 1930s the shipbuilding industry in the North-East has enjoyed periodic revivals but the long-term trend has always been downwards. The yards of Japan and then Korea and Taiwan became to the late twentieth century what Newcastle was to the nineteenth. Unions were blamed, governments were blamed, but in the end it was simply the wheel of history turning relentlessly on.

Until the 1830s Hull had about as much fishing as any other coastal town, neither more nor less. It was certainly not a centre for the industry. What brought the smacks to Hull around this time was the propensity of London's high society to migrate annually to Scarborough. The Brixham men had already transferred a number of their beam trawlers to Ramsgate in order to supply sole and turbot to 'the quality', so when the customers moved north it was natural to take the boats with them. Initially the fishing was from Scarborough itself but gradually the advantages of Hull came to be seen and acted upon. By the late 1840s there was a sizeable deep-water fishing fleet, largely trawling the grounds off Greenland.

In 1845 there were twenty-nine smacks of around twenty tons each. Thirty years later there were very close to 400 and the size of each individual boat had trebled. Moreover, the use of ice to freeze catches, coupled with swift cutters to bring a portion of the catch back to market, meant that fleets of smacks would stay at sea for almost the whole summer.

Fish were so plentiful over the Dogger Bank in the middle of the nineteenth century that with the railway companies charging twelve shillings per basket to move prime fish to London, lesser species such as haddock and plaice were thrown back overboard by the trawlermen. As the railways spread all over northern England, freight rates came down and the poorer people were soon able to buy 'Offal fish', as plaice and haddock became known, from the new fishmongers opening up everywhere. Grimsby and Hull supplied nearly all of this trade.

In the 1860s there were no large-scale commercial operators. Most smacks were owned by men who had begun on the deck, handling the trawl, qualified as skipper and then borrowed money to buy their own boats. There was an interesting degree of primitive credit union, in that much of the finance to buy new boats came from friends and colleagues already in an industry which seemed capable of expanding without limit.

The main artery of the fishing industry was the Hessle Road, off which most of the owners and crews lived. It was west of the River Hull and near to the fish dock, and soon became a very distinct district of the city of Hull. It was a notably prosperous part of the city in Victorian times. On Saturday nights Hessle Road was described by contemporaries as having a fairground atmosphere.

By the 1880s the industry was employing around 20,000 people and far more of those were ashore than at sea. There were blacksmiths, icemakers, yards building trawlers and at least sixty companies smoking fish.

One peculiarity of the system was the dependence upon bound apprentices for deck labour. When they refused to go to sea, as they increasingly did towards the end of the nineteenth century, the owners would seek to have them imprisoned. In Hull this was generally without success, although Grimsby magistrates were harsher and more inclined to gaol the boys – who often came from orphanages. The sight of boys of twelve and thirteen being led aboard trawlers in handcuffs and chains became, eventually, a national scandal.

The appalling conditions aboard the trawlers and the great dangers inherent in the job were the main reasons for desertion. Measured in deaths per 1,000 men employed, fishing out of Hull and Grimsby was ten times more dangerous than Victorian coal-mining, a trade that was scarcely one for faint hearts.

The change to steam trawling began in the early 1880s and ten years later the new ships formed more than half the fleets in both major North Sea ports. This was the real end of the owner/skipper. Because of the increased capital cost of the steam vessels, shore grandees with money in the bank but no knowledge of the industry became the main investors in trawling. By 1900 there were over 6,000 arrivals a year of steam trawlers in Hull's fishing dock and just a handful of smacks. It had taken barely sixty years for a way of life to rise and die.

Grimsby was always a more specialized fishing port than Hull. In the early 1500s there are records of scores of Grimsby boats heading off to the cod waters of Iceland, and the trade persisted down the years. What brought modern Grimsby into existence was the Manchester, Sheffield and Lincolnshire Railways. When bad blood arose between the Hull Docks Company and the fishermen, the former group toured the east coast trying to tempt fishermen to base themselves in Grimsby at the new Fish Dock.

In the 1950s Hull was one of the premier fishing ports in the country.

By 1887 the number of smacks reached its zenith, with nearly 900 based in the port. Twenty years later it was 500 steam trawlers and just thirty smacks struggling to stave off bankruptcy.

Financial loss was probably not as common as the grim, monotonous loss of life in the fishing industry. Few fishermen could swim and in the event of being knocked overboard by a line or a net, they would soon be dragged under by their heavy protective clothing. The ships themselves were lost almost weekly, and it was a rare day that did not see a wife and young family down at the docks anxious for news of a trawler two or three weeks overdue from a trip. Between 1879 and 1913 1,100 smacks and steam trawlers were lost from Grimsby, with very few survivors from the crews.

By the inter-war period of the twentieth century some 30,000 people in Grimsby depended on the fishing industry, most of them ashore. Despite contrary claims from Hull, in the 1920s Grimsby had achieved the status of the world's biggest and most prosperous fishing port. The Grimsby Ice Company was the largest such undertaking anywhere, and rendered obsolete the swift barques which had previously brought the ice down from Norway.

The Second World War was a resented interruption to the real work of both Hull and Grimsby. When fishing resumed in 1946 as many as 500 trawlers could be seen leaving on one tide. It was a gold-rush that lasted until the 1970s, with many fortunes being made and vessels becoming ever larger, better equipped and more sophisticated.

Iceland first began to extend her fishing limits in the 1950s and the process continued until, in 1975, it culminated in the infamous 'Cod Wars'. Being banned from these grounds was the nail in the industry's coffin, but in concert with nations such as Russia, France and Germany, the deep-water grounds of the North Atlantic had been over-fished for decades and catches were dropping annually.

Iceland's assumption of a 200-mile limit off her own coast was accepted, reluctantly, by Britain in 1977, after two years of warp-cutting and ramming between Icelandic coastguards and British trawlers – it was a miracle that no one was killed. In the same period of history Britain's accession to the EEC gave other European countries access to sixty-five per cent of the fish swimming in British waters. The two blows together have reduced fishing to a very minor role indeed in Britain's industrial landscape and left towns like Hull and Grimsby with only a fabled and barely credible past to look back on.

——— GAZETTEER ———

The North-East from Berwick to Grimsby

From Berwick south to Spurn Head – some 170 miles (274 km) – there is a total lack of natural harbours. Up until the Industrial Revolution boats had to be designed which could land safely on to exposed beaches in the worst weather. The coble (from the Celtic *ceubal*) is unique because it can be beached stern first.

BERWICK-UPON-TWEED, England's northernmost town, seems almost to turn its back to the sea and face instead the River Tweed, which has served as a natural moat in the past and now provides a port at Tweedsmouth for Berwick's small fishing fleet. The Tweed is one of Britain's premier salmon rivers and during the netting season (15 Feb – 14 Sept) Berwick's salmon fishermen may be seen dropping their nets in an arc from their boats. The sea swirls around Holy Island or Lindisfarne, making it an island at high tide. The first record of a raid in England by Vikings was in 793 when they looted the Lindisfarne monastery on Holy Island.

BAMBURGH was the birthplace of Grace Darling, (see inset).

GRACE DARLING MUSEUM
Radcliffe Road, Bamburgh.
The exhibition centres on the coble used in the rescue, It is 23 ft (7 m) long and was built at Berwick-upon-Tweed in 1828. It is the oldest surviving coble and has one important difference from those built in the nineteenth century in that the top plank of the side is straight up, like traditional boats, not as in the case of a true coble, turned in to form a curved side.

LONGSTONE LIGHTHOUSE is on Longstone, one of the principal islands in the Farnes. A lonely and isolated spot lying off the north Northumberland coast, it is famous for its Grace Darling connection.

CRASTER is famous for its kippers, which are smoked in sheds above the little harbour. Craster is a quiet unspoilt fishing village. The exceptionally hard whinstone used to be quarried behind the village, loaded on to barges and taken to London to be used for kerbstones.

BOULMER has a community virtually dependent on boats fishing off an open beach, and is one of the few remaining places where this is so. All the coble men still live in the village. Boulmer's fishing community has survived triumphant. In the early 20s there were 15 cobles, while in 1981, there were 8, but motor cobles are much larger than the old sailing ones. In the Fishing Boat Inn at Boulmer there is a romantic Victorian painting showing the women dragging the lifeboat into the water. This was a true scene – women helped with hard work in these fishing communities so that the men would go to sea fresh. Lifeboats needed hours of heavy rowing to reach the rescue and the men therefore needed all their strength for this and a safe return.

At **ALNMOUTH**, the sheltered estuary of the River Aln is now a yachting haven, although before the river changed its course in 1806, it was an important port.

AMBLE harbour at one time was bustling with

ships loading coal from local mines, but Amble has now adjusted to a quieter routine as a fishing and manufacturing town.

BLYTH'S main harbour is busy with ships loading coal and unloading timber. In the south harbour are fishing and sailing boats, cruisers and the headquarters of the Royal Northumberland Yacht Club, housed in a redundant wooden lightship. An early coal harbour of 1660 can be seen at Seaton Sluice where a sluice gate held the river water back at low tide and then horse-drawn ploughs were used to disturb the silt bed of the harbour. The water was then released from the sluice to wash the silt away.

Off **WHITLEY BAY** is the high tide island of St Mary's or Bates Island where there is a lighthouse, the first 'light' was a lamp kept burning in the sanctuary of a chapel.

On the hill above Prior's Haven in **TYN-MOUTH** is the timber watch house of Tynmouth

Age of the clipper, Tyne dock 1909.

Volunteer Life Brigade set up in 1864. The watch house contains a little museum with mementoes of wrecks and rescues off the coast near by. Beyond the watch house, a statue of Admiral Collingwood, Nelson's contemporary, stands on a column facing the river.

SOUTH SHIELD'S MUSEUM AND ART GALLERY
Ocean Road, South Shields.
Houses the town's maritime and navy associations and the lifeboat *Tyne* built in 1833. It is one of the oldest lifeboats in existence having saved 1,024 lives. At the foot of the cliffs, is a pub called The Grotto built into the caves in 1782 by a miner who lived in the caves with his family.
Open daily.

NEWCASTLE

MUSEUM OF SCIENCE AND ENGINEERING
Blandford House, West Blandford Street.
Permanent maritime gallery showing development and diversity of steam merchant ship 1880-1930. 150 builders' models of Tyneside ships. Two north-coast fishing vessels *Blossom* and

Peggy can be seen. Also the steam launch *Turbinia* is housed near the museum and can be viewed by written appointment to the above.
Open Tues to Fri.

LAING ART GALLERY
Highham Place, Newcastle.
Many fine marine paintings.

SUNDERLAND: There has been a port at the mouth of the Wear for 1,000 years. Sunderland remains a major shipbuilding centre. The public are not allowed in the shipyards but the parapet of the Wearmouth Bridge gives a good view of ships being fitted out on the Wear riverside.

GRINDON MUSEUM
Grindon Lane.
Displays relating to history of town's merchant navy connections which include ship models and marine paintings.

MUSEUM AND ART GALLERY
Borough Road.
Marine paintings, large collection of builders' models of sail, steam and motor vessels constructed on Wearside, particularly 19 Doxford Yard turret steamers.

HARTLEPOOL: The old town of Hartlepool retains glimpses of its interesting past. Part of the town wall has an archway leading to a beach through which Crusader knights passed on their way to the Holy Land. In the docks complex a fish market is held early every morning.

MARITIME MUSEUM
Northgate.
Maritime history of the town depicting its growth from a small fishing village to its present status as a major port. Includes fishing, shipbuilding, marine engineering, etc. Displays of simulated fisherman's cottage; ship's bridge and an early gas-lit lighthouse lantern, net store; boat-builder and models of pointed stern cobles.
Open Mon – Sat.

MIDDLESBROUGH: Captain James Cook, the greatest explorer of his age, was born in the village of Marton, south of Middlesbrough in 1728.

CAPTAIN COOK BIRTHPLACE MUSEUM
Stewart Park, Marton, Middlesbrough.
This illustrates Captain Cook's early life and voyages of exploration. Displays relate to Cook's personality, natural history and ethnography of the many countries he visited. At Middles-

brough's indoor shopping area there is a large-scale replica of HMS *Endeavour*.
Open daily.

On the seafront at **REDCAR** is the *Zetland*, the oldest lifeboat in the world which was built in 1800 and saved 500 lives before being taken out of service in 1887.

ZETLAND MUSEUM
5 King Street, Redcar.
Has a number of displays relating to lifesaving and local fishing industry.

MARSKE-BY-THE-SEA is an attractive fishing village which has the grave of Captain Cook's father who, buried in 1779, was unaware that his son had died 6 weeks earlier.

The cliffs along this stretch are breached by valleys that shelter fishing villages and relics of Britain's first chemical industry – the mining and purification of alum that took place along the north Yorkshire coast between 1600 and 1870.

At **BOULBY** the cliffs stand 666 ft (200 m) above the sea, making them the highest cliffs on England's east coast.

STAITHES with its steep sides, has a harbour which has remained much as James Cook would have known it in 1744. It is smaller than in his day but a fleet of fishing cobles still works from the port. Boat-building and sailmaking once thrived alongside fishing and the loading of iron ore. In 1867 there were 120 cobles working from Staithes. However, its prominence as a fishing centre was reduced by steam trawlers and drifters working in deep-water harbours. The harbour at nearby **PORT MULGRAVE** is dilapidated and it seems strange that anyone should build one in such an inaccessible place. However, it was once used to ship iron ore (conveyed via a tunnel emerging at the foot of the cliff) to Jarrow.

RUNSWICK BAY: Jet was formerly mined here. Like most villages on this coastline Runswick has a history going back to the Norse invasions. Local families can still trace their Viking descent. Kettle Ness, the headland at the east end of the bay, has the remains of a Roman lighthouse.

WHITBY: High above Whitby harbour, on the East Cliff stands the church of St Mary, designed inside by eighteenth-century shipbuilders to re-

GRACE DARLING – HEROINE OF HARKER'S ROCK

Had Grace Darling lived in the late twentieth century she would have become an international celebrity; the Hollywood movie rights to her tale of courage and nobility auctioned for millions. Instead, this young woman born at Bamburgh on the Northumberland coast, has stayed 'a name imperishable in the annals of the sea'.

Grace was twenty-three and living with her family when the *Forfarshire*, a 300-ton paddle-steamer was wrecked on her doorstep. William Darling, the heroine's father, was keeper of the Longstone lighthouse, an isolated beacon on the Farne Islands ten miles (sixteen kilometres) east of Bamburgh. Like most early steamships *Forfarshire* was plagued with breakdowns. Her boilers failed on a voyage from Hull to Dundee and she drifted helpless in a northerly gale. Just before dawn on the morning of 7 September she hit Harker's Rock, a reef just visible from the lighthouse despite the blinding windborne-spray.

With her father Grace launched the twenty-one-foot (six-metre) coble (the traditional double-ended Northumbrian beach craft) and rowed through mountainous seas to the wreck. They found four men and women clinging to floating debris and hauled them aboard. After an exhausting haul back to the Longstone, Grace pushed off again with two of the survivors and went back to the wreck. Another four survivors were pulled aboard the coble and returned to safety.

Forty-three passengers and crew died that night. But for the unflinching bravery of Miss Darling there would probably have been more. One consequence of that bitter night's work was an outcry which led to the regular Board of Trade inspection of all passenger-carrying steamships. Another was the award to William and Grace of the Royal Humane Society gold medal.

The Victorian equivalent of the Fleet Street tabloid press descended on the village of Bamburgh. Father and daughter were endlessly interviewed and – this was the age before photography – in one twelve-day period they sat for seven portraits. The Adelphi theatre in London offered the young heroine ten pounds per week, possibly the equivalent of a thousand pounds nowadays, to row across the stage each night in the boat used for the rescue.

None of this appealed to the shy, if determined, Northumbrian lass and she stayed on at the

semble the 'tween decks of a wooden sailing ship!

Whitby still remains a centre of coble building, the skills of wooden-boat construction have been kept alive by the Whitby Bay Building Co and the men who trained in this yard and started their own enterprises, such as William Clarkson, Gordon Clarkson and JN Lowther.

Captain Cook started his nautical career aboard Whitby's colliers in 1746. On West Cliff top stands the monument to Cook, a huge statue of him surveying the harbour which was the birthplace of three ships, *Endeavour*, *Resolution* and *Adventure*, that carried him round the world on his three great voyages of exploration. Just below the Cook monument is an arch made from the jawbone of a whale, a reminder of Whitby's history as a whaling port.

Whitby's most famous whaling captain was William Scoresby, the inventor of the 'crows nest' who accounted for 533 whales, of a total 2,761 landed at Whitby.

CAPTAIN COOK MEMORIAL MUSEUM
Grape Lane.

Housed in Cook's home, this museum is full of authentic manuscripts, furniture, watercolours and drawings.
Open 1 May – 31 Oct, (Tues to Sat).

WHITBY MUSEUM OF WHITBY LITERARY AND PHILOSOPHICAL SOCIETY
Pannett Park.
Local history, shipping gallery, Captain Cook mementoes. 150 ship models from earliest times to steam.
Open daily all year.

LIFEBOAT MUSEUM
Scotch Head, Pier Road.
Contains last rowing lifeboat in the country.
Open daily, May – Sept.

ROBIN HOOD'S BAY: Fishing and smuggling were once the main pursuits of this picturesque resort on the north-east coast. Local legend has it that Robin Hood came to Whitby to help the abbot to repel Danish invaders.

Tiny fishermen's cottages line the steep twisting street leading to the shore. A network of tunnels

lighthouse with her father. However, the experiences of that tumultuous night had taken their toll on her frail body and four years later Grace Darling died of consumption.

The Museum in Bamburgh contains many evocative items from her distinguished and tragically short life. Pride of place goes to the coble used in the rescue. It continued in everyday use until 1873 and was then preserved. Less dramatic but equally affecting is Grace Darling's copy book from her schooldays in the village school. On one page she has copied out the phrase 'Friends in adversity are not often found'.

The heroic Darlings in the rescue of Harker's Rock.

with others branching from it, through which King's Beck discharges into the sea, was used by smugglers – it was said that a smuggled bale of silk could pass from one end of the village to the other without appearing above the ground. Some of the old houses have interconnecting doors disguised as cupboards through which smugglers could escape from the revenue men.

This coast is lined with soft clay cliffs which crumble with every storm. The loss of land has been going on steadily for centuries and it is believed that since medieval times up to 30 villages have gone into the sea and the coast has moved inland 3 miles (5 km). For example at Hornsea and Withernsea, very few houses are older than nineteenth century as the original towns of these names are under the sea.

SCARBOROUGH: The Romans built a signal station on the headland here but it was settled by Vikings. The discovery of springs in 1620 and its subsequent development as a spa gives Scarbor-

Scarborough fishermen just before the First World War.

ough the distinction of being the first seaside resort in Britain.

ROTUNDA MUSEUM
Vernon Road.
Local history and maritime exhibits.
Open Tue – Sun.

LIGHTHOUSE AND FISHERIES MUSEUM
Vincent Pier.
Various specimens and exhibits. A climb to the lighthouse top.
Open daily, May – Sept.

FILEY MUSEUM
8-10 Queen Street.
Seven rooms of exhibits housed in old cottages, some of which relate to seashore and fishing and the lifeboat service in Filey.
Open daily (except Sat), May – Sept.

FLAMBOROUGH HEAD juts out into the North Sea dominating the coast. South of it the land slopes down to the lowlands of Holderness. Riddled with caves and crowned by a lighthouse that stands 214 ft (65 m) above the sea, it has

defied winds and weather since 1806 and has a present beam of 29 miles (47 km). It is considered to be one of the most magnificent of British lighthouses. It is open to the public in the afternoon. About 3,000 years ago the headland was fortified by the building of a huge earthern rampart still visible west of Flamborough village. Although it is known as Dane's Dyke the Viking settlers did not land until the ninth century.

BRIDLINGTON is a busy tidal harbour and home of the Royal York Yacht Club. There has been a harbour here for 900 years and its history can be found on the north side of the harbour where a Maritime Museum displays the harbour's history as well as sea-fishing methods and the lifeboat *Oakley* on display, which is open daily in summer.

The *Three Brothers* is the last of the sailing cobles at Bridlington, built in 1912, it can be hired for sailing within the bay.

Bridlington's famous pleasure steamer the *Yorkshire Belle* sails daily from the North Pier. A two-hour cruise around Flamborough Head affords a good view of the cliffs but also views of the local inshore fishing fleet in action. Now here was wrecked the *Bonhomme Richard*, the famous

Pleasure trips at Bridlington.

ship commanded by John Paul Jones, the American privateer who became a folk hero.

SPURN HEAD is a 3½-mile (5.6-km) curving peninsula into the Humber estuary that has built up over the centuries. Because the shipping lanes into the Humber are narrow and difficult, all ships entering and leaving the estuary are accompanied by pilots who speed out from the jetty on Spurn Head. During the First World War soldiers manned a gun on its tip – a little railway connected them to civilization 3½ miles away – on the railway ran a truck propelled by a sail. Moored off the jetty is the Humber lifeboat, one of only three in the country manned by a full-time crew.

The lighthouse on Spurn Head was the second recorded lighthouse in Britain. It was first built in 1428 by a hermit who was granted permission by Henry VI to do so and thus 'have a compassion and pitee on the Xtian people that ofte tymes there perished'. Later beacon and hermitage were engulfed by the sea. Several more were built over the years with varying success until J Smeaton (builder of one of the Eddystone lighthouses) built 2 towers – one inevitably washed down and is now lying with many others beneath the sea.

KINGSTON-UPON-HULL: The River Hull, where the port's prosperity began, is still a busy harbour for river barges and small coasters. At the river's mouth a huge tidal surge barrier has been built with concrete towers supporting a steel gate like a guillotine which can be dropped to prevent the city from being flooded.

HULL is also the home of the Humber Keel and Sloop Preservation Society which renovates and restores local boats. The *Amy Howson* (sloop) and the keel *Comrade* are both restored and sailing. Contact: 135 Waterside Road, Barton-on-Humberside.

On the Boulevard stands a statue of George Smith, skipper of the trawler *Crane* which was involved in a bizarre incident in 1904 known as the 'Russian Outrage'. Russia was at war with Japan and on 22 Oct the Russian fleet opened fire on Hull trawlers fishing on the Dogger Bank mistaking them for Japanese torpedo boats. George Smith was killed and his trawler sunk.

GOOLE MUSEUM AND ART GALLERY (a few miles inland from Hull)
Goole Library, Market Square, Carlisle Street (0405) 2187.
Collections illustrating the early history of the area and the formation and development of Goole as a port and its connecting waterways. Maritime paintings.
Open Mon – Sat.

The former Dock's Authority office is now a maritime museum and there is a Maritime Heritage Trail – a walking tour round all the relevant sights in Hull.

TOWN DOCK'S MUSEUM
Queen Victoria Square.
Displays cover whales and whaling; fishing and trawling; Hull and the Humber; ships and shipping and extensive collections of scrimshaw – the carvings done by nineteenth-century seamen on whales' teeth or walrus tusks.
Open all week.

TRANSPORT AND ARCHEOLOGY MUSEUM
36 High Street, Kingston-upon-Hull.
Navigation of the Humber, ships, barges and keels.

WILBERFORCE HOUSE AND GEORGIAN HOUSES AND MUSEUM
23-25 High Street.
The birthplace of William Wilberforce in 1759, this is a museum to his memory, with many contemporary grim relics of the slave trade, telling the history of slavery and its abolition. There is a monument to Wilberforce in Queen's Gardens, next to the museum.
Open daily.

GRIMSBY: Fish have been vital to Grimsby since a Danish fisherman named Grim landed there 1,000 years ago and began selling fish to locals. Around the perimeter of the dock is the long covered arcade of the fish market, but the contraction in the fishing industry has hit Grimsby and the fleet's decline has left empty moorings along the quayside.

Grimsby remains an important commercial dock trading in Danish dairy produce. The Victorian buildings of 4 docks are presided over by a 309-ft (94-m) folly called Dock Tower: it is modelled on the Palazzo Publico in Sienna.

WELHOLME GALLERIES
Welholme Road.
Model ships, marine paintings, among other costume and folk items. Comprehensive collection of builders' models of trawlers covering period 1886-1935; passenger liners, 19 ft (6 m) builder's model of P & O liner *Narkunda*. Documents, books and a wide variety of artefacts relating to the fishing industry and navigation.
Open Tues – Sat.

East Anglia

**Beach-launched crab boats at Cromer,
north Norfolk**

EAST ANGLIA

EAST ANGLIA'S maritime history has been governed more than most parts of Britain's coast by the ebb and flow of larger historical forces. In certain periods when this country's interests, commercial or military, have focussed on Continental Europe, then the proximity of England's eastern bulge to Germany and the Low Countries has given the region huge importance and consequent wealth. During these cyclical peaks, trade, shipping, passenger traffic and naval activity have projected East Anglia to national prominence and wealth. When the focus has shifted away, to the exploration of North America or the later development of the British Empire, then ports and industries on the south and west coasts of the British Isles have flourished and the flat grey coasts of the southern North Sea have slept awhile. Now, as 1992 and the prospect of an integrated Europe beckons, East Anglia heads towards the peak of yet another cycle of maritime importance.

As if in an unwitting reflection of these cyclical tides of fortune, so too the coastline of East Anglia has come and gone. Any low-lying shore composed entirely of sedimentary rocks and mud is prone to significant changes as the centuries pass. Sometimes the time-scale is much shorter; tens of years rather than hundreds. In Norfolk there are villages with a Georgian quayside now over a mile inland from the sea. Less than 100 miles away in Suffolk, cliff-top churches have toppled and crumbled beneath the waves within living memory. At Kessingland, just south of Lowestoft, a shipwrecked family were landed on the beach by lifeboat. As they waited for further assistance from the locals the ever-crumbling cliff staged a mini-avalanche and the mariners were buried and killed.

Another factor which will not be reversed is the virtual disappearance of the shallow-water fishing industry. For nearly 400 years the Dogger Bank and its rich neighbours were a happy hunting ground for the towns-folk of Yarmouth and Lowestoft. The produce was known around the world. Such was the scale of the industry that its elimination seemed unthinkable. Yet the Yarmouth bloater and the salt herrings of Lowestoft are now items in history books, not entries on any contemporary shopping list.

Archaeological studies rather than written records have revealed that in pre-Roman times there were four regular and well-travelled sea-routes linking the British Isles with the mainland of Continental Europe. Three of these either crossed the Channel or followed the Atlantic coast down to Spain, Portugal and, ultimately, the Mediterranean. The fourth was from East Anglia to Denmark and the Low Countries; a migration route that was to determine much in the nation's future.

In the second millennium before Christ it was the highway into the British Isles for the Beaker people. Twenty-five centuries later the Anglo-Saxons followed the seaway blazed by the intrepid cave dwellers. Between those groups came possibly the most significant invaders of all: the Romans. Their beach-head was at Colchester, in the southern-most portion of Essex. The oldest recorded town in these isles became a Roman fortress in AD 43 and grew from there. Troopships and supply galleys could come up the River Colne to a dock at The Hythe, still in commercial operation.

The formerly barbarous town of Camulodunum, where British chieftains had ruled for generations, became the chief port and administrative centre of Roman Britain – civilized Colchester, where to this day the main streets follow the Roman plan. The emperor Claudius took the surrender from no fewer than eleven British kings here. The vast Norman castle stands on the site of a temple dedicated to Claudius and his conquering fleet.

When Boudicca sacked the city in AD 61 little survived of Roman civilization bar the massive city walls. An exception is the oyster industry in the lower reaches of the River Colne and the creeks around Mersea Island. Claudius began the industry and it thrives 2,000 years later. In September the coming of the oyster season is heralded by the mayor who sails downstream to dredge the first molluscs and declare the beds open. In a curious ceremony first recorded in the reign of Charles II but possibly dating back to the Middle Ages, the mayor passes his voyage drinking gin to toast the Queen's health while nibbling on gingerbread.

The estuaries of the Blackwater and Colne are still the best places to catch sight of the traditional Colchester oyster smacks. These gaff-rigged sloops needed a powerful sail plan if they were to haul the dredges, which were full of oysters and thick black mud, along the sea-bed. A fleet of similar working oyster boats still survives at Falmouth. In Essex some are still working but many more have been turned into private yachts and can be spotted at the marinas and pile moorings which surround Mersea.

Yachting is not the recreation, indeed industry, in eastern Britain that it is on the south and west coasts. The shoal waters, shifting sandbanks and sheer unpredictable nastiness of the North Sea make it the preserve of the commercial mariner and the dedicated small-boat enthusiast. However, there is a corner of sporting pleasure focussed around Burnham-on-Crouch. In the early years of the century the yacht races of Burnham Week used to rival, in both entries and calibre, its now more famous sister event at Cowes. Today there is no comparison in size, but the chummy intimacy of Burnham village, where the river can be glimpsed

almost all the way down the High Street and spar-makers jostle against shoe shops, is a welcome reminder of the days before competitive sailing meant titanium rigging and aerospace-inspired technology.

In fact, the whole saga of yachting – that is sailing boats for pleasure rather than profit – began in East Anglia. At Harwich in the mid-seventeenth century Charles II took one of the first recorded sailing trips entirely for the fun of it. A memento from that time is preserved in the shape of a treadmill crane on the Green to the south of the harbour. The rise and decline of Harwich is the story of the region in miniature. As the finest natural harbour on the east coast, it possessed a natural strategic importance in the years before the Royal Navy commenced blue-water operations. In 1340 it was the assembly point for Edward III's fleet which defeated the French at Sluys, the first major battle of the Hundred Years War. Henry VIII based his navy largely in Harwich and his daughter Elizabeth described it thus: 'Pretty little town and wants nothing.'

The vast expanses of sheltered deep water inside Orwell Haven made it of great naval importance from Elizabethan times to the end of the Napoleonic wars, the greatest developments coinciding with the time when Holland was Britain's chief maritime rival – if not actual enemy. Raleigh, Drake, Frobisher and Nelson were all based at times with the town, the latter lodging at the Three Cups Inn which is still proud of the fact.

People are often surprised that Britain's best-known and most charismatic naval hero, Lord Nelson, should have come from rural East Anglia (Burnham Thorpe, 100 miles north of Harwich near the Norfolk coast) rather than the hinterlands of Plymouth or Portsmouth with their traditions of war at sea. But once one understands the former importance of Harwich, Nelson's career begins to make more sense. For many years all boy sailors entering the Royal Navy were trained at a vast shore establishment, HMS *Ganges*, across the river from the town.

Parson House, pastoral birthplace of Admiral Nelson.

Military glory is over now but the 300-year-old tradition of the mail link to Holland and Germany persists. Since the mid-1600s Harwich men have run a packet service to the Low Countries. The mail struggled through in the Dutch Wars and still flowed when the French began to fight. Designed for speed and built without guns the mail-boats were supposed to outrun their opponents. Captains were briefed that they should 'Run when you can, fight when you must and when you can fight no longer destroy the mail before you strike the colours.' Consequently the mail was stowed in a lead-weighted bag and kept near a porthole. If defeat looked imminent a sailor tossed it over the ship's side.

The ferry services that still sail frequently from Harwich to the ports at the mouth of the Rhine are the direct inheritors of this tradition. The 100-mile (160-kilometre) run to the Hook of Holland can now be managed in five hours but the voyage still retains infinitely more glamour and texture than the 'bus-ride'

Rail link to Holland via the Harwich-Hook ferry.

Thames barge with hay off Greenwich, 1830s.

trip between Dover and the French channel ports.

Further up the Orwell lies the town of Ipswich. As Harwich lies at the bottom of its cycle of decline, so the more established county town of Suffolk passed through its dog-days during the nineteenth century and is once more a booming port and maritime centre. Ipswich was a significant trading harbour in Roman times and by the arrival of the Anglo-Saxon era was this country's busiest port. Exporting wool and other agricultural products from the rich farmland surrounding the city made Ipswich wealthy.

Shipbuilding inevitably sprang up here in the days of wooden ships, before the time when proximity to iron and coal was essential to the industry. At one time yards extended six miles (9.6 kilometres) downstream from the town wharfs to the riverside beauty spot of Pin Mill.

Many of the once prosaic but now coveted Thames sailing barges were built in this area.

The broad, shallow-draft hulls were ideal for the shallow waters of the coast and the Thames estuary. With the lee-boards in place of a conventional keel, they owe much more to the Dutch commercial craft than to the English tradition. Their regular trade was bricks, hay and foodstuffs down to London – usually returning with horse manure to fertilize the East Anglian farmlands.

Pin Mill stages a Barge Match each July when dozens of the well-preserved 'old gaffers' can be seen racing on the River Orwell. In their working lives the crew would most likely be one seamen and a boy but their popularity today is such that a much larger body of voluntary seamen is required. Throughout the rivers and estuaries of southern East Anglia the preserved barges can be seen sailing in the summer months. There is even a Spritsail Barge Research Society, based in Ipswich.

Lowestoft had a military shipbuilding tradition as well as the famous herring fishery. Throughout the twentieth century frigates and fast naval craft were built at the yards of what is now Brooke International. That work dwindled to a halt as the Royal Navy itself shrank and the yard now has a growing reputation as a centre for the construction of luxury motor yachts. Repairing and re-fitting those already afloat is another part of the work and some of the most luxurious and extravagant craft afloat, the toys of Arab princes and American tycoons, can be glimpsed occasionally on the quay beside Brooke.

The tradition of safe seamanship in small boats was handed on from the Lowestoft fishermen to the Royal Naval Patrol Service during the Second World War. Up to 60,000 officers and men manned the tugs, trawlers and drifters of what was the navy's equivalent of Dad's Army. The RNPS and its remarkable story is remembered in a small museum (see Gazetteer) but those who love small military craft may wish to head fifty miles (eighty kilometres) inland to the Imperial War Museum outstation at Duxford, Cambridgeshire.

During the naval stalemate of 1915 three young lieutenants stationed in Harwich devised the concept of fast hit-and-run torpedo boats which could dart into the Heligoland Bight and attack the German 'battlewagons'. Light cruisers would carry them to within sixty miles (100 kilometres) of the target and then the motor torpedo-boat (MTB) would streak off at thirty knots to attack the target. It was revolutionary in terms of naval architecture but Thorneycrofts adapted the hull from a racing hydroplane named *Miranda* and achieved the brief.

Over 100 of these boats, the direct forerunners of the MTB of the Second World War and the patrol boats used by Iranian forces to harass tankers in the Gulf War, were built. One survives on display at Duxford. CMB104 is the forty-foot (twelve-metre) craft in which Lt Augustus Agar won the Victoria Cross in 1919 when he sank a Russian cruiser sheltering in Kronstadt.

Great Yarmouth shared in Lowestoft's fishing prosperity and then in its decline.

Yarmouth's annual autumn event, the Free Herring Fair, was one of medieval Europe's great celebrations, known to seafarers the length and breadth of the North Sea and the Baltic. But by 1963 the last Yarmouth drifter was sold. By one of those strokes of fortune which guide the lucky, this coincided with the earliest exploration of what is now known as the North Sea oil and gas fields. Yarmouth became the chosen base for the tugs, tenders and rigs of the southern North Sea and its maritime tradition was assured, albeit in a new direction.

At the East Anglian Maritime Museum in Yarmouth one finds what is probably the most comprehensive display in Britain on rescue from shipwreck. The museum is housed in the former Home & Refuge for the Shipwrecked, the end product of a vigorous campaign fought by Captain George Manby, Barrack Master in Yarmouth during the early nineteenth century. Manby was an odd kind of philanthropist. He fought duels and managed to get himself shot in the head. He could not keep a wife and plagued the powerful at Court for a knighthood. But he did invent the breeches-buoy system of rescue.

The museum has a model of the mortar line-throwing system that Manby devised to make contact with foundering or beached ships to bring off their crews. His mortar was first used in earnest in 1808 at the wreck of the brig *Elizabeth*. In recent years the coastguard service has decided that the advent of helicopters and rugged inshore lifeboats has rendered the rescue by rocket, line and breeches-buoy obsolete, but the Yarmouth museum is a fascinating tribute to a system that saved many lives in what seemed like impossible circumstances.

It is no accident that some of the earliest recorded mentions of lifeboat rescues come from the east coast. In a region bereft of good natural harbours, boats for the early inshore fishermen had to be beach-launched and capable of making safe progress through heavy surf. It made them natural craft to go out into storm and tempest, though it may be prudent not to enquire too closely whether a desire for booty or humanitarian motives drove the crews.

In north Norfolk the centuries-old tradition of using boats based on a bare shingle beach for crab and lobster fishing continues to this day. In 1724 that indefatigable traveller of shorelines and harbours, Daniel Defoe, wrote of Cromer: 'I know nothing it is famous for – besides being the terror of sailors – except good lobsters which are taken off the coast in great numbers and carried to Norwich, and in such numbers as to be carried to London too.'

The clinker-built double-ended crab boats of Sheringham and Cromer bear a striking resemblance to both the Viking ships and the Saxon vessel found preserved at Sutton Hoo, just off the River Deben in mid-Suffolk. What our ancestors found seaworthy, so too do their twentieth-century descendants.

Along this long flat coast nothing indicates the fickleness of the sea more than the changes to long-established villages, as the ocean retreats and advances through the centuries. Cley-next-the-Sea is now anything but. Although a busy fishing port in the Middle Ages it is now half-a-mile inland from the marshy shoreline. Cromer, by contrast, stood some way inland during the Middle Ages, but as the sea gradually swallowed its adjacent harbour of Shipden, so Cromer found itself a port.

At Blythburgh, inland from Southwold on the Suffolk coast, the cathedral-like scale of the village church gives another clue to the tricks of the North Sea. In the fifteenth century, when the church was built, the River Blyth took deep-water ships and the big bustling town was among the most significant wool-exporting towns on the east coast. Then the river silted and the sea receded leaving a virtual ghost-town. Southwold itself repays attention. Although never an important port

Peaceful Southwold as a 1920's seaside resort.

The Battle of Sole Bay, with HMS *Royal James* on fire.

this delightful Georgian town is the piece of England nearest Holland.

In the third Dutch War the Battle of Sole Bay in 1672 was decisive. The bay, an indentation long since removed by the waves, was the anchorage of the Anglo-French fleet. Their headquarters was in Sutherland House, still standing in the High Street, where the Duke of York made his battle plans. However shrewd their lordship's strategies, it all came to naught on the morning of the battle. The Allied fleet was still at anchor and many of the sailors still in their hammocks when the Dutch fleet came in, blazing broadsides through the helpless British ships. Still unexplained is the action of many of the French men-of-war who sneaked off to the south during the night, leaving their English allies to take the brunt of the one-sided fighting.

From the Seaman's Reading Room on Southwold's grassy seafront it is an easier trick than one might imagine to cast a mental picture of the battle out on to the empty pewter sea beyond the shingle beach. The Reading Room itself is a delightful jumble of models, old books and maps, plus a few armchairs. It conveys the feeling of an old seaman's attic where memories and keepsakes are stored higgledy-piggledy.

Although the Norfolk Broads are strictly speaking inland waterways, they do come down to the sea at Yarmouth. In the era preceding rail transport these vast flooded peat diggings were the primary route for moving Norfolk's grain and other produce down to the quays of Yarmouth and thence the export market. This county produced a rich crop of purely local craft, of which the wherry is the best-known example. They were around sixty feet (eighteen metres) long, with a draught of around four feet (1.2 metres) and a capacity of forty tons. Unlike the Thames sailing barges, with their mizzen rig, the wherries had a single mast. It was

Wherry moving cargo through the Norfolk broads.

delicately counter-balanced with over a ton of lead so that the owner could lower it single-handedly to pass under bridges. Only one example, the *Albion*, survives, preserved by a group of enthusiasts in Norwich.

At the margin of East Anglia, easing away into the low grey horizon of Lincolnshire, lies The Wash. It seems to belong to a different age. Neither the stoical boom and bust of the East Anglian coastal cycle nor the gritty industrialism of the shores to the north of it, appear to relate to The Wash. Boston and King's Lynn, its chief ports in medieval times, bear the aura of retired dowagers looking back to more sparkling times and entirely divorced from the here-and-now. In 1347 King's Lynn was prosperous enough to contribute nineteen ships to the English fleet at a time when London could manage only twenty-four. Such is the town's remoteness from modern road and rail routes that much of its atmosphere and richness of the maritime past has survived – which is true of East Anglia generally.

———— GAZETTEER ————

EAST ANGLIA FROM BOSTON TO BURNHAM-ON-CROUCH

BOSTON was one of Britain's most important ports in the fourteenth century. The old town clusters on the east bank of the River Witham by the old docks. Many houses have flood steps, a reminder of the fenland floods of the fifteenth century to seventeenth century. Climb the 272-ft (83-m) 'stump' – the tower of St Botolph's fitted with a navigation light for mariners in The Wash. In 1607, the earliest Pilgrim Fathers set sail from Scotia Creek a short way downstream from the town. They were arrested and brought back in open boats. Pilgrims' Pillar, a memorial to the Pilgrims erected in 1957, can be seen on the bank of the Haven. In 1630 a second group successfully set sail from here and founded the city of Boston, Massachusetts.

In the eighteenth century trade revived with the building of the Grand Sluice and the deepening of the river. In 1882 the docks were built and a straight channel cut to The Wash. Boston is now a modern port trading in timbers, fertilizers, fruits and potatoes. It is a shell-fishing centre, with fishing smacks unloading on to quays in the middle of the town.

GUILDHALL MUSEUM
South Street. Tel: (0205) 65954.
The museum houses the original prison cells in which the early Pilgrim Fathers were imprisoned after their abortive attempt to leave England searching for religious freedom. The Maritime Room contains an interesting display of models and customs artefacts.
Open all year.

KING'S LYNN sits at the foot of The Wash, built on the eastern bank of the Great Ouse; it was already a harbour at the time of the Domesday Book (when it was known as Lena or Lun). In 1204 King John granted it a charter and was entertained here before his last journey to Newark Castle where he died. His baggage train was caught by an October high tide and was lost crossing The Wash. People still look for the treasure. Medieval streets run down to the quays. Merchants' houses with their private warehouses still present an aspect of considerable wealth, and two guildhalls still function.

CUSTOM HOUSE
Purfleet Place.
A graceful classical building stands overlooking the River Ouse. Designed in 1683 by Henry Bell, twice Mayor of Lynn.

THE LYNN MUSEUM
Old Market Street. Tel: (0553) 775001.
Local maritime history. Several relics from the eighteenth-century whaling industry at King's Lynn are preserved here. There are harpoons, some fine scrimshaw, and a picture of the old Blubber House. Four whalers were known to have been based in the town.
Open all year.

HUNSTANTON is the only west-facing resort in East Anglia (with unique red and white striped cliffs of alternate chalk and carr stone layers). Local landowners were the Le Strange family who, as hereditary Lord High Admirals of The Wash, could claim possession over anything on the beach (or in the sea as far as a man could ride his horse into it at low tide and then throw his spear). Half a mile to the north is Old Hunstanton, a village with red-roofed cottages of fishing days. A hut beside the track, running from the cliff-top, Lighthouse Lane, houses the inshore rescue boat. The public are admitted on request to see the collection of historic photographs and lifeboat relics.

BURNHAM THORPE, 2 miles (3.2 km) inland, is the birthplace of Horatio Nelson in 1758. All Saints Church houses the font where he was christened, a crucifix made of wood from the *Victory* and a bust of Nelson in the chancel. Nelson Hall has his medicine chest, silver goblets and mementoes of his career. The Lord Nelson public house is full of Nelson prints and memorabilia. Legend has it that Nelson was born in the huge flint barn next to the pub.

BURNHAM OVERY STAITHE is a delightful little sailing village and nearest harbour to Nelson's birthplace. At low tide the sea goes far out, revealing tracks on the marshes. One of them, 'The Cockle Path' has been restored and leads to Scolt Head Island National Nature Reserve.

A plaque on a house by the harbour reads 'Richard Woodget, master of the *Cutty Sark* lived here 1899-1926'.

WELLS-NEXT-THE-SEA still maintains its status as a fishing port supplying most of the whelks eaten in Britain. Quayside stalls sell local cockles, dressed crabs and samphire. The prized cockles known as 'Stewkey blues' are gathered from nearby Stiffkey.

BLAKENEY is typical of the villages along this coast, where the sea is separated from dry land by a wide expanse of sand, and the quay flanked by miles of salt marshes. It has a superb natural harbour, now crowded with yachts. The church has a beacon tower which still shines every night as a landmark for ships at sea.

CLEY-NEXT-THE-SEA is now more than a mile away from the sea but was once a busy fishing port and important wool port. The eighteenth-century custom house is evidence of a once flourishing wool trade.

SHELL MUSEUM
Glandford (3m NW Holt on B1156).
Shells from all over the world and a tapestry of the Norfolk coast.
Open all year.

SHERINGHAM has a small fleet of crab fishing boats and a lifeboat station.

CROMER is an old fishing port whose former importance is shown by the size of its church, whose perpendicular tower at 160 ft (48 m) high, is the tallest in Norfolk. Today Cromer is known for its crab fishing and the bravery of its lifeboatmen, who during the Second World War saved 450 lives. The famous lifeboatman Henry Blogg, coxswain from 1909-1947, is commemorated by a bronze bust which gazes out to sea from North Lodge Park, not far from the old lifeboat house, now a LIFEBOAT MUSEUM with models, pictures, and photographs.

Whelks coming ashore at Wells-next-the-Sea, 1929.

Horatio Nelson aged eighteen.

The lifeboat, *Ruby & Arthur Read II* can be viewed free at the LIFEBOAT HOUSE at the end of the pier from 1 May – 31 Sept. Talks and film shows can be arranged.
1 May – 31 Sept, daily.

CROMER LIGHTHOUSE (33 Hillside): Before the erection of a lighthouse here lights for guidance at sea were shown from the tower of the church. The original lighthouse of 1690 was destroyed by the sea in the eighteenth century and the present one, a white eight-sided tower, was built in 1833. It is 58 ft (18 m) high, has a light range of 23 miles (37 km) and is open to the public on weekday afternoons. Reached on foot from Cromer along cliffs or by entrance to Royal Cromer Golf Club.

CROMER MUSEUM
East Cottages, Tucker Street. Tel: (0263) 513543.
Late Victorian fishermen's cottages with maritime exhibits displayed among local history, geology,

archaeology and natural history of the Cromer area.
Open all year.

HAPPISBURGH: For centuries the bodies of shipwrecked sailors have been buried in the churchyard. The large green mound north of the church is said to be the mass grave of 119 members of the crew of HMS *Invincible*, wrecked on the sands in 1801 when on her way to join Nelson's fleet at Copenhagen. The church has a 110 ft (33 m) tower, perhaps built to serve as a beacon for sailors.

Ten miles south is the tiny smuggling hamlet of Horsey where contraband was loaded on to wherries and taken inland by boat to Norwich. Horsey Mere just west of the village is an offshoot of the Broads, where Nelson is said to have learnt to sail.

WINTERTON ON SEA: Inside the enormous tower of Winterton church is a reminder of the destructive power of the North Sea. The 'fisherman's corner' is a memorial to all those lost at sea. Almost everything there has been to sea: the cross is made of ship's timbers; other items include ropes, an anchor and ship's lamp.

Fragments from wrecks on the notorious Hazelborough Sands are often washed up on Winterton shore. When Daniel Defoe went there in 1725, he wrote that half the houses in the village were built of timber from wrecks.

GREAT YARMOUTH, which is mentioned in the Domesday Book, grew up along the east bank of the Yare. Throughout the Middle Ages it developed as a harbour and shipbuilding centre. Between the town wall and the river the houses were squeezed together into 145 narrow lanes known as Rows, one of them only 30 ft (9 m) wide. A few can still be seen.

Nelson, whose portrait hangs in the Town Hall, landed at Yarmouth after his victories at the Battle of the Nile (1798) and Copenhagen (1801).

Behind the South Beach is the NORFOLK PILLAR or NELSON'S MONUMENT
South Beach Parade. Tel: (0493) 858900.
Erected in Nelson's honour in 1819, it can be climbed (217 steps to the top). Open during the summer and Trafalgar Day (21 Oct).

The whole of the waterways at the Broads empty into the sea at Great Yarmouth. They lie within a wedge-shape formed by Beccles, Lowestoft, Great

Lifesavers at Caister, 1903.

Yarmouth, Horsey Mere, Wroxham and Nor-wich. There are 30 in all which make up 200 miles (320 km) of waterways. The term Broad – meaning an open expanse of water with navigable approach channels – has been in use since the 1500s.

RNLI LIFEBOAT STATION (south of harbour mouth)
Since 1986 a team of volunteers has been restoring the *John & Mary Meiklam*, a 1922 motor lifeboat. It saw active service on the east coast from 1922 to 1946, saving 211 lives. The restoration is open to the public in the summer months and work is half complete.

THE MARITIME MUSEUM FOR EAST ANGLIA
Marine Parade. Tel: (0493) 842267.
Historic shipwrecked sailor's home built in 1861 and functioning as such until 1965. It now contains exhibits covering all aspects of maritime history, including herring fisheries, life saving and shipbuilding. Boats include early Broads yacht *Maria* and a Yarmouth beach boat. Sailors' trophies include a Red Indian scalp and several fine Maori carvings.
Open all year.

NORWICH

BRIDEWELL MUSUEM OF LOCAL INDUSTRIES
Bridewell Alley. Tel: (06030) 611377.
Displays include maritime paintings illustrating the history of trades and industry in Norwich from the seventeenth century and Broads boats and wherries.
Open all year.

The Norfolk sailing wherry *Albion* constructed in 1898, the last one in existence can be chartered from the Norfolk Wherry Trust:
63 Whitehall Road, Norwich. Tel: (0603) 624642.

BRUNDALL (7 miles (11 km) east of Norwich on River Yare)
1st Blofield and Brundall Sea Scouts have restored as their HQ a 43-knot motor torpedo-boat built by Vospers in 1938. The single torpedo tube is in place and the hull, wheelhouse and deck are original. Visits by arrangement with the scouts.

LOWESTOFT is eight miles (13 km) south of Yarmouth and her maritime rival for centuries.

LOWESTOFT & EAST SUFFOLK MARITIME MUSEUM
Hapload Road. Tel: (0502) 61963.

Models of fishing and commercial boats, old and new. Paintings, shipwrights' tools and fishing gear.
Open during the summer.

ROYAL NAVAL PATROL SERVICE MUSEUM
Tel: (0502) 86250.
Sparrow's Nest (Sparrow's Nest was the central depot for the embarkation and return of the men and officers who manned the minesweepers, drifters and trawlers 1939-46): ship models, naval documents, uniforms, photographs and certificates.
Open during the summer.
Hydroplane racing May – Sept.

LOWESTOFT FISHING INDUSTRY AND HARBOUR TOUR
A tour of the working harbour and fishing industry, on board a trawler. Tour from Monday to Friday 7.15 am – 10.30 am by appointment. Further information from (0502) 565989 Ext 125. Inland at Oulton Broad the tests of the first hovercraft were carried out.

LOWESTOFT LIGHTHOUSE: A lighthouse was established in 1609 (present tower 1676) and became known as the Pepys Tower, from the inscription that it was erected during the mastership of Samuel Pepys. Open to the public on weekday afternoons. FREE.

SOUTHWOLD: Domesday Book records that Southwold was a prosperous fishing port in the eleventh century. Built virtually on an island cut off to the north by Buss Creek, named after the herring 'busses' or boats that once used the waterway, and to the south by river Blyth. It is lined with boatyards and huts selling fresh fish.

Guns were given to the town in the 1630s by Charles 1 to protect ships against the 'Dunkirkers' – privateers operating from Dunkirk. The battle of Sole Bay was fought in 1672 between the English and Dutch. Six cannon now stand on Gun Hill, south of the town, given by George II in 1745 for 'protection against the insults of the Common Enemys'.

SOUTHWOLD LIFEBOAT MUSEUM
Bartholomews Green. Tel: (Southwold 722422).
RNLI models, photographs, certificates and relics from old boats. One section devoted to Battle of Sole Bay.
Open during the summer.

SOUTHWOLD SAILORS READING ROOM
On the seafront.

Seafaring relics, models of ships including famous yawl *Bittern*.
Open all year.

WALBERSWICK was once a thriving fishing village and shipbuilding centre, and was used by Icelandic fishing fleets in Tudor times.

HERITAGE COAST CENTRE
The Green. Tel: (0473) 5580.
Displays on the Heritage Coast and Walberswick village. For centuries this long stretch of coast has been at the mercy of wind and tide which can change the seashore.

DUNWICH, established in Saxon times on the River Blyth, was once the most prosperous town of Norman Suffolk. The fifth busiest port in Suffolk is now under the sea. A solitary gravestone near the edge of a shallow cliff is the last survivor of All Saints Church which collapsed into the sea in about 1920, following Saxon, Norman and Medieval Dunwich. It is said that at times the submerged church bells can be heard ringing out a warning of an approaching storm.

In January 1326 in the course of a single night's storm, one million tons of sand and shingle were banked across the harbour mouth cutting it off from the sea and diverting the River Blyth north. This effectively killed the town's trade.

DUNWICH MUSEUM (4m SW Southwold)
St James Street. Tel: Westleton (072873) 358.
Chronicles the town's strange past from Roman times.
Open during the summer.

At **ALDEBURGH** the village pub, The Ship, is dimly lit and exudes a nautical atmosphere.

In 1983 Aldeburgh had the largest fleet of any beach landing in East Anglia. With its off-lying shallows creating short-breaking seas, it can be very dangerous for landing, but a map of 1588 clearly shows boats and crab capstans on the beach, so beach fishery appears well established here. Herring and sprat have been the backbone of Aldeburgh fishing in the autumn since medieval times. South of Aldeburgh at Slaughden is a Martello tower, the northern most in the chain built against Napoleon in the 1800s.

ORFORD: In the twelfth century Henry 11 built a great castle to protect the busy port of Orford. The 90-ft (27-m) keep survives and is used as a navigation mark by local shipping. Over the centuries the long shingle spit of Orford grew, cutting off the port from the sea. Today Orford survives as a small fishing village.

WOODBRIDGE was, at one time, an important trading centre, it still has a thriving boat-building industry. The quayside, reached by way of a level crossing, is an attractive jumble of boatyards and chandleries. Here on the River Deben and over-looking the Sutton Hoo Burial Ship Site is situated the white weatherboarded TIDE MILL. First built in 1170, the present one dates from 1790 and is now restored to working condition and powered by the tide's ebb and flow.
Open during the summer.

WOODBRIDGE MUSEUM
Market Hill. Tel: (0394) 2548.
Local history and a display of a Sutton Hoo ship burial (main display in British Museum).
Open during the summer.

FELIXSTOWE is now a busy container port, one of the largest in Europe with ferries from Sweden and Belgium. At the south end of the town a track leads to Landguard Fort, first built in the 1540s to guard the eastern entrance to Harwich Harbour. The present fort dates from 1718.

Felixstowe: booming Continental gateway.

LANDGUARD FORT MUSEUM
New View Road. Tel: (Fel) 286403.
Houses items relevant to the history of the fort. HMS *Beehive* Room (nautical).
Open during the summer.

FQ TOWER
South Hill. Tel: (0394) 285735.
Martello tower built in 1810 as coastal defence against expected invasion by Napoleon. Exhibition.
Open during the summer.

WALTON HERITAGE CENTRE
Interpretative museum of local history, rural and maritime in former lifeboat house.
Open during the summer.

Upstream towards Ipswich is **NACTON** on the east side of Orwell Park. In the eighteenth-century Orwell Park was the home of Admiral Sir Edward Vernon (1684-1757). His nickname 'Old Grog' given him because of his suit of coarse grogram cloth, was applied to the 'grog' introduced by him to the navy – a daily ration of rum mixed with water.

IPSWICH: In 1404 the town was made a 'staple port' – one of the ports from which wool could be legally exported (the port also traded in skins,

leather and fish). For centuries Ipswich was a centre of shipbuilding. The town's official seal dating from 1200 is the earliest known depiction of a ship with a modern rudder instead of the traditional steering oar.

By 1800 the harbour was almost choked and it took half a century of dredging and dock-building before trade recovered. From this period is dated the fine porticoed OLD CUSTOM HOUSE.

PIN MILL hamlet juts out into a section of the Orwell estuary 6 miles (9.6 km) downstream from Ipswich. Its name derives possibly from the wooden pegs or 'pins' made there and used in boat-building. Apart from all sorts of popular sailing craft, the last of the old red-sailed sailing barges may be seen here.

SHOTLEY GATE: At the end of the promontory that separates the Orwell and Stour are the rows of buildings and towering fully rigged ships' masts that until 1977 made up HMS *Ganges*, a naval training base named after the training warship that formed the original base.

MANNINGTREE, once a busy port, this little Georgian town has now lost its trade to Mistley. At the end of July there is a regatta for local punts – often home-made and originally fitted with wide bore 'punt guns' for shooting wild fowl.

HARWICH: Contrary to popular belief it was from Harwich and not from Plymouth that the *Mayflower* set out for America in 1620. She was a Harwich-registered ship and called in at Plymouth because of bad weather. Christopher Jones, her Master, was born in Harwich and lived in a house in Kings Head Street. Likewise, the diarist Samuel Pepys, who was MP for Harwich and Secretary of the Admiralty is commemorated by a plaque on the Town Hall.

HARWICH MARITIME MUSEUM
Low Lighthouse, The Green.
Housed in a disused lighthouse on the edge of Harwich Green, with special displays on RNLI, Royal Navy and commercial shipping, guided tours. Fine views over unending shipping movements in the harbour.
Open during the summer.

HARWICH REDOUBT
Main Road (car-parking in Harbour Crescent).
190ft (58 m) diameter circular fort built in 1808 to defend port against Napoleonic invasion. Moat cells, cannon, local finds.

Easter – end Oct weekdays; winter, Suns only.

BRIGHTLINGSEA stands on its own 'island' surrounded by water on three sides. As the possessor of the finest boat-landing ramp for miles around, Brightlingsea is a centre for boats of every description. Fishing and boat-building have been staple industries for centuries and the town was once famous for oysters. In the Middle Ages, Brightlingsea was an important port and the only 'limb' or associate member of the Cinque Ports outside Kent and Sussex. The town's officials still swear allegiance to the Mayor of Sandwich.

The parish church has more than 200 memorial tiles commemorating local men who died at sea. The town is the HQ of the Smack Preservation Society, devoted to preserving the fine old Essex fishing boats. Each September there is a race from Brightlingsea to Clacton and back. (Most of the participating boats were built at the beginning of the century.)

MERSEA ISLAND, joined to the mainland by The Strood, is famous for the *Ostrea edulis* or common British oyster. West Mersea is the main resort and boating area; here oysters known as 'West Mersea Natives' can be bought and eaten at stalls beside the old storage pools, some of which are still in use.

WEST MERSEA ISLAND MUSEUM has local history exhibitions and boat-making techniques, nineteenth-century marine equipment and RNLI display.
Open during the summer.

COLCHESTER OYSTER FISHERY CO
North Farm, E Mersea. Tel: (W Mersea) 4141.
Visitors can see oyster production at work.

TOLLSHUNT D'ARCY (B1026 7 miles (11 km) SW of Colchester) is a large village with a marina and some fine examples of boathouses and old sail lofts dating back to the turn of century when Tollshunt d'Arcy had a fishing fleet of more than 100 sailing smacks.

MALDON, although 12 miles (19 km) from the sea, has strong sea-faring traditions. Two Maldon ships fought at the Siege of Calais in 1348. A little downstream by the Norman St Mary's Church can be seen carefully restored nineteenth-century Thames sailing barges. In the nineteenth century Maldon produced a type of barge known as

Maldon, barge port.

HERRING DAYS

The age of sail would never have seemed romantic to the herring fishermen of Yarmouth and Lowestoft. The latter has been an important fishing centre since the Domesday Book. Before the walled harbour was constructed in 1830 the fishing boats operated from the beach; indeed, many continued the practice afterwards in order to avoid harbour dues. Herring, millions upon millions of them, made the fortunes of these two ports. The migrating fish swam in shoals up to four miles (six kilometres) wide down the North Sea from the Arctic Circle.

From the late nineteenth century until the mid-1930s, the vast swarms of small bony fish seemed inexhaustible. In 1913 over a thousand drifters worked out of Yarmouth and nearly the same number based themselves in Lowestoft.

Herring fleet at Lowestoft.

These small sailing craft would shoot a wall of net up to a mile long and just drift with the wind and tide. The mesh was broad and only the bigger fish that swam into the net were trapped. It was a conservation-minded process before the word was thought of. The boats spent eight weeks at sea and then two weeks at home, an average of five trips per year. They fished in fleets up to 100-strong under a skipper who was designated 'the Admiral'. He would decide what tack to sail on, when to shoot the nets and how long to fish. Each day a large fish-carrier would sail up from Billingsgate Market to collect the catch so that the fleet could stay at sea continuously.

The fishermen hated it. For two months they would only remove their boots and oilskins for sleeping, and not always then. Cooking had to be done in saltwater and could often be rendered impossible by bad weather. Rowing the catch to

the fish-carrier – precursor of the modern factory ship – in a small open dinghy was a horrendously dangerous job that claimed countless lives over the industry's fifty-year heyday.

The fishermen of Suffolk, particularly Lowestoft, became renowned as the finest seamen in the North Sea. They needed to be. Once you track north of Yarmouth there are 'No harbours but plenty of lifeboats' as the locals are fond of observing. Throughout the country they became known as 'The Roaring Boys'. It came not from their 100 per cent attitude to work and play but from the business of salting herring in the seventeenth century. The blunt wooden spade that turned the fish over was known as a 'roaring shovel' and this provided the nickname.

It was the coming of the steam trawler that ended the vast fishing fleets of Suffolk. At first the new technology was embraced with vigour. In 1897 every Lowestoft and Yarmouth drifter was still under sail but by 1914 they had universally embraced steam. Over-fishing became a serious problem after the Great War when the steam trawler fleets began to 'vacuum clean' the traditional fishing grounds. In 1909 the average catch for a sailing drifter was 350 pounds (130 kilos) per day. By the 1930s a well-equipped steam trawler was scooping forty tons a day from the Dogger Bank.

Nor was it just over-fishing that threatened and eventually overwhelmed the Suffolk industry. Regional disadvatages were magnified by the coming of steam. Hull and Grimsby were not only nearer the deep-water grounds that trawling, as opposed to drifting, required, but they had ready access to the coal for powering the new vessels. There was no coal in East Anglia and transport costs were still high.

Moreover, the manufacture of ice for preserving the catch was another large consumer of coal, giving the northern ports a double advantage. In 1912 Lowestoft was registered as having 5,400 full-time fishermen, twenty per cent more than Hull. But within twenty years the northern port had eclipsed every rival on the east coast. Only one herring drifter, and that a steam boat, survives from the Yarmouth and Lowestoft fleets. The *Lydia Eva* was launched at King's Lynn in 1930 and rolled down the slip into a fishing depression. She is now owned by the Maritime Trust and can be seen in London's West India Dock, an exhibition of the past fishing trade in her fish-hold.

'stackies' – shallow and broad which carried complete corn stacks 12-ft (3.6 m) high up the narrow inland creeks. Sailing-barge races are held in July.

MALDON MARITIME CENTRE
The Hythe.
Plans, photographs, models and artefacts of local maritime interest.
Open during the summer.

BURNHAM-ON-CROUCH, often referred to as the 'pearl' or 'Cowes of the east coast', was once a centre of the oyster, whelk and cockle trade. Its yachting clubs are known throughout the sailing world. (The Royal Burnham YC mounted the British challenge in the 1983 America's Cup competition.)

Highlights of the racing season are 'Cadet Week' held annually in July drawing teams from as far afield as Australia, and 'Burnham Week' held in the last week of August with over 400 boats of all classes competing.

BURNHAM MUSEUM
Providence (opposite the Clock Tower).
Local history, particularly maritime and agricultural.
Open all year.

LONDON AND THE THAMES ESTUARY

**HMS *Belfast* surrounded by square-riggers
in the Pool of London**

LONDON AND THE THAMES ESTUARY

LONDON today seems many things. To the visiting Japanese businessman it might be the square mile around Throgmorton Street and the Stock Exchange. For the history-starved schoolchild from Milton Keynes it could be the standard 'Heritage List', from the Tower of London to the V & A Museum. A sophisticated New Yorker on a week's 'culture grab' might be oblivious to all but the bustle and glamour of the West End theatres. Yet one can safely assert that very few modern visitors perceive the capital as the maritime hub of a great seafaring nation – and, at one time, the centre of the greatest empire the world has yet seen. One needs a little knowledge and a vivid imagination to recall the days when the lines of ships moored in the centre of the Thames were more essential to London's well-being than almost anything happening ashore. To a modern Londoner or visitor, dodging motor-cycles and cars and cursing the clogged traffic, it seems almost inconceivable that congestion on the river and the level of accidental drownings in the weir beneath London Bridge were the principal transport worries of eighteenth-century London.

Of course, its history as a port goes back far beyond those relatively recent times. It is impossible to know whether there was any pre-Christian outpost at the navigable head of the Thames, but most authorities agree that the origins of London as a continuous city settlement begin with the arrival of the Romans in the middle of the first century AD.

Whether the Romans perceived their new outpost as a military venture or merely a convenient landing stage for transporting goods and personnel into the new colony is unclear. Certainly it never had anywhere near equivalent status to the Roman capital at Verulamium, now St Albans. It was probably a rather grubby and utilitarian landing stage in the minds of the emperors, convenient for their great city twenty miles to the north but of no real significance.

The Roman port was entirely on the north bank of the river. A city wall built around AD 100 runs on three sides of a square, from the Tower to Aldgate, east to the Barbican and down to meet the river bank again at Blackfriars. The wall actually ran along the water's edge with two fortified gates to grant access to the quays. The two entrances were at Billingsgate, later the site of the world-famous fish market, and Dowgate (directly below what is now Cannon Street station). The river bank ran considerably north of its current line, making the Thames both wider and shallower. Roman barges were of impressive size but minimal draft. Remains of one found in the mud at Blackfriars have been reconstructed in cross-section at the Museum of London.

Yet for all their convenient ability to negotiate sandbars and the twists and turns of the river, Roman merchants and captains shipped cargoes of corn and military goods only as far down the Thames as Gravesend. The shoals and channels of the Thames estuary, plus its perennial fogs, were too risky for these early coastal navigators. From Gravesend the cargoes were moved by ox-cart overland to Richborough, the major south coast port.

Moreover, the outer estuary was not safe in a military sense. As the centuries of Roman occupation progressed, raids from tribes in the Low Countries opposite the mouth of the Thames became more frequent. In AD 296 a particularly bold enemy fleet sailed up to the City itself and there was hand-to-hand fighting in the streets. In an early precursor of the Royal Navy, the Roman governor

London Bridge, the western limit for big ships.

appointed a 'Count of the Saxon shore' with a fleet of vessels and up to 10,000 men to call on. His job was to defend the estuary and the coast up as far as Ipswich against incursion.

The Roman efforts to defend the city were trying to stop the ebb of history. The legions were gone by AD 410 and the occupation by Angles, Jutes and Saxons began. By AD 605 the Saxon tribes and chieftains were in complete control of London, inheriting from their predecessors a sophisticated system of wharfage and dredged channels. No record of the nature or volume of London's trade in Saxon times exists but that invaluable early chronicler the Venerable Bede, who lived from 673-735, recorded that 'London was the mart of many nations, resorting to it by sea and land'.

The years and centuries that followed were jumbled and confused from the point of view of rulers and occupiers of the city on the river; but the trading patterns survived each change of authority. London's position opposite the mouths of the Rhine and Maas was immutable and as Europe became more civilized and settled, so these direct trade routes into the heart of Belgium and Germany, as we now know them, became established and well travelled by vessels from London.

By 1066 and the crowning of William, Duke of Normandy, there were already established colonies of both German and Norman merchant traders in the heart of London. They had permanent offices and homes on either side of the Wall Brook where it ran into the river. Although the Thames estuary had not become any safer to navigators, familiarity had brought together a body of knowledge that made the North Sea crossings a little less of an adventure. More importantly, London was developing the network of financiers, shipowners and merchants who would be so important in the centuries to come.

Among William's first major projects in the land he had conquered was the creation of his permanent fortress, the Tower of London. Barge loads of stone from Kent and Caen in Normandy were brought in throughout the construction period – which lasted from 1070 until 1300 – and greatly increased the volume of river traffic. During the same period building work began on the first St Paul's cathedral, again with most of its stone and timbers being brought down the Thames. During those years of growth and frenzied building, probably not paralleled on the London riverside until the creation of the enclosed docks in the Victorian era, work also began (in 1176) on the first London Bridge, an incredible mercantile centre of shops, offices, homes and even a church. Since it effectively closed the river above its arches to sea-going ships, the construction of the bridge was the first real delineation of what became known throughout the world as the 'Pool of London'.

During the period 1100 to 1600 the river traffic expanded until the whole of the river bank, from the River Fleet (which is now culverted but used to join the Thames at the site of the current Blackfriars Bridge) to the Tower was lined with quays and warehouses. The carracks – those distinctive ships of the Middle Ages with a 'castle' fore and aft and displacement of about 600 tons – would fill the river as far as the eye could see. The principal cargo into London was coal from the North-East, the first recorded instance being in 1306. An invariable guide to significant volumes of trade is the attention of the taxman. Edward I ordered his revenue officers to levy a six pence toll on each shipload of coal passing up to or under London Bridge.

As far as exports were concerned, foreign merchants known as 'easterlings' were more successful than the English. The king granted these foreigners rights to live in London because of their access to European markets for English wool. Most of the fibre went to Flanders or northern Italy. However, the natives did eventually pick up the necessary skills to organize their own sea-borne trading and in 1315 there is the first record of a London-owned trading ship leaving the Pool for a Continental voyage. It took 125 sacks of wool valued at £1,400 to Antwerp.

The river was the most visible indicator of England's expansion into a great trading nation. The volume of activity on the Thames was staggering. For every sea-going cargo vessel there would be ten or a dozen small rivercraft skittering around with victuals, crews and small cargoes. In the reign of Elizabeth I a primitive attempt at a census by profession revealed that there were around 40,000 watermen working on the Thames between Windsor and Gravesend.

In this era the specialization which is another of the signs of rapid and sustained growth began to show itself on the river. In the mid-1600s over twenty 'legal quays' had been established along the two miles (three kilometres) of London bank. Each of these was designated to handle a particular cargo, ranging from spices to coal. The phrase 'legal quays' was used because they were sanctified by law for the payment of customs dues and were strictly patrolled by the revenue men.

In this buoyant mood of commercial optimism the East India company was founded in 1599. Dutch and Portuguese navigators were beginning to bring back to Europe products from the Orient for which there was a vast demand and an even bigger profit potential. These patriotic Englishmen could not see why much of it should not accrue to themselves. At a meeting of merchants in Founders Hall in 1599, 215 knights, aldermen and other worthies of the City of London voted to create a fully funded venture for trade with the east. They subscribed £72,000 in shares of £25.

The first voyage began from Woolwich in 1601. The East India Company was more influential that any other factor in the growth of trade and wharfage eastwards downstream and out of the Pool of London. Its decision to base both the company's clerical offices and its dockyard at Blackwall, a landmark event in 1612, was a leap forward in London's expansion. That first voyage comprised five ships and 480 men, having been two years in planning and recruitment. It was an enormous success, the ships returning full of 'spices' – the term in general use at that time for any exotic Eastern dry goods. As an example of the profits to be made, in 1620 the East India Company imported 250,000 pounds (93,000 kilograms) of pepper to England from Bombay. It cost £26,041 and was sold on the London market for £208,333. Small wonder that the shareholders turned up in droves and sang lustily at the Thanksgiving

Foreshore near Shadwell, 1914.

service held every two years to mark the safe home-coming of the fleet.

The establishment of the East India yard at Blackwall was the beginning of large-scale commercial shipbuilding on the Thames. Just over 100 years earlier, in the late fifteenth century, the forces of the Crown – not yet formally divided into army and navy – had begun to construct vessels downriver from the Tower. In 1475 King Edward fitted out a fleet big enough to carry 15,000 archers to France and shortly afterwards Henry VII built the first ever military ship of over 1,000 tons, the *Henri Grace à Dieu*.

By 1515 the infrastructure and skills in place along the banks of the Thames enabled Henry VIII to set up Royal Dockyards at Deptford and Woolwich. These supplemented the principal yard built some years earlier at Woolwich. In addition, and probably most significantly, the king created the Admiralty to oversee the whole mercantile arm of his forces. His Majesty lived long enough to see a workmanlike navy of forty-five vessels established, including the earliest galleons (a fighting version of the carrack).

Throughout the sixteenth century the City thrived and prospered, with a population of over 200,000. If there was a false note, it was the endless search for the north-east and north-west passages to the East. These voyages swallowed up millions of pounds and cost the lives of many scarce mariners. Meanwhile the Spanish and Portuguese traders and explorers were using less fanciful routes and flourishing in the spice trade. It was not until 1588 and the defeat of the Armada that the seas were truly wide open for British commerce. Sir Francis Drake's role in that episode has been widely canvassed but he should not be thought of entirely as a military hero. The divisions between war and trade were far less clear cut in the Elizabethan period. When Drake returned from his epochal circumnavigation in 1580 he was met at Deptford by the Queen and knighted on the banks of the Thames. To the City merchants his voyage had far more commer-cial than military significance, not that the two were easily separated when it came to the question of new colonies.

During the seventeenth century London boomed on its overseas trade. The earliest North American settlements – the Virginias, Carolinas and Massachusetts – were beginning to thrive and the Navigation Acts ensured a monopoly of their trade to British ships, mostly London-based. However, this booming century did have its setbacks; notably the Plague and the Great Fire. The latter was to have major implications for the way the capital organized its sea trade.

Generally speaking the merchants and their financiers were much keener on trading and exploring than creating wharfside facilities. The docks, quays and warehouses were a chaotic jumble of piling and wooden warehouses that had merely been added to piecemeal over 300 years. When the fire came the vast quantities of brandy, pitch and sulphur stored in the warehouses created a firestorm. Virtually nothing was left standing between the Tower and Temple church. When the facilities were rebuilt it was downstream of London Bridge, in Wapping, Shadwell and Hay's Wharf, that the new quays were built.

A second but in the long term vital change was the burgeoning insurance market for ships and cargoes. In 1571 the Royal Exchange, directly modelled on its counterpart in Antwerp, had opened in the heart of the City. Marine assurers met there to discuss, assess and assign risk until the Great Fire destroyed the building. Temporarily homeless they gathered in Mr Lloyd's coffee house in Lombard Street. Intelligence of vessels' movements was collected and pinned up on the walls. The modern marine insurance industry had begun to take root. A future world centre of excellence had been established.

For all the setbacks of the 1600s it had been a century of astonishing and permanent growth. By 1700 (when a rudimentary survey was carried out) the Port of London handled

Launch of HMS *Cambridge* at Deptford, 1757.

seventy-seven per cent by value of all Britain's foreign trade. There were nearly 600 ships registered with the capital as home port and 10,000 sailors called it home. London was already four times bigger than the country's next biggest port, Bristol.

A modern-day visitor to London can stand in the bow-window of the Prospect of Whitby pub at Wapping, look out over the river and struggle to conceive the frantic anarchy that existed there three centuries before. The Thames was chaos. There was no organized mooring or anchoring system; it ran on a 'first come, first served' principle. A visitor would find the East India ships clustered around Blackwall, the West India ships near Deptford, Baltic schooners discharging rafts of timber straight into the river, and up to 300 collier brigs a week arriving from the north-east of England. These were, in turn, serviced by over 2,000 coal barges and countless other non-classifiable vessels and passenger wherries.

The future growth of the port – if it was to move beyond terminal congestion – had to come from enclosed, artificially excavated, pools just off the river. The East India Company's pioneering effort at Blackwall was not repeated until 1700 when Howland Great Dock at Bermondsey was created to give over ten acres of sheltered water. In the mid-eighteenth century it was adapted to become a specialized centre for the whaling and blubber trade, rather than dealing with general cargo, but it remained a beacon for the future.

In the 1790s a parliamentary committee considering the construction of 'wet docks' at St Katharine's and Wapping was told that there had been over 1,300 ships packed into the river on a single day – and that took no account of the small craft servicing their needs. It was the exact equivalent of the modern public debate over the need for a new airport. Many factions argued their point but something had to change.

In July 1800 the foundation stone of the West India Dock was laid. There were to be two parallel basins, each half-a-mile long and 400 feet (120 metres) wide, labelled for Import and Export. Pilferage had already become a problem in the London of Fagin and the Artful Dodger so a thirty-foot (nine-metre) wall and six-foot (1.8-metre) deep moat were installed to provide security. This project began a thirty-year period of seemingly endless excavation and expansion. Trade was the driving force but a huge technological change had a powerful effect.

SS *Marjory* was the first steam vessel to visit the Pool of London, arriving in 1814. A ship powered by engines could now reach London docks from the open sea on a single tide – although unloading would prove no faster. For the ordinary working people of the East End, holiday trips on steamers plying between St Katharine's and Gravesend became the fashion. Skippers tended to become involved in impromptu races and there were several terrible accidents resulting in mass drownings.

On land, the arrival of James Watt's steam engine in factories and workplaces had led to a seemingly exponential rise in the demand for coal. And, of course, the steam-powered little ships built in Newcastle and Sunderland were able to make up to five trips a month compared to the single voyage of a sailing brig. Colliers began to be the biggest single cause of overcrowding on the river.

As the Victorian era reached its zenith London became the mercantile hub of the greatest empire the world had yet seen. The capital had a monopoly on trade with India and the East Indies, over half the trade to North and South America and the West Indies. Within Europe there was a huge trade with Russia – this country's biggest source of tallow in an age when candles were a constant purchase. To all these markets we exported our burgeoning technology, everything from steam engines to grocer's scales.

The boom in traffic encouraged the building of the vast Royal Victoria Dock on land to the east of the Isle of Dogs. It was to be the world's first dock with a direct rail link on to

Excavating the Royal Victoria Docks in the 1850s.

the wharves. Hydraulic cranes were another innovation, making the unloading of ships a much quicker affair than when hand-powered windlasses would swing the cargoes up out of the dark, cramped holds. By 1860 the Royal Victoria was taking 2,600 ships a year, more than double its biggest rival, the Indies docks.

Even this gargantuan capacity was quickly to become inadequate. In 1875 work began on the Royal Albert complex, 1.75 miles long (2.8 kilometres) with a water area of eighty-six acres (thirty-five hectares). Its excavation was one of the wonders of the Victorian world. As evidence of that era's utter belief in progress towards the bigger and better, the docks were designed to take ships of up to 12,000 tons – bigger by far than any vessel then afloat.

However, these were not boom years in every sector of the marine industry. As iron ships became the industry norm, both for trade and naval vessels, the shipyards of the lower Thames began to die out. They had no simple access to the iron and steel products that were on the doorstep for the Tyne and the Clyde and there were fewer and fewer customers for wooden ships. The great shipyard at Blackwall struggled on into the early years of the twentieth century but by 1907, it too was gone.

This was a small sector of gloom. Elsewhere it was onwards and upwards. Rivalry with the Royal Albert dock led, in 1882, to work starting on the biggest complex of all, downstream at Tilbury. Access to the vast complex was possible at all states of the tide through a lock 700 feet (213 metres) by eighty feet (twenty-four metres) and over thirty-three feet (ten metres) deep. It was a stupendous feat of engineering that excited the entire world of shipping.

From the turn of the century to the outbreak of the First World War was the absolute heyday for London docks. The Victoria and Albert complex had 180 separate cranes and the world's largest frozen meat store. From Tilbury liners set out daily for Australia, New Zealand and the colonies of the Far East. There was a hotel inside the docks specially to cater for passengers waiting overnight for a ship. Surrey Commercial Docks became the global centre for the timber trade. There was not a type of wood known to man that could not be found in its vast open sheds. The beautiful Georgian warehouses of St Katharine's specialized in the wool trade. There was always a minimum of half a million bales in stock. Next door was the Ivory House. Tusks up to nine feet (2.7 metres) high lay stacked to the rafters. Buyers came four times a year to purchase ivory for billiard balls and piano keys.

The stupendous growth of maritime London had not simply been a commercial affair, although that was its heart. As world trade grew navigation needed to grow into a science rather than a vague and shadowy craft handed down from father to son. In 1675 Charles II established the Royal Observatory at Greenwich. Its purpose was strictly in the realm of applied science, to provide information for ships to determine their position at sea. Accurate timekeeping was a major contribution. Once chronometers had been developed to a reasonable point, ships could anchor in the river below the Observatory and take their time for the voyage from the dropping of a red ball on the roof at 1.00 pm precisely. The development of a global 'grid' system with Greenwich at its heart on the nought meridian was the fundamental backbone of navigation – although it took several centuries to become accepted on a genuinely international basis.

A less theoretical but equally vital branch of navigation was growing downstream from Greenwich at Deptford. In medieval times the men with skill to pilot a ship were known as lodesmen (from the Middle English word 'lode', meaning a course) and in 1512 the Guild of Lodesman, based at Deptford, applied to Henry VIII for a charter. Two years later it was granted and Trinity House came into being, responsible for marking, buoying and lighting 2,350 miles (3780

Greenwich Hospital by Canaletto.

kilometres) of English and Welsh coast, as well as pilotage. The board of Trinity House consists of ten Elder Brethren and a secretary. Quaint titles still abound, the superintendant at Gravesend – the largest pilot station in the world – is to this day known as the Ruler of Pilots. Until 1899 his men wore frock coats and silk hats while on duty, now they stick to dark blue jackets with eight brass buttons and a simple cap badge.

Whenever the sovereign goes afloat in her official capacity, the Elder Brethren have the privilege of leading her. Thus when the Royal Yacht *Britannia* attends an event such as the Fleet Review at Spithead, the Trinity House vessel *Patricia* will steam ahead of her. The Trinity House headquarters has moved from Deptford to an office block overlooking the Tower of London in recent years but it is still the primary agency for everything from lighthouses to channel markers around Britain's coast.

While Britain's merchant fleet grew by leaps and bounds, so to did her navy, controlled throughout from the Admiralty building on Whitehall. Although one tends to think in terms of the primary naval dockyards being at Portsmouth and Plymouth, in the early years of the standing navy the bases along the southern shore of the Thames were at least as important. The distance between London and Portsmouth led Henry VIII to establish additional bases at Deptford, Woolwich and Chatham. Since all the ordnance was stored in London the yards on the Thames began to grow in importance. In 1550 it was decided to transfer all of the Portsmouth vessels to the Medway at Chatham and in 1570 the Kent port became a full royal dockyard.

However, after 1688 and the achievement of a settled peace with the Dutch it became obvious that the French were to be the long-term threat to the Crown. By virtue of its position opposite the Normandy coast, Portsmouth once more came to naval pre-eminence – a situation that was to remain unchanged for three centuries.

The history of the Thames has tended to be wrapped in commerce and affairs of state, but one notable area of pleasure at sea is linked to the estuary.

Katherine, the first yacht ever to be built in England was constructed for Charles II at Deptford in 1661. He had acquired a taste for the Dutch sport of yacht-racing during his exile in Holland. The King had been given a sail-boat, the *Mary*, by the government in The Hague but *Katherine* was found to be faster. Not to be outdone by his monarch, the Lord High Admiral built his own yacht, the *Anne*, at Woolwich.

GAZETTEER

LONDON AND THE THAMES ESTUARY FROM LONDON TO RAMSGATE

As one approaches London from the sea, with marshland on both sides, there is little to indicate the extent of the port's size – to the north is the low coast of Essex, to the south, the rising land of Kent. Somewhat inevitably, the London area tends to have the lion's share of what has been preserved of our nautical past.

CENTRAL LONDON: The stretch of the Thames above the Pool of London has little shipping today, but it was on these reaches that the Romans established the settlement that preceded London. Two Roman boats have been discovered in this area: one on the County Hall site in 1910 and another was discovered during the building of the Blackfriars underpass in 1962. The Blackfriars barge dates from the year AD 200 and is the oldest sailing vessel yet found in Northern Europe. These and other interesting maritime items are on display at MUSEUM OF LONDON, London Wall EC2.

SCIENCE MUSEUM
Exhibition Road.
Wide collection of model ships illustrating the history of navigation. This includes most types of vessels from liners and battleships to local work boats. Large model of Port of London.

LLOYDS OF LONDON has a Nelson Room filled with mementoes of the Admiral.

MADAM TUSSAUDS has a tableau recalling what it must have been like on board Nelson's flagship *Victory* during the Battle of Trafalgar. Of London's memorials to its maritime past, the best known must be the 185 ft (56 m) Nelson's Column in Trafalgar Square. Further down Whitehall, the old Admiralty is still a part of the Navy Department. There in the Ripley Building, is the Admiralty Board Room with its great table – a round section cut out, to fit the figure of a rotund former Secretary to the Admiralty. This room also still has the original wind indicator, directly connected to a weather vane on the roof which kept the Sea Lords informed of the likely course of shipping in the Channel. The building also houses the Nelson Room where Nelson's body rested prior to internment.

There are many statues, sites and houses in London which have close links with a number of famous English seamen: Nelson lived for a time at 96 (now 103) New Bond St and also at 5 Cavendish Square; he is buried in St Paul's Cathedral.

Captain Christopher Jones, the Master of the *Mayflower*, is buried in the churchyard of St Mary's Rotherhithe. There is a statue of Drake in front of Deptford Town Hall. Memorials to Raleigh include one in Whitehall and a window dedicated to him in St Margaret's Westminster. He frequented the Mermaid Tavern, was held prisoner in the Bloody Tower of the Tower of London and was finally executed in front of the Palace of Westminster in 1618.

Captain Scott lived at 56 Oakley Street, Chelsea: his last diary and the record of his polar expedition are held in the British Library. Captain Cook lived at 88 Mile End Rd. Samuel Plimsoll 'The Seaman's Friend' is remembered with a statue in the Embankment Gardens, Victoria Embankment.

THAMES EMBANKMENT, on the north side of the

Thames, is home to a number of ships permanently berthed, but not normally open to the public. They include the paddle-steamer *Princess Elizabeth, Hispaniola, The Tattershall Castle,* the *Chrysanthemum; President* and *Wellington* – both former naval sloops.

SOUTHWARK (on south side)
Imperial War Museum, Lambeth Rd SE1.
Displays include ship models, naval uniforms and ordnance, paintings and photographs. Also on display is 15-ft (4.5-m) clinker boat *Tamzine* used to ferry troops off beaches during the Dunkirk evacuation.

KATHLEEN & MAY
Cathedral St (near Southwark Cathedral) SE1.
Britain's last remaining wooden 3-masted topsail schooner (1900) is afloat in St Mary Overy Dock.
Coastal sailing trade exhibition on board.
Open daily throughout the year.

HMS *BELFAST*
Symons Wharf, Vine Lane (off Tooley St).
Part of the Imperial War Museum, HMS *Belfast* is the last survivor of the Royal Navy's big-gun ships and is now permanently housed in the Pool of London as a floating naval museum.

She is the first warship since HMS *Victory* to be preserved for the nation. During the Second World War, the 11,500-ton *Belfast* was one of the most powerful cruisers afloat and took part in the last battleship action in European waters.
Open every day except 24-26 Dec and Jan.

BILLINGSGATE, the principal fish market in London and the oldest market, is located on a spot that was probably a small harbour in Roman times. By 1773, a Dutch historian reported that 'it is the only port for fish in London'. The fine frontage is of especial architectural and historic interest and has been restored. The market is now sited in West India Dock.

The MARINER'S CHAPEL at All Hallows-by-the-Tower, is an important religious centre with strong maritime traditions. It is hung with many ship models: by tradition, sailors went there to be blessed before setting sail and when they returned, offered models of their ships as thanks for their safe passage.

ST KATHARINE'S DOCK: This redeveloped area next to Tower Bridge, has a notable gathering of Thames barges. The St Katharine by the Tower Co has encouraged other traditional craft to make their base here, including, the steam tug *Challenge* (1931) and the *Nore Light Vessel* (1931).

CUTTY SARK – 'LAST OF THE CLIPPERS'

Against the sublime backdrop of the Christopher Wren and Inigo Jones buildings of Greenwich, the tea clipper *Cutty Sark* sits like a swallow upon an elm tree. She is the evolutionary crescendo of around 3,000 years of merchant sailing ships: fast, elegant and – it has to be said – obsolete before she was launched.

Cutty Sark was built primarily from a love of speed and a desire to win the race from China with the new season's tea. The first cargo to reach London could be assured of the highest prices. Moreover, the victor enjoyed a prestige with the public and among the shipping fraternity that was not to be equalled until the next century and the arrival of the Blue Riband trophy for transatlantic liners.

She was built for John 'White Hat' Willis, a former sailing-ship master who had left the sea and devoted his time to running the family

The *Cutty Sark*, permanently in dry-dock at Greenwich.

shipping business in London. With his patriarchal white beard and the distinctive headgear that gave him his nickname, Willis cut an impressive figure as he threaded his way down Leadenhall Street in the heart of the City's maritime district. His efforts to keep building costs down were so successful that when *Cutty Sark* was launched in October 1869 at Dumbarton, Scotland, the young partnership that had designed and built her promptly went into liquidation.

The ship's name comes from a poem by Robbie Burns about a befuddled Scots farmer pursued at midnight by a voluptuous young witch wearing only a 'cutty sark', the dialect phrase for a scanty chemise that revealed a great deal more than a drunken farmer expects to see on his way home. The ship's figurehead shows the young witch, arm outstretched, clutching the tail from the fugitive's horse in her fingers.

While White Hat Willis might have been careful with his pennies, the Clydeside shipwrights stinted nothing on the 930-ton ship. Her condition today, nearly a century and a quarter after construction, illustrates how well-found *Cutty Sark* was. It was a change in both geography and technology that rendered her lack of commercial success inevitable.

In 1869 the Suez Canal opened. With a shorter route and more regular sailings the new steamships could place enormous time pressure on the big clipper ships which still had to ride the Roaring Forties around Cape Horn. The difference in distance was close to 5,000 miles (8000 kilometres). More important still was the development of the triple-expansion steam engine which gave enormous increases in horsepower per ton of coal burned.

The *Cutty Sark* and her sisters, *Thermopylae, Ariel, Taeping, Sir Lancelot* and *Leander*, were an esoteric breed. They existed as racehorses among a vast army of working animals. In 1860, 420,000 tons of sailing shipping was registered in Britain and less than one per cent of that represented the tea clippers, ships designed expressly for speed.

As a tea clipper *Cutty Sark* was never lucky. She raced home against the *Thermopylae* only once, in 1872. But while over 400 miles (640 kilometres) ahead of her rival, *Cutty Sark* lost her rudder in the heavy swells of the Pacific Ocean. A jury rig got her back to Portland 120 days out of Shanghai but she lost the race to *Thermopylae*. In 1877 she carried her last cargo of tea: 1,334,000 pounds (605,125 kilograms) from Hankow to Scilly in 122

days. The prosaic but profitable ships of new lines such as Blue Funnel and Glen were already bringing the 'opium of the masses' back at half the cost and twice the speed.

Six years of virtual 'tramping' came to an end in 1883 when *Cutty Sark* ventured into the Australian wool trade. The newly prosperous colony was sending its wool home to the textile mills of Yorkshire and, as once with tea, time was money. *Cutty Sark* made her first trip from Newcastle, New South Wales, to Deal, Kent in a breathless eighty-two days. Every year from 1885 to 1895 *Cutty Sark* beat her rivals home to England, the record trip being an astonishing sixty-seven days from Sydney to Ushant in 1885.

Just before the close of the century Willis decided he could no longer make a relatively small clipper like *Cutty Sark* pay on the deep-sea trade. She was sold to Portuguese interests and traded out of Lisbon for twenty-seven years. In 1922 Captain William Dowman, a master-mariner who had known the *Cutty Sark* in his youth, saw the bedraggled ship in Falmouth harbour, near his retirement home. He bought her for £3,750 and had the old lady towed up from Portugal in order to start restoration work.

Cutty Sark's progress into the public domain began in 1938 when the Dowman family presented her to the Thames Nautical Training College which moored her at Rotherhithe. During the Festival of Britain in 1951 she was moved to a mooring off Greenwich and generally tidied up. The Duke of Edinburgh headed a fund-raising drive to find £250,000 to preserve Britain's only square-rigged merchant ship and keep her in the dock where she now rests.

Of the ten million people who have visited the ship since then, only the stone-hearted and the obtuse can fail to have been thrilled by her power to evoke the excitement and grandeur of life aboard the most dynamic commercial sailing vessel ever seen. With her three towering masts and three-quarters of an acre of canvas capable of driving her at over seventeen knots, *Cutty Sark* at full-bore must have been a sight we can only wonder at.

The poet John Masefield is probably best known for his word-sketch of the 'dirty little tramp-steamer' but he also responded in verse to the glories of the clipper ships:

They mark our passage as a race of men
Earth will not see such ships as those agen.

LONDON UNDERWATER MUSEUM
MV *Celtic Surveyor*, North Quay, West India Dock.

Housed on board an ex P & O 1930s vintage ferry now permanently berthed in London's West India Dock. Displays include ancient and modern diving equipment, salvaged treasures and arte-facts including authentic items from the *Mary Rose* and the more recent HMS *Edinburgh* gold bullion salvage.

WEST INDIA DOCK
Here the Maritime Trust has concentrated its smaller London vessels. They include: *Lydia Eva*, a 1930s steam drifter for Yarmouth herring fisheries; *Portwey*, a Dartmouth steam tug, and *Robin*, a steam coaster built in 1890.

GREENWICH

NATIONAL MARITIME MUSEUM
Romney Rd, Greenwich SE10.

Situated in the heart of historic Greenwich, the museum holds the world's greatest maritime collections of paintings, prints, ship models, relics of distinguished sailors and events, fine collections of manuscripts, navigational instruments and charts, medals, a large library with reference sections, inter-Continental migrations and Arctic exploration. It comprises 4 parts:

West Wing: houses permanent gallery with exhibitions on Nelson, Cook and 'The Ship at War' – a spectacular permanent display of the museum's models, illustrating the development of the Royal Naval warship through the great age of fighting sail 1650–1810.

East Wing: where special exhibitions are mounted.

Queen's House: designed by Inigo Jones for Anne of Denmark, wife of James I, and lived in by Queen Henrietta Maria, wife of Charles II.

Old Royal Observatory: on the hill above the museum, in Greenwich Park. It was started by Charles II to help discover a method of finding longitude. In 1884, the Greenwich longitude was accepted by the world as the prime meridian from which all other time is calculated. The Observa-tory now houses the largest refracting telescope in the UK and an extensive collection of historic time-keepers and astronomical instruments. The

Above: Figurehead from HMS *Ajax*, National Maritime Museum.

Below: Old Royal Observatory clock.

South Building of the Observatory, at the Greenwich Planetarium, gives educational and public performances.
Open daily.

THE CUTTY SARK
King William Walk, Greenwich.
The last of the China Tea Clippers built in 1869. Exhibition on board includes famous Long John Silver figurehead collection.
Open daily.

GIPSY MOTH IV, close by in Cutty Sark Gardens, is open only in the summer. Francis Chichester sailed around the world aboard her in 1966.

THAMES BARRIER VISITOR'S CENTRE
Unity Way, Woolwich.
Multi-media exhibition of photos, models, video film and slides about history of the Thames Barrier.
Open daily, Mon – Fri.

TILBURY, downstream, is the probable site of the camp where Elizabeth 1 reviewed her troops in August 1588 before the onslaught of the Spanish Armada. Tilbury's giant container port has the largest lock in England. The first docks were constructed here in 1884 and it has expanded ever since.

GRAVESEND: Here the Thames is still a recognizable river rather than a wide estuary which it becomes a few miles downstream. It faces Tilbury across à few hundred yards of water.

For centuries Gravesend has been a centre of activity on the Thames. As early as the fourteenth century Gravesend's ferrymen had the monopoly of waterborne passenger traffic to London on a ferry which still runs every half hour. There is a bronze statue of the Red Indian princess Pocahontas, in St Giles' churchyard in Gravesend. She saved the life of Capt J Smith, one of the earlier Virginia colonists and married another settler John Rolfe who brought her back to England. She died of fever before setting out on return to America and was buried here. Gravesend is also the northern end of the Saxon Shore Way, a walking route which follows the coast line for 140 miles (225 km) to Rye in Sussex.

ROCHESTER: When the Romans came, there was already a British stronghold guarding the Medway Crossing. Among the maritime traditions of Kent is the so-called 'Admirals Court' held annually on the Medway at Rochester. While afloat on a barge, the 'Admiral', the Mayor of Rochester, holds his court making laws 'regulating the Oyster Fishery and the taking of floating fish'.

ROCHESTER GUILDHALL MUSEUM
High Street.
Local history including a collection of ship models, plus some French prisoner-of-war models made in Rochester Castle: there are also models of barges and a fishing bawley.

CHATHAM, the first Royal Dockyard of the Medway, was founded in 1570, by Elizabeth I. In 1620 the site was enlarged and by 1860 it covered 71 acres (28 hectares). Down the centuries the great names of maritime history, Drake, Hawkins and Nelson, have all sailed from here. It was the birthplace of many of the navy's great ships including Nelson's *Victory*.

CHATHAM HISTORIC DOCKYARD
Old Pay Office, Church Lane.
Includes an audio-visual presentation, a visitor centre and a museum; an ordnance collection, a good collection of ships' figureheads, all telling the story of the dockyard. Guided tours include the Commissioner's House (1703) (the oldest intact naval building in Britain), Mould Loft (1753), Dockyard Church and Mast House and Covered Slips. HMS *Gannet* (1878) is a composite auxilary steam sloop designed to carry out patrols over great ocean distances for many years at a time. Recently restored, it can be viewed and boarded.
Open Wed – Sun and bank holidays.

PADDLE-STEAMER *KINGSWEAR CASTLE* is Britain's last coal-fired passenger paddle-steamer, built in 1924 with a 2-cylinder compound diagonal engine. Owned by the Paddle-Steamer Preservation Society, it has regular sailings from Chatham Historic Dockyard and Strood Pier up and down the River Medway.
Open mid May – early Oct.

MEDWAY HERITAGE CENTRE
Dock Road.
Housed in the old parish church of St Mary's Chatham, the Centre has displays telling the story of the river from Sheerness to the limit of tidal waters at Allington Lock.

FORT AMHERST
Barrier Road off Dock Road.
Commenced in 1756 as part of defence works to protect the dockyard, it was extended in the

HMS *Royal Charles* under attack in the first Dutch War.

nineteenth century and is today the most complete Georgian fortress in the country. There are 6,560 ft (2000 m) of tunnels, gun batteries, casemates and a reconstruction of a Second World War operation's room.
Open Apr – June & Oct Wed, Sat & Sun. July – Sept daily.

SITTINGBOURNE was once a busy harbour town where the creek used to be lined with brick and cement works. Works all now closed.

DOLPHIN SAILING BARGE MUSEUM
Crown Quay Lane.
The museum occupies former barge building and repair yard of Charles Burley Ltd active 1880s – 1965. Displays in former sail loft. Ground floor: photographs, models, shipwright tools and shop. Forge opposite has old barge tillers used to support roof: barge ironwork displayed. Barge repairs carried out at the yard. Maritime Trust Thames barge *Cambria* (1906) moored here.

SHEERNESS, on the north-west tip of the Isle of Sheppey, is a busy container ship and car-ferry port. The first Sheerness dockyard was built in 1665 under the supervision of Samuel Pepys,

Charles II's Secretary to the Admiralty. In 1797 it was the scene of the notorious Nore Mutiny when sailors of the Nore Command rebelled against the inhuman conditions in which they lived – it resulted in a general improvement in sailor's lifestyle.

FAVERSHAM, on the creek of the Swale, was an ancient port and still has sailing barges moored at Iron Wharf; its medieval warehouses at Standard Quay are still in use. The fifteenth-century Fleur Lys Heritage Centre has displays relating to Faversham's colourful history as a shipbuilding, trading, brewing, oyster-fishing and gunpowder centre.
Open daily all year.

In Roman times the Isle of Thanet was a real island separated from the mainland by a mile-wide stretch of water, the Wantsum Channel, which silted up over the centuries. The coast from Herne Bay to Margate is now mainly resorts:

HERNE BAY was originally a fishing village and is now a resort. Further eastwards the twin towers of Reculver's ruined church, nicknamed the two sisters, are the principal landmark of the 10-mile (16-km) stretch of coast between Herne Bay and Margate. The sea washed away much of the rest of the church in the nineteenth century, but the towers were retained and restored because of the visibility from seawards.

MARGATE

MARGATE has, with its famous pier designed by the Scottish engineer John Rennie, a few attractions of a specifically maritime character:

SHELL GROTTO

Grotto Hill, off Northdown Rd.

Discovered in 1835, believed to be a temple of ancient but unknown origin, has 2,000 sq ft (186 sq m) of interiors decorated from floor to ceiling with intricate shell designs.

Open Apr – Oct.

MARGATE CAVES

Northdown Rd.

These were hewn out of chalk more than 1,000 years ago and have served as dungeons and a smuggler's hideout.

Caves open daily in summer (Easter – end Sept) 10.00am – 5.30pm.

TUDOR HOUSE AND MUSEUM

King St.

Exhibitions covering the human occupation of Thanet to end of Tudor period. Included is a collection of tools once used locally in ship-building.

LIFEBOAT HOUSE

The Rendezvous, Margate Harbour.

The lifeboat *Silver Jubilee* can be viewed and other items connected with lifesaving at sea.

Open end May – end Sept, daily.

NORTH FORELAND LIGHTHOUSE

A light has been shining on this spot since 1505 to warn ships away from the treacherous Goodwin Sands, 7 miles (11 km) off the coast. The present North Foreland lighthouse is 85 ft (26 m) high. Its beam is visible at night for 20 miles (32 km).

Open to public weekdays (operational duties permitting) Easter – Sept.

BROADSTAIRS

BROADSTAIRS: Bleak House, where Dickens wrote *David Copperfield*, stands high on the north side of the town overlooking the sands of Viking Bay which is sheltered by a sixteenth century pier. It is now the DICKENS & MARITIME CENTRE. Open daily, April – Oct.

CRAMPTON TOWER MUSEUM

High St.

Housed in old waterworks building designed by eminent Victorian engineer Thomas Crampton. The museum commemorates his work and in-

cludes submarine telegraphic communications display.

RAMSGATE

RAMSGATE: The harbour is one of the busiest on the south coast since the introduction of the cross-channel ferry to Dunkirk in 1981. An obelisk on the East Pier commemorates George IV's landing at Ramsgate in 1822, since when the harbour has had the title of Royal Harbour.

One of the most heroic rescues in the history of the RNLI took place in January 1881 when the Ramsgate lifeboat *Bradford* rescued 11 men from the *Indian Chief*, a 1,238-ton ship that had left Middlesbrough bound for Japan. It took *Bradford* and the steam tug *Vulcan* five hours to reach the burning wreck. Despite the enormous seas sweeping over the lifeboat, the crew managed to rescue the 11 survivors. Coxswain Fish, a national hero, was awarded the RNLI gold medal.

There is a Historic Harbour trail with 36 points of interest from the modern lifeboat to the dry dock of 1791.

RAMSGATE MUSEUM

Ramsgate Library, Guildford Lawn.

Collection and displays relating to civic life and history of Ramsgate and the harbour including prints, pictures and holiday souvenirs.

Open Mon – Thurs & Sat.

MARITIME MUSEUM

The Clock House, Pier Yard, Ramsgate Royal Harbour.

The museum is housed in an early nineteenth-century Clock House with 4 galleries displaying various aspects of maritime heritage of the area including artefacts from the *Stirling Castle* which along with 3 battleships foundered on the Goodwin Sands in the Great Gale of 1703, and other RNLI memorabilia. In times of war, Ramsgate is a front-line town and there are many exhibits relating to it as a coastal forces base. Also displayed are the trades and activities of bygone Thanet shipbuilders, sailmakers and fishermen, navigational instruments from 1700 to the present day and a mock ship's bridge. The dry dock, restored to its original 1791 walls and flooring, has several interesting craft on display, for example the motor-yacht *Sundowner* (1912). This Admiralty launch is famous for its trip to Dunkirk in 1940 when despite her previous maximum number of passengers being 21, she returned dodging the Luftwaffe with 130 embarked. Also on display is the 233-ton steam tug *Cervia* (1946) and the south Devon fishing smack *Vanessa* (1899).

Open all year.

THE SOUTH-EAST

Dover harbour: gateway to England

THE SOUTH-EAST

MAINLAND Europeans have always seen the south-eastern corner of England as the natural gateway into the country. From Caesar to Hitler few of the visitors, actual and potential, have been exactly welcome but the successful invaders, most notably the Romans and the Normans, arrived that way. Hordes of others tried. Interestingly, for all their technically advanced forts and disciplined military skills, the Romans were no more able to protect this low-lying shingle coastline than their unwilling British subjects.

Around 1050 Edward the Confessor introduced a novel defence concept for the shores of Kent and Sussex: ship service. Five seaports – Hastings, Romney, Hythe, Dover and Sandwich – were nominated as responsible for providing ships and men to the Crown for the purpose of coastal defence. In the French that was the contemporary language of Court, they became 'the Cinque Ports'. Their return for this loyal support of the monarch was a considerable degree of local self-government. Each town possessed a good harbour and a considerable fishing fleet – and therefore a pool of skilled mariners.

They had three principal duties. First, the defence of the coastline against seaborne invasion. Secondly, to take part in larger naval operations initiated by the king and often involving his own ships. Thirdly, transporting the king and the royal household to and from mainland Europe as often as required.

At first glance the Norman invasion of 1066 might seem an instance where the Cinque Ports had failed abysmally in their duties. In fact, the fleet from Kent and Sussex was already at war on the north-east coast, where King Harold had successfully resisted an opportunistic incursion by Tostig, King of Norway. Had they been on station at their home ports, acting under the first of their duties rather than the second, the Kent sailors with their fast, manoeuvrable craft would probably have sent the heavy Norman transports to the bottom of the Channel, altering the course of English history more than somewhat.

As it was, William Duke of Normandy sacked Romney and then advanced on Dover, taking the castle after a short siege. He beheaded the Saxon chief Ashburnham and his son at the gateway, before moving on to an orgy of murder, rape and pillage before burning the town to the ground. Dover was rebuilt fairly speedily and the inhabitants seemed eager to make peace with William on advantageous terms. Although the Cinque Ports had failed, through no fault of their own, to repel his own invasion the new king realized the value of this marauding, unconventional Channel fleet and quickly reconfirmed the rights and duties they had been granted by Edward. Above all, William needed to protect his supply and communication routes back to Normandy. His famous Domesday Book contains an entry for Dover: 'The burgesses supplied the king once in the year 20 ships for 15 days and in each ship were 21 men.'

During the thirteenth century the Cinque Ports reached the zenith of their maritime power. Their ships, home-built on the Kent beaches, had won the freedom to do what they pleased on the short seas between England and France. The ships were small, between twenty and twenty-five tons, and propelled by oars, thus necessitating a large crew of between twenty and twenty-one plus a captain. There was a square sail for use when the wind was near astern and the vessel was steered by an oar hung over the stern, rather than by a rudder.

Norman battle tactics focussed on ramming

the enemy with the knife-edged metal beak at the bow of the boat. If a set-piece battle was expected and soldiers were going to be embarked then castles would be fitted fore and aft to give archers the necessary height to rain arrows down upon their enemies. The primary cause of the increased military activity involving the Cinque Ports during the thirteenth century was England's loss of Normandy in 1204. The Channel ceased to be a lake between two linked provinces and became once more an international frontier between hostile nation states.

Although the English ships had habitually fought as the individualistic privateers that they were at heart, this period of conflict gave rise to an event that was profoundly to influence the future of naval warfare as practised by the English. In 1216 a French expeditionary force landed and laid siege to Dover Castle. Eventually the defenders triumphed and Hubert de Burgh, castle commander, gave chase out into the Channel at the head of large Cinque Ports fleet.

Off Sandwich they encountered the French fleet and for the first time the British vessels manoeuvred and fought as one military eche-

Henry VIII leaves Dover for the Field of the Cloth of Gold, 1520.

lon, bringing their total firepower to bear on small units of the enemy force. It was a milestone in naval warfare that was to echo on down the centuries as the Battle of Sandwich. After de Burgh's success it became clear to the king that a unified command between Dover Castle and the Cinque Ports would be advantageous. The post of Lord Warden was created and de Burgh became the first commander. It was a position to equal the importance of the modern Chief of the Defence Staff, although in recent centuries it became more of an honorary position occupied by such distinguished figures as the Duke of Wellington, Winston Churchill and the Queen Mother.

If the Battle of Sandwich was the high spot for the ships of the Cinque Ports it was also the beginning of the end for their distinctive style of operations. Success had brought its own death warrant. By the mid-fourteenth century the marauding style of the individual privateers was over and they were never again to be more than a single component of the king's forces in large set-piece battles. Fifty years later the French were more powerful than ever and natural forces in the shape of drifting shingle were ruining the ports. Sandwich was sacked by the French and Dover

was so silted and clogged that shipping was operating from the beach. The last offensive operation carried out by the military arm of the Cinque Ports was to contribute half a dozen ships and crews to the English fleet fighting the Armada in 1588.

While Dover stood for several centuries as *primus inter pares* among the Cinque Ports it has always had a long-term significance surpassing that particular organization. Before either Bristol or the Port of London existed, Dover stood sentinel between the high hills enfolding the River Dour. Dover's position, twenty-two miles (thirty-five kilometres) from Calais, twenty-six miles (forty-two kilometres) from Boulogne and sixty-two miles (100 kilometres) from Ostend gave it inherent advantages at a time when sea travel was both dangerous and expensive.

Julius Caesar made the first recorded comments on Dover in 55 BC as he reconnoitred the Kent coast seeking a landing spot for his invasion force. 'The sea was confined by mountains so close to it that a dart could be thrown from their summit on to the shore,' the future emperor observed. Seeing the tactical advantages Dover gave to the massed defenders, Caesar veered off and went elsewhere to land.

In the centuries that followed, Dover was the backdrop for every medieval spectacular from the departure of Richard Coeur de Lion for the Holy Land to the return of Henry V after Agincourt, carried shoulder high through the surf. The origins of the harbour can be traced back to small craft which made use of the sheltered mouth of the Dour. In late Saxon times it was still navigable but it silted up fast and became an impenetrable delta of small channels. In 1495 the largely silted-up haven under Castle Cliff was abandoned in favour of the Archcliff indentation on the other side of the bay. With the addition of a breakwater it became Paradise Bay but the problems of silting remained.

As late as 1676 the sound of a drum at low water would rouse the citizens armed with shovels to clear the harbour. The process of enlargement and development continued, fuelled by the demand for conveyance to the Continent. Between 1720 and 1820 the cutters of the Passage Fleet became the swiftest and most sought-after little ships in Europe. They were regularly making the Channel crossing in three and a half hours.

In 1909 the then Prince of Wales opened the modern harbour. It remains largely unchanged today. Over 11,000 feet (3350 metres) of stone breakwater encloses 650 acres (260 hectares) of sea, giving access to both ferry and cargo docks. In the nineteenth century the emphasis was on ferries and mail packets that met and, in some cases, embarked trains for the Continent. But the most significant date in our own century was 1928 when Captain SM Townsend started the first ferry service for accompanied cars. In the first year he carried just 6,000 cars, but by the outbreak of war in 1939 the total had risen to 31,000. In 1988 Dover's car ferries carried very nearly two million passenger vehicles and over 12.5 million people across the Channel making it the busiest sea-crossing in the world.

As this distinctive and specialized trade has expanded, beyond the physical capacity of Dover at peak periods of the year, so the ferry business has expanded laterally to involve neighbouring ports such as Folkestone, Ramsgate and even Sheerness. What impact the arrival of the Channel tunnel will have on a regular ferry service with roots going back nearly 1,000 years remains to be seen.

The only other commercial port of any real significance on the south coast is, of course, Southampton. It is sheltered by the massive bulk of the Isle of Wight, has the benefit of double high tides because of the Solent's 'funnel' effect and is opposite the Cherbourg peninsula and the mouth of the Seine, gateway to inland France. However, Southampton's fortunes have always been enormously cyclical. Despite its natural advantages the port seems capable of periods of regular decline and torpor lasting whole centuries.

Landing at Dover from the steam packet.

Southampton's first recorded existence as a harbour was the Romano/British town of Clausentum on the eastern bank of the River Itchen, opposite where the new Ocean Village marina is now taking shape. Little is known of its fate until the years immediately following the Norman conquest. Nearby Winchester was still the capital of southern England and so Southampton became an important route between the Court and the nobles' homes in Normandy. In the twelfth century Henry II's marriage to Eleanor of Aquitaine gave England possession of the Gascony region and the wine trade began to flourish, almost entirely imported through Southampton. By the fifteenth century there was also a considerable trade with the Italian city states, notably Genoa, and a small but commercially vigorous Italian community grew up in the town.

But by the middle of the next century Southampton's trade had collapsed, due to three factors. The improved windward ability of ships provided by a better rig enabled them to proceed up Channel and round the North Foreland with confidence. When they arrived in the Thames estuary there was the new facility of Trinity House pilots. Finally, in Italy the city states were at war and virtually ceased international trade. The outbreak of war with France in 1543 was the final nail in the coffin and this most favoured of ports fell into a decline which was to last nearly 300 years.

With the close of the Napoleonic Wars in the early nineteenth century Southampton began to lift itself off the floor. In 1823 a regular steam-packet service to Le Havre was established and within five years it was carrying 2,000 passengers a week at a fare of ten shillings. The first stone of the modern docks was laid in 1838 and the facility opened in 1843. It was immediately put into heavy use by the P & O Line which had secured the contract for mail to India. Southampton became the post office to the burgeoning British Empire.

Passengers began to reason that if their ship was stopping anyway they might as well proceed to London by land. In 1838 there were thirteen regular coaches a day linking the capital with Southampton via the turnpike, the fastest of them taking only eight hours. For a time, until the coming of the railway, it was the most densely travelled stagecoach route in England.

In 1895 the Prince of Wales Dry Dock, at the time the largest on earth, opened. Southampton was the principal port of embarkation for men and material during the Boer War, making the docks enormously busy. Success breeding success, both the White Star and American Line chose that year to move their transatlantic terminus from Liverpool to Southampton.

The White Star Line is, of course, famous for one ship above all others – the *Titanic*. She sailed on her maiden voyage in 1912 with a largely Southampton-based crew and the shock when she was lost in the north Atlantic was a savage blow to the port's growing optimism. In the city's East Marland Park there is a monument commemorating the heroism of the crew, particularly the engineers who worked so hard to keep the ship afloat so that passengers could escape. Not one stoker, artificer or engineer survived.

Nevertheless, the growing liner traffic on the Atlantic route survived the tragedy and expanded year by year. For the next forty years, until the advent of jet air travel, Southampton seemed to lie at the crossroads of the world. The magnificent Ocean Terminal, opened in 1950, is a stunning wood-panelled tribute to a world that was about to end. Not all the people travelling through the port were pursuing pleasure or commerce. During the Second World War the city acquired a new name, Area C, the greatest military and naval base the world had yet seen as the build-up to the invasion of Europe began.

The bulk of the invasion forces were living in tents on the Common just prior to June 1944 and as D-Day approached every road and lane into the city was jammed with tanks, jeeps and trucks. Two-thirds of the total personnel landed on the Normandy beaches sailed from Southampton Water and in the docks a plaque commemorates the bravery of the two million American military personnel who embarked from the port between 1944 and the end of the European war.

Although Southampton enjoyed a temporary military celebrity during the preparations for and aftermath of D-Day, it is its neighbour twenty miles to the east, Portsmouth, that is significant in terms of national defence. For most of Britain's recorded history Portsmouth has been the focus of naval power, a centre of warship design, construction and repair as well as providing the huge logistical support necessary for what has been, at various times, a Royal Navy capable of global deployment.

It was in 1194 that Richard I took the decision to create a naval and military base at Portsmouth from which he could attack France. Early in the next century King John decided to station all of his war galleys at the new naval base – not that such a concept would have been understood at this time – and in 1212 the mayor was instructed to build a high, strong wall around the dock at Portsmouth 'so that we may avoid damage to our vessels and their appurtenances'. In 1215 a Master of Ships was appointed to serve at Portsmouth Harbour, where the numerous mud banks and large tidal range gave ideal conditions for ship repair.

There is an important distinction to be made between a naval base of this period and the new concept of a naval dockyard. The former could be any commercial harbour or yard where Crown ships were repaired or victualled; the latter was defended Crown property where the sole purpose was the repair or construction of warships. Portsmouth was undoubtedly the first example of the latter in Britain. In 1496 the kingdom's

Southampton docks in the liners' heyday.

first dry-dock for warships was constructed inside the dockyard there. Although Henry VIII may be seen as having detracted from Portsmouth with his decision to open additional yards at Deptford and Woolwich, this was a decision based purely on transport difficulties from London. His vision for the country's maritime defence was of a standing navy based at Portsmouth. Henry VIII ordered the *Mary Rose* and *Peter Pomegranate*, state-of-the-art warships, to be constructed at Portsmouth and the yard established a position held for centuries as the 'prototype yard'. The first examples of any new type of ship – particularly battleships – were built there before repeat orders were contracted out to commercial shipyards.

From around 1550 to the mid-seventeenth century Portsmouth went into eclipse. The Thames and Medway yards had greater military significance because of their proximity to the hostile Low Countries. However, following peace with the Dutch the French became the main threat and Portsmouth came into its own, never to lose its pre-eminence.

During the reign of Charles II a huge ropery, nearly 1,200 feet (365 metres) long, was built in the dockyard. It was an amazingly large structure for its day but the ropery had to be as long as the biggest rope on the vessel and a seventy-four-gun ship of the line would have over thirty miles (forty-eight kilometres) of cordage and rigging. After the Nine Years War (1689–97) it was decided to replace naval losses with new ships built at Portsmouth. As the programme took wing in the early years of the eighteenth century, Portsmouth Dockyard emerged as probably the largest industrial enterprise in Britain. Scores of new buildings were erected, many of which survive as one of the finest collections of Georgian industrial architecture in the country.

For the city and the dockyard the eighteenth century and the Napoleonic Wars was a period of boom and unrestricted expansion. Thousands of artisans flocked to the dockyard from all over England and Scotland, guaranteed well-paid and secure employment. Other trades flourished, not least timber haulage. It took sixty acres (twenty-four hectares) of felled Sussex woodland to build an English

HMS *Britannia* entering Portsmouth, 1835.

first-rater – the most efficient fighting machine in the world during this era. Every oak trunk was fetched by teams of horses and bullocks to meet the dockyard's seemingly insatiable demand for timber.

By 1760 employees at the dockyard were enjoying high wages and perks such as injury benefits and superannuation – conditions not to be found in any other employment for a craftsman or manual worker. Small wonder that when, during the American War of Independence, Yankee sympathizer John Aitken fired the dockyard and managed to destroy the ropery, thousands turned out to see him hanged within sight of the dockyard gates.

During the Crimean War it was shown in the most cruel and dramatic way possible that timber ships were too vulnerable to modern artillery. The Admiralty ordered HMS *Warrior*, the first iron warship; she was built at Blackwall, on the Thames, in 1859. Portsmouth needed to learn new skills if she was to survive as the navy's premier shipbuilding centre. The dockyard responded magnificently, changing over to iron construction with a speed that was startling for such a traditional organization. In the 1860s new docks and basins were excavated by the forced labour of convicts, the spoil being taken to extend nearby Whale Island which was to become the Royal Navy's world-famous gunnery school HMS *Excellent*.

By the 1890s the dockyard had a labour force of slightly over 8,000 and was one of the world's most advanced technology centres – the Silicon Valley of its day. Her finest hour was the construction of HMS *Dreadnought*, launched in 1906. This battleship was the most powerful ship afloat and represented a quantum leap over her rivals. Her ten twelve-inch guns meant she could fight from beyond the range of any existing enemy and should she be unlucky enough to incur a direct hit

Terpsicore, Ilyrica, and *Britannia* off Cowes, 1923.

her eleven-inch armour plating (no other ship had more than seven inches) would protect her. Radical steam turbine engines designed by the Tyneside firm of Parsons gave her twenty-one knots of speed, enough to outrun any warship afloat.

King Edward himself conducted the launch and thousands gathered beside the slipways to see a ship that rendered all other battleships in service obsolete overnight. Portsmouth went on to build thirteen more dreadnoughts between 1907 and 1914, reinforcing its position as the world's leading naval base.

Two world wars pushed Portsmouth once more into prominence but Britain's naval story during the twentieth century had been essentially one of fewer ships and declining importance. The shallow waters of the Channel and its busy commercial traffic made the base unsuitable for operating the modern dreadnought, the missile-carrying submarine. Portsmouth is now best known for its preservation role: the superb dockyard buildings, HMS *Victory* and HMS *Warrior* and the *Mary Rose*.

Directly across the Solent at Cowes a very different form of sailing ship predominates. This snug little town, split east and west by the River Medina, is the ancestral home of yachting. The world's oldest and most prestigious clubs are here, headed by the Royal Yacht Squadron (RYS) – founded in 1815 as the Royal Yacht Club. The first recorded sailing match at Cowes was in 1788 for a thirty-guinea purse. In the earliest days of yachting, wagers were as much a part of the scene as they have always been in horse-racing.

The promenade beneath the walls of Cowes Castle, home of the RYS, has many times been thronged with eager crowds watching the big boats race. The very first America's Cup was started from here in 1851. The schooner *America* had sailed over from New York to challenge the best that Britain had to offer. She had no trouble disposing of the opposition in a sixty-mile (ninety-six kilometre) race around the Isle of Wight. The 100 Guineas Cup, as it was originally known, was taken back to the New York Yacht Club by the victors. Despite its subsequent travels to Australia, California and back to New York, the silver Victorian ewer has never returned to Cowes.

GAZETTEER
THE SOUTH-EAST
FROM PEGWELL BAY TO LYME REGIS

PEGWELL BAY: In AD 597 St Augustine landed at Ebbsfleet on the wide sands on virtually the same spot as the Saxon invaders, Hengist and Horsa, had arrived at 150 years earlier. To commemorate the arrival of the Saxons, a replica of a dragon prowed Viking longboat, the *Hugin*, sailed from Denmark to Pegwell Bay in 1949, where it still stands.

A mile further inland is Richborough Castle on the site of 2 forts built by the Romans to guard the important mile-wide waterway Wantsum Channel which, in the first century AD, separated the Isle of Thanet from the mainland. Later in AD 285, the castle was built as one of the chain of fortresses, the Forts of the Saxon Shore, erected to deter North Sea raiders. The enormous triumphal arch

Replica longboat at Pegwell Bay.

which still stands would have been an important landmark for mariners.

SANDWICH: Because of the silting up of the River Stour, Sandwich is now over 2 miles (3.2 km) from the sea but its former maritime importance is still visible. In the Middle Ages, Sandwich vied with Hastings as being the most illustrious of the Cinque Ports, acting as a gateway to Europe for kings, princes and merchants.

The Great Storm of 1287 changed the coastline and mouth of the Rother and, with the silting up of the river, made many harbours unusable.

GUILDHALL MUSEUM
Cattle Market.
Local history and Cinque Ports' treasures.
Open Mon & Thurs.

GOODWIN SANDS, which lies 4 miles (6.4 km) off Deal, is one of the world's most notorious menaces to shipping – a sand-bar measuring 12 miles (19 km) long and 5 miles (8 km) wide resting on a chalk bed. Countless vessels have foundered here never to be seen again, hence its nickname 'The Ship Swallower'. At low tide the remains of these wrecked ships are visible. There is a more ghostly sighting every 50 years of the 3-masted schooner *Lady Lovibond* which went aground on 13 February 1748, and has been reported as reappearing every 50 years since.

Ships still founder and 7 lifeboat stations are on call making this the most extensive lifeboat coverage for a single area.

DEAL: From the time of Julius Caesar's landing near here in 55 BC (commemorated by a plaque in Marine Road south of Deal Castle), Deal became increasingly important in defence and naval terms.

TIME BALL TOWER
Victoria Parade.
It was used to semaphore messages to London and ships at anchor in the Downs could check their chronometers. At 1.00 pm GMT every day the black ball on top of the tower connected electrically to Greenwich dropped down the central shaft.
Open Spring bank holiday to end of Sept, Tues to Sat.

MARITIME AND LOCAL HISTORY MUSEUM
22 St George's Road.
Houses many maritime relics and boats, among them the Deal galley *Saxon King*, a narrow pulling boat which worked off the beach attending anchored ships. In 1801, when Nelson was stationed in the Downs, he wrote how a galley had come through the surf on to the beach in conditions which could have swamped an Admiralty-built boat. Because of the good reputation of the Deal galleys, naval captains used to buy them and they greatly advanced small craft design.
Open daily, May – Sept.

ST GEORGE'S CHURCH was built in 1709 to administer to the spiritual needs of the sea-faring community. In the churchyard lies the tomb of Nelson's beloved Capt Parker.

TOWN HALL
St George's Road.
Houses a small museum containing a full set of robes of a Baron of the Cinque Ports.
Open by appointment.

Just along the coast from Deal is WALMER CASTLE coastal fort, built by Henry VIII in about 1540. It has been the official residence of the Lord Warden of the Cinque Ports since 1708.

ST MARGARET'S BAY: Above the cliffs north-east of the village is a granite obelisk of the Dover Patrol Memorial commemorating the men who died in 2 world wars, while patrolling the Channel. The bay itself, 21 miles (34 km) distant from France, is the traditional starting or finishing point for cross-channel swimmers.

DOVER: The world's busiest passenger port, is the only one of the Cinque Ports, when it was known as the 'Key of England', to remain a major port today. The Roman pharos or lighthouse was built in the first century AD to guide Roman vessels into the sheltered anchorage of Dubris, the headquarters of the *Classis Britannica*. At a height of 40 ft (12 m) it is the tallest surviving Roman structure in Britain.

There is an exhibition of the Cinque Ports in the castle. On the promenade is the statue of Capt Matthew Webb who in 1875 became the first man to swim the channel.

DOVER MUSEUM
Ladywell.
Local history including ship models, clocks, etc. Dover's defences exhibition.
Open daily except Wed & Sun.

FOLKESTONE is unusual because it has no proper sea front but is a major harbour and cross-channel port. Along the huge stretch of open grassland above East Cliff Sands are 3 Martello towers.

FOLKESTONE MUSEUM AND ART GALLERY
Grace Hill.
Local history including maritime displays.
Open daily (closed Bank holidays and Sundays).

THE EXHIBITION CENTRE
St Martin's Plain, Cheriton High St.
The Euro Tunnel Exhibition showing the up-to-date progress of this huge engineering project, connecting the road and rail networks of Europe.
Open Tues – Sun.

HYTHE: The first written reference to Hythe was in 732 when Ethelbert, King of Kent gave it a charter. Its chief feature is the Royal Military Canal which was constructed as part of the sea defences against French invasion.

HYTHE LOCAL HISTORY ROOM
Oaklands, Stade St (nr Library).
Local history including Cinque Port Baron's robes.
Open daily except Sun and bank holidays.

CHURCH OF ST LEONARD
Churchyard has grave of Lionel Lukin, who in 1786 converted a Northumberland fishing boat into the first shore-based lifeboat.

LYMPNE, 3 miles north of Hythe, was once a port used by Roman legions occupying the fortress now called Stutfall Castle. Shepway (or Shipway – way of ships) Cross is a monument commemorating the centuries of administration of the ancient Cinque Ports' Court of Justice.

DYMNCHURCH: This small resort is strung out behind a grass-covered sea wall – Dymnchurch wall dating from Roman times built to guard the sluices which control the water level of Romney Marsh which lies 7½ ft (2.3 m) below sea level. On either side of the town there are 2 Martello towers built to guard the town. One of these, No 24, is open to the public with displays illustrating England's Napoleonic defences. Dymnchurch was also the home of the author Russell Thorndike, whose evocative stories of Dr Syn and the exploits of Romney Marsh smugglers are commemorated today in the biennially held festival 'Day of Syn' in August.

OLD ROMNEY: Although diminutive in size now, it was an important port until the great storms of the late thirteenth century which diverted the River Rother.

SNARGATE: 4 miles (6.4 km) into the marsh from Old Romney contains a mere handful of cottages. The south aisle of its capacious church used to be sealed off and used as a hideout for smugglers. On the west end of the north wall there is an ancient wall-painting of a fifteenth century galleon.

DUNGENESS: The various lighthouses on the vast shingle promontory of Dungeness have helped provide safe passage for ships since 1615 when it was stated that '1,000 person perished there from want of light every year.' The earliest light was a simple open fire and there are the remains of a further 3. The oldest is the base of Samuel Wyatt's lighthouse of 1792, now used as a lighthouse keeper's home. Nearby is the Old Lighthouse, 33 yd (30 m) from the sea, which with 167 steps to the top of its brick tower (1904) is the highest in the UK.
Open during the summer.

RYE: The fact that the sea receded from the town 400 years ago has not diminished Rye's status.

During the Middle Ages, Rye contributed 5 ships to the Royal Fleet, so earning the right to supply fish direct to the king's table. It still has a small fishing fleet. Despite silting up, Rye continued as a centre for building sailing coasters including the barge *Convoy* (1900) which is still sailing; fishing and sailing boats are still based here.

Like the other Cinque Ports, Rye was constantly under attack by the French and in 1377 it was almost completely destroyed. The medieval Mermaid Inn (1420) was the haunt of a notorious gang of smugglers known as the Hawkhurst Gang. Many of the houses still have inter-connecting attics, through which smugglers could dodge to escape the excise men.

Marsh barges at Rye.

RYE MUSEUM
Ypres Tower.
Local collections are housed in this thirteenth century tower with several displays of Cinque Port material and shipping.
Open Easter – mid Oct, Mon – Sat.

WINCHELSEA: The town was laid out towards the end of the thirteenth century to replace the original port which was washed away in the Great Storm and lies under the waters of the Channel somewhere out in Rye Bay.

'Modern' Winchelsea developed into an important port with a lucrative wine trade and became a Cinque Port suffering countless attacks from the French. With the build-up of shingle along the shore which gradually cut off Winchelsea from the sea, its prestige declined, though it remained a hotbed of smugglers.

WINCHELSEA MUSEUM
Court Hall.
Collection illustrating history of Winchelsea and

Beach-fishing boats at Hastings.

the Cinque Ports. Models, maps, documents.
Open May – Sept.

HASTINGS: When William landed in 1066, Hastings was already an important port with its harbour at the eastern end of modern Hastings, where fishermen still winch their boats ashore. Hastings is one of the few places to have decked beach craft. They are very beamy which gives them buoyancy for coming through the breaking waves. Hastings became the premier port of the whole confederation of the Cinque Ports until the Great Storm ruined its harbour. The old town is hemmed in on both sides by steep cliffs. West Hill is honeycombed with caves including:

ST CLEMENTS' CAVES: used by smugglers in the eighteenth century for storing contraband.
Open daily.

THE FISHERMAN'S MUSEUM
Rock-a-Nore Road.
Housed in what was once the fishermen's church, alongside the old net sheds which, dating back to Elizabeth 1's day, are such a distinctive and unique feature of the beach. Displays include

local fishing, fishing nets, old photographs, ship-models, including a 1922 model of *Henri Grace à Dieu* and a horse-capstan used to haul the luggers up the beach until the Second World War. Also housed here is the Hastings lugger *Enterprise* (1909) which was the last Hastings boat built for sail only.

SHIPWRECK HERITAGE CENTRE
Rock-a-Nore Road (east end of sea front).
An exhibition '3000 Years of Shipwrecks' with an excellent audio-visual presentation 'Medieval Shipwreck Adventure'. Visitors can monitor the shipping in the Channel with working radar. Major exhibits are objects from 3 important local wrecks, the warship *Anne* (1690), the Dutch ship *Amsterdam* (1749) and a Danish ship (1861). These contain muskets, brandy, wine and a tomb stone.
Open daily from Easter to Oct.

MUSEUM OF LOCAL HISTORY
Old Town Hall, High St.
Displays on maritime history, the Cinque Ports, smuggling, fishing and models of ships such as the Dutch East India *Amsterdam* whose wreck is exposed at very low tides on the foreshore. Among the maritime traditions is the ancient annual custom of 'Blessing the Sea', held in the late spring at Rogationtide.

ROYAL NATIONAL LIFEBOAT MUSEUM
Grand Parade.
Many types of lifeboats from the earliest date to present time. Various items used in lifeboat service.
Open mid March – New Year's Day.

BEACHY HEAD: Rising sheer from the rocky foreshore to a height of 534 ft (163 m), Beachy Head has at its foot the famous red and white lighthouse. The coastline here presents the magnificent scalloped white wall of the Seven Sisters, breaking at Cuckmere Haven (an important 'gap' used by eighteenth century smugglers for their cargoes) before rising up again to the huge bulk of Seaford Head.

NEWHAVEN: Built 400 years ago to replace the blocked harbour of Seaford it has never expanded like Southampton, Dover and the other cross-channel ports. In the churchyard of St Michael's parish church there is a memorial to 105 officers and men who drowned when their ship HMS *Brazen* was wrecked beneath the Newhaven cliffs in 1800.

ROTTINGDENE is a smuggling centre of old. Rudyard Kipling wrote *The Smugglers Song* here.

BRIGHTON was once a major fishing centre but the expansion of the pleasure resort slowly strangled the industry. To the east of Brighton the marina opened in 1979, the first man-made harbour reclaimed on a large scale solely for yachts.

SHOREHAM-BY-SEA, where the River Adur makes a right-angled turn to the east, forming a natural harbour one mile long and running parallel to the shore line, has a strong maritime flavour. In the mid-Victorian period, wooden brigs and barques were built here for general ocean trades. Although the commercial centre has shifted eastwards towards Hove, there is plenty of sailing activity in the harbour, and reminders of maritime past in the town.

On the South Lancing side of Shoreham harbour, there is an interesting collection of Second World War naval MTB and similar craft, now converted into house boats.

MARLIPINS MUSEUM
High Street.
A fascinating display relating to local history of shipping and Shoreham Harbour including water-colours and ship models. Housed in an early twelfth-century secular building.
Open May – Sept, (Mon – Sat).

WORTHING was once a beach-fishing station until residential interests discouraged fishermen.

WORTHING MUSEUM
Chapel Road.
Has a small display of the history of lives saved by 3 Worthing lifeboats since 1868 until 1930 when Worthing ceased to be an active lifeboat station.

LITTLEHAMPTON: There has been a settlement at the mouth of the River Arun since Saxon times – fishermen's cottages known first as Arundel Haven. Its harbour was already flourishing in the Middle Ages as the main port of entry for Caen stone and it was the home of ocean-going ships in the age of sail. Harveys, renowned for wooden sailing ships of great quality, had a yard on the west bank of the Arun.

THE LITTLEHAMPTON MUSEUM
12a River Road.
The museum was built by a notable local sea captain, Arthur Robinson as his home in 1904.

D-Day preparations, Portsmouth.

From the eighteenth century all the men of his family had been master-mariners and the museum has records and paintings of their 40 sailing ships that traded across the world. There is a painting of one of these, *Trossachs*, which sailed from Little-hampton taking the first sheep to the Falkland Islands. There are some fine marine paintings by RH Nibbs, Claude Muncaster and Leslie Wilcox. On his coming ashore in the 1920s, Capt Robinson created a garden summer-house and the Long Gallery using old ship's timbers.
Open Apr – Oct, (Tues – Sat).

The narrow entrance to **CHICHESTER** harbour opens into a landlocked lagoon, where peninsulas split the main channel into many tidal creeks which, with 27 square miles (70 sq km) makes one of the biggest sailing harbours on the south coast. Until the nineteenth century many of the pretty waterside villages were busy commercial harbours (Dell Quay was the main harbour for Chichester and once the seventh most important port in England) but are now boating centres.

The Saxon church at **BOSHAM** features on one of the earliest panels of the Bayeux Tapestry. It was from Bosham, an important harbour in Saxon times, that Harold set out on his fateful journey to Normandy to swear loyalty to William. **BIRD-**

HAM was the building site for ships in Williams's time and was also a source of salt, hence the local name 'Salterns'.

EMSWORTH in the time of Henry II was a thriving fishing and trading port. It was a landing place for smugglers until well into the twentieth century. It once had a substantial oyster fleet, but deaths through pollution of the beds led to its decline from 1900. There is also the remains of the *Echo*, the largest ship of the oyster fleet, launched in 1903, but which never put to sea because of the Emsworth oyster being banned due to pollution from 1903 – 1914. The 'Ark', a great box-like construction intended for storing oyster catches at sea, but grounded upon launching, can be seen.

LANGSTONE is the original port for Havant at the head of the ancient waterway to Hayling Island and as late as the last century it served as a coasting port. There are water tours of the harbour from Itchenor on traditional passenger boats similar to the *African Queen*.

PORTSMOUTH has a long and distinguished record as the home of the Royal Navy, (see inset). It and its immediate environs have an unparalleled collection of naval reminders and exhibits. The walls of a Roman fort still overlook the harbour which saw Henry V depart for Agincourt and allied troops leave for the Normandy beaches.

Portsmouth's Naval Heritage

Portsmouth dockyard may have shrunk in importance from the days when it employed 25,000 workmen and headquartered a Royal Navy that spanned the world, but it now has a new role – as Britain's pre-eminent centre of naval heritage. Three historic warships – HMS *Victory*, HMS *Warrior* and the *Mary Rose* – are on display there, plus the bonus of the comprehensive and vivid Naval Museum.

HMS *Victory* is still a commissioned warship, with a commanding officer and naval ratings to man her – they also guide the tour parties. It is this fact that gives her an atmosphere way beyond anything that a museum can generate. To peep into Nelson's cabin, to stand on the spot in the orlop deck where England's hero breathed his last and to stumble in the stygian gloom of the lower gun deck where 800 ratings existed on salt beef and maggoty biscuits – plus the blessed rum, of course – is to feel the centuries drop away and imagine oneself at sea in the eighteenth-century navy.

Victory, the world's last remaining ship-of-the-line, was laid down in 1759 at the Royal Dockyard, Chatham. With 104 guns she was the largest and most expensive ship the navy had ever ordered, creating public controversy and debate similar to the arguments over the desirability of the modern Trident submarine fleet. She was launched in 1765 – one reason why HMS *Victory* has lasted so well is that her oak timbers had the opportunity to season as she lay in dry dock while the politicians wrangled.

It was thirty-five years before Nelson took command of the *Victory*, well past the operational life of a modern warship. Her finest hour came on 21 October 1805, when the allied fleets of France and Spain were sighted off Cape Trafalgar in south-western Spain. At 12.40 pm the *Victory* fired her first colossal broadside into the French

Nelson falls mortally wounded, hit by a sniper's bullet, at Trafalgar.

flagship *Bucentaure*, smashing her stern, dismounting twenty guns and killing over 200 sailors and marines. Nelson's tactic of punching a hole through the enemy line of battle was to prove crucial. Although he was struck down by a sniper's bullet twenty minutes later, Trafalgar was already going to the British. Of thirty-three Royal Navy ships that went into battle all returned safely, although damaged to a greater or lesser degree. Out of the forty enemy ships only four returned to their home ports; the rest were either destroyed or taken as prizes.

Nelson died in the orlop deck of the *Victory*. His body was preserved in a cask of brandy – which the sailors later wanted to drink as a sign of respect – and taken back to London since the Admiral had requested that he not be buried at sea. The funeral barge which took Nelson up the Thames to his last resting place in St Paul's is the centre-piece exhibit in the main gallery of the museum. The plaque records that the Thames was wild and rough, weather which the perpetually seasick Nelson would have hated.

HMS *Warrior* was a ship that changed the navy almost as much as did the *Victory*. While iron-hulled steamers had become common on commercial routes during the 1850s, the Lords of the Admiralty remained convinced that warships would always be built of oak. When the French navy launched *la Gloire*, a battleship with five inches (twelve centimetres) of iron cladding around her hull, they began to change their minds. HMS *Warrior* was the response. Launched in 1860 with the most powerful steam engines available, *Warrior* was twice the length of the *Victory*, packed four times the firepower, had twice the speed and used far fewer crew.

Aloft, the *Warrior* still had the full rigging of a square-rigged warship since there was still relatively little confidence in engines. On patrol she would tend to sail because at high speeds her coal consumption became prodigious.

Like the nuclear submarines of today, the mere presence of the *Warrior* in the Channel kept the peace between Britain and France. She never fired a shot in anger. *Warrior* spent nearly 100 years stripped of guns and engines as a depot ship or a fuelling hulk; the last fifty as Oil Fuel Hulk C77 in Pembroke dock, west Wales.

With the growing interest in old ships a movement began in the late 1970s to save the *Warrior*. She was towed to Hartlepool, one of the cradles of iron shipbuilding, and spent seven years alongside there undergoing a £7 million stem-to-stern restoration that culminated in her triumphant return to Portsmouth in 1987.

That concern with maritime heritage also provided the impetus for the dramatic discovery and eventual recovery of the Tudor warship *Mary Rose*, now on display just a few hundred yards from HMS *Victory*. Henry VIII ordered this ship to be built shortly after he became king in 1509. *Mary Rose* was constructed in the world's first dry dock, close to where she is now housed. She capsized and sank during an engagement with a French invasion fleet just a mile from the entrance to Portsmouth Harbour.

Powerful Solent tides covered the wreck with silt and mud. This provided the preservative medium that kept the starboard side of the hull virtually intact for over 400 years. She was discovered, as a consequence of a planned exploration programme, in 1971 and the next eleven years were spent cataloguing, measuring and excavating. A task performed by hundreds of volunteer divers and archaeologists.

In 1982 came the big lift, an extraordinary feat watched live on television by millions of viewers.

Mary Rose under a protective moisture spray.

Mary Rose was transferred in a steel cradle to a low-temperature (five degrees centigrade) high-humidity building constructed above the dry dock next to the *Victory*.

There she sits today, marvelled at by thousands of visitors, 'the flower of all ships that ever sailed,' as Sir Edward Howard described her to Henry VIII in a letter concerning the flagship on which he had been so proud to serve.

SOUTHSEA CASTLE is built from where 3 sea forts are visible (between the 2 eastern forts lay the wreck of the *Mary Rose* until she was raised in 1982). The castle contains displays illustrating Portsmouth's development as a military fortress and aspects of naval history.
Open all year (except Dec 24–26).

ROYAL MARINES MUSEUM
Royal Marines Barracks, Eastney, Southsea sea front.
Housed in the old officers' mess, this display spans all aspects of the Marine's history from 1604: the great heyday of sail, to the Falklands campaign, with uniforms, medals, colours and audio-visual displays. There is a special display of various musical instruments used by the Royal Marine Bands throughout the centuries.
Open all year.

D-DAY MUSEUM
Clarence Esplanade.
The only museum in the country devoted to the Normandy landings. Magnificent Overlord embroidery is its centre-piece.
Open all year.

On the beach between Clarence Pier and the

HMS *Holland No 1*, the Royal Navy's first submarine.

Royal Navy War Memorial, is the original anchor of HMS *Victory*.

DOCKYARD APPRENTICE MUSEUM
Just outside the Naval Base's Unicorn Gate, it concentrates on the industrial side of building and repairing naval vessels. Contains ship models, documents and photos of the old dockyard.
Open weekdays, Apr – Sept.

BLUE BOAT TRIPS
Clarence Esplanade (next to Hovercraft Terminal).
50-minute harbour tour by boat leaving from Esplanade – takes you past historic harbour fortifications built from pre-Elizabethan to Napoleonic times and through the narrow harbour entrance passing the naval base where modern British and foreign warships lie.
Operates Easter – Oct daily.

ROYAL NAVY SUBMARINE MUSEUM
South of the ferry, near the submarine training base of HMS *Dolphin* at Fort Blockhouse, it records the history of the 'silent service' from its origins at the end of the nineteenth century to the present day. The chief attractions are HMS *Alliance*, one of the last Second World War A-class submarines, fully restored to her service condition. The other is HMS *Holland No 1* which

Trains and boats at the Ocean Terminal, Southampton.

was the navy's first submarine, launched in 1901. Open all year.

GOSPORT MUSEUM
Walpole Road (a short walk up the high street from the RN Submarine Museum).
Tells the story of Gosport's developments from a fishing village to the 'storehouse' of the navy. Local maritime crafts are included.
Open Tues – Sat.

NAVAL ARMAMENTS MUSEUM
Priddy's Hard, Hardway, Gosport.
A unique collection of naval armaments spanning maritime history, all housed in a vast eighteenth-century gunpowder store.
Open on application to curator.

HAMBLE village on Southampton Water is one of the most concentrated yachting centres in Britain, with 5 yacht marinas and a passenger ferry across the Hamble. At the head of South-ampton Water lie the sprawling docks that made SOUTHAMPTON Britain's major passenger port and the home of the Atlantic liners of the Cunard company. Its history goes back more than 1,000 years: it started out as the Roman port of Clausentum and was William the Conqueror's port for his ships from Normandy. There are 6 miles (10 km) of quay including the Ocean Dock, where the *Mauretania*, *Queen Elizabeth* and *Queen Mary* once berthed.

MARITIME MUSEUM
Wool House, Bugler Street.
Once a medieval wool warehouse, in which French prisoners of war were housed in the eighteenth and nineteenth century, it is now a museum of merchant shipping with a large model of the *Queen Mary*.
Open Tues – Fri.

The tiny village of BUCKLER'S HARD on the banks of the Beaulieu River, although originally planned as a base for importing sugar from the West Indies, became an important shipbuilding centre from 1698 to 1827. For almost a century work was under the control of the family and descendants of the master builder Henry Adams

A six-metre yacht off Cowes.

who built more vessels for the navy in 80 years than any other of the private Hampshire yards. Giant oaks felled in the nearby New Forest were cut and shaped into the massive timbers of 64-gun ships of the line, such as Nelson's favourite HMS *Agamemnon*, and the *Euryalus*.

THE MARITIME MUSEUM recalls the past achievements of Buckler's Hard with models of many of the ships built for Nelson's fleet. Other exhibits include a replica of the figurehead from HMS *Gladiator*, launched in 1782, but which never saw action as she served as a home for convalescent seamen at Portsmouth until she was broken up in 1817.

Also included is the memorabilia of Sir Francis Chichester who used the Beaulieu River as his sailing base prior to circumnavigating the globe single-handed. Also the eighteenth-century homes of a master shipbuilder, shipwright and labourer have been recreated in the original cottages.
Open daily.

The importance of defending the Solent and the approaches to Portsmouth and Southampton has always involved the **ISLE OF WIGHT** in any defensive schemes since Roman times. 22 brass cannon point from **COWES CASTLE** out over one of the world's most famous yachting harbours, scene of the annual regatta (Aug 1–9). There are 9 yacht clubs at Cowes with the castle acting as base for the exclusive Royal Yacht Squadron founded in 1815.

COWES MARITIME MUSEUM
Beckford Road Library.
Collection contains models, photos and plans of shipbuilding that took place in the Cowes shipyard of JS White, including warships from the late nineteenth century to the Second World War. Small craft include: Prince Philip's Flying 15 *Cowslip*, and an Uffa Fox dinghy.
Open Mon – Fri.

BEMBRIDGE MARITIME MUSEUM (on the east coast)
Sherborne Street.
6 galleries of ship models, wreck items, material from Second World War submarine HMS

Swordfish. Early diving equipment, deep-water sail, paddle-steamers, work of Trinity House.
Open Easter – Oct, daily.

In the south, St Catherine's lighthouse, built in 1838 is open to the public at the discretion of the keeper. Just inland off the coastal path on the 780-ft (238-m) summit of St Catherine's Hill stands an octagonal tower known as 'the Pepper Pot'. It is the relic of a lighthouse built in about 1323 by Walter De Godeston as an act of penance for having received casks of wine looted from a wrecked ship.

The huge natural harbour of **POOLE** nearly 100 miles (160 km) around, has a double high tide, a characteristic of this stretch of coast, so the harbour has 14 hours of high water each day. In Poole many of the buildings are of maritime interest. A 15-acre (6-hectare) site beside the harbour includes the custom house, the old harbour office and a fifteenth-century wool house which is now the

MARITIME MUSEUM
Paradise Street, Poole Quay.
Displays illustrate Poole's link with the sea from prehistoric times until the early twentieth century. The life and work of merchants, seamen, fishermen, shipwrights and allied craftsmen and tradesmen of the port are illustrated through the tools they used. Examples of local boats, contemporary accounts and ship models. Also has a display of original works of art by notable local artists such as Bernard Gribble and Leslie Ward, through whose work we see the last days of sailing in the old port of Poole.
Open all year.

PORTLAND and **PURBECK** frame a stretch of coast where Dorset's chalk downs meet the English Channel in sheer white cliffs which have been cut into by the sea forming magnificent natural sculptures like Durdle Door, or isolated caves where smugglers once stored their contraband.

WEYMOUTH was once a prominent 'South County' port sending ships to Newfoundland and was active in the coastal trade. It is through Weymouth that the Black Death entered England in 1348. It is now an important cross-channel ferry port. A Tudor cottage in Trinity Street is a museum showing a typical Elizabethan house of a ship's captain. Splendid cliffs dominate Lyme Bay and reach 626 ft (190 m) at Golden Cap, the highest point on England's south coast.

WEYMOUTH LOCAL HISTORY MUSEUM
Westham Road.
Has among its display, George III's bathing machine.
Open May – Sept.

At **BRIDPORT** the broad pavements were once drying tables for the thousands of miles of rope demanded of the town by the Royal Navy ever since the time of King John. Much of the old industry, introduced by the Romans, has disappeared and the town is now given over to net-making and is the biggest producer of industrial fishing and multi-purpose netting in Europe and probably the world.

BRIDPORT MUSEUM AND ART GALLERY
South Street.
Items connected with the town's historic rope and net-making trade.
Open weekday ams throughout the year and Mon, Tues, Wed and Fri pms, 1 June – 30 Sept.

The harbour at **LYME REGIS** is protected by the Cobb, a massive breakwater. Though silted up it is still used for lobster fishing boats and pleasure craft. Five local ships helped to defeat the Spanish Armada in 1588, but the most notable event in Lyme Regis's history was when the Duke of Monmouth landed in 1685, raising his standard against James II.

THE WEST COUNTRY

Secret harbour: Polperro, Cornwall

THE WEST COUNTRY

OF ALL ENGLAND's varied coast-line, nothing appeals quite so much to the romantic in all of us as the scrambled loveliness where Devon and Cornwall come down to the water's edge. From the intimacy of verdant little creeks in the South Hams district of Devon to the vast rolling perspectives of Falmouth harbour, there is a variety in this coast that is hard to find elsewhere in Britain. Moreover, it is an intensely domestic shore. Fishermen, coastal traders and those whose business does not bear too much official looking-into, have been active here for millennia. Because of the absence of raw materials such as coal and iron, industrial shipbuilding never took hold in the West Country – with the possible exception of warships at Devonport and the specialized constructions of Appledore and Bideford in North Devon.

The region's popularity with holidaymakers since the earliest days of mass travel has undoubtedly been based on the attractions of harbour and beach. Almost every marine activity in Devon and Cornwall is small scale and accessible. One can hardly imagine a tourist strolling the Grimsby quay to watch a stern-trawler put to sea, but from the mole at Coverack there is infinite pleasure in watching the tiny lobster boats go out to tend the pots. Or seeing the graceful, gaff-rigged oyster boats of Falmouth, probably the last working sailing boats in Britain, trawl for the succulent and lucrative bivalves.

In the Middle Ages seagoing ships were infinitely smaller than now. Devon and Cornwall's indented coastline, full of tiny creeks and river harbours between large, solid headlands, was a godsend to mariners who could get their light, shallow-draft vessels into hundreds of towns and villages. Nowadays only Plymouth and Dartmouth, plus Falmouth to the west, have the room and depth of water for modern tonnages. On the north coast there is only the port of Barnstaple, which is full of shoals and guarded by a dangerous bar. Yet what are now hazards for navigation were positive advantages in the days of small-ship warfare and piracy.

In the ninth century Danish marauding fleets began to appear along Devon's shores. There were major recorded battles between native defenders and the invaders at both Wembury, near Plymouth, and Exeter. Rich farmland coming almost down to the water's edge and prosperous, unfortified villages made this region a fat and juicy target for the Danes. King Alfred's response, when his ad hoc navy of chartered merchant ships with soldiers in charge cleared the Danes out in AD 897, was one of the earliest known examples of the British crown's use of sea power. Alfred's remedy was effective for over a century although in the late tenth century the Danes returned and in AD 1003 Swein, King of Denmark, was able to storm Exeter – at that time a major port. With the arrival of William the Conqueror on England's throne, naval attention switched to the Cinque Ports, with their quick sea access to Normandy. The West Country settled down to intra-coastal trading and fishing, although Dartmouth retained status as a major European port and Crusade fleets sailed from there in 1147 and 1190.

The high-minded Christian exertions of the Crusades were an aberration for Dartmouth. From the twelfth century and for the next 500 years the South Devon coast became a haven for piracy to rival anything later seen on the Spanish Main or the Barbary Shore. The region's strategic position on the maritime highway into Europe and its distance – in the days before roads – from the civilizing and regulating influences of London, meant that its skilled and self-willed sailors roamed the

Channel as they pleased, seizing the ships and crews from many other nations; 'to the shame and scandal of the whole realm,' wrote the anguished Edward II, whose Italian bankers had just been captured, robbed and murdered by the Dartmouth pirates.

As if in search of respectability the pirates gradually became known more as privateers, attacking the king's enemies to fill their own pockets. Seamen that now stand in the pantheon of national heroes – Drake, Hawkins and Grenville, for example – were often acting in a great West Country tradition that owed more to self-help with gun and cutlass than noble patriotism.

By Tudor times Dartmouth had emerged as the most well-defended harbour fortress on England's south coast. Two castles commanded the entrance to the Dart – as they do to this day – and a chain could be stretched between them. In 1522 the Earl of Surrey reported to the king that he had never seen 'a goodlier haven after all our opinions'. Thirty miles (forty-eight kilometres) to the west Plymouth Hoe was studded with bastions and inter-connected defence works. According to one contemporary letter-writer there were so many privateers and pirates at sea from South Devon ports during the sixteenth century that many of the fishing boats were being manned by women. A Spanish agent, living under cover in Dartmouth, wrote back to his spymasters in Madrid that 'the inhabitants are warlike and constantly at sea'.

By the time of Elizabeth's accession to the throne the pirates of South Devon had become a national scandal. The new Queen was determined to come down hard on these maritime entrepreneurs. In 1577 one John Plomleigh, the Mayor of Dartmouth and not a person to be trifled with by a Crown anxious to defend its shores, was fined £100 for piracy, the second highest fine Devon had ever seen. In the previous year the monarch had been shamed by the news that up to a dozen Dutch pirates were based in Torquay and being given support and victuals in an informal alliance with the townspeople.

Of course, the Crown's perspective changed as relations with Spain deteriorated and the risk of an invasion grew. To have a fleet of brave, skilful, if anarchic, seafarers commanding the Western Approaches might be an international embarrassment in peacetime but as war became inevitable the swashbuckling Devon captains became a national asset. Elizabeth's father, Henry VIII, had conducted a shipping census in 1560 that for the first time showed the West Country's maritime importance. Devon had 1,268 full-time seafarers and eighteen vessels of over 100 tons, five in Plymouth and nine in Dartmouth. Devon was ahead of every other county and only two ships behind London.

By reason of its geographic and strategic position Plymouth had always been a crucial point for the assembly, arming and victualling of whatever fleet the Crown choose to put together in time of naval emergency. Yet, possibly because of its remoteness from London, no navy yard was established in the city at the time when the royal dockyards of Portsmouth and Chatham were forging ahead. In the early sixteenth century Sir Walter Raleigh had proposed the great sheltered Hamoaze as a naval harbour but the Queen had baulked at the cost.

It was not until William of Orange came to the throne nearly a century later that work commenced on what was to become Devonport Dockyard. The site was on the eastern side of the estuary and separated from the town centre by a marshy river near what is now Union Street. Access was easiest by sea, despite it being a two-mile (three-kilometre) row from the Barbican. The first docks were ready in 1693 and within five years ancillary work such as officers' housing and a 1,000-foot (300-metre) long covered ropewalk had been added.

The town of Devonport grew so rapidly through the well-paid work being offered to tradesmen and labourers that it became the boom town of early eighteenth-century England. At that time it was still called Plymouth Dock. That indefatigable chronicler of the

Devonport Dockyard, 1798.

time Daniel Defoe marvelled that it had grown to half the size of its elder sister in a mere fifty years. At the turn of the century the dockyard had overtaken Plymouth in size and in 1821 their respective populations were 35,000 and 21,000. Once each quarter there were vast celebrations in the dockyard area, fit to rival any fiesta in a Spanish town. These marked the arrival of the pay frigate from London, wages being sent by sea to avoid the considerable risk of highwaymen.

As the century advanced Britain seemed to be routinely at war with almost every country to the south and west. Spain, France and the emerging United States all provided protagonists and opportunities for Plymouth Dockyard to grow. One of the most interesting developments, still largely unchanged today, was the naval hospital at Stonehouse. Completed in 1762 it was revolutionary in its concept of putting groups of patients into small ward blocks – fifteen all told – which were conveniently grouped in a square but allowed the free circulation of air. Patients could be delivered direct by boat to a hospital jetty in Stonehouse creek. The hospital became a legend in European medical circles

and many French and German hospitals were to have their designs based upon it.

Although a superb natural harbour, Plymouth Sound was wide mouthed and exposed to the prevailing south-westerly wind. A breakwater was needed, despite the considerable engineering challenge such a construction would present.

The first rock in over seven million tons of limestone and granite was placed in 1817. It would be over twenty-five years before the work was totally complete. The mile-long structure, the central 3,000 feet (915 kilometres) completely straight, still stands today and dominates the wonderful seascape from the Hoe.

An even more outstanding engineering achievement, fourteen miles (22.5 kilometres) further out to sea than the breakwater, was the creation over a century earlier of the first lighthouse on the Eddystone reef, a hazard that had claimed ships and lives since West Country men first put out in ships. Work began to build a tower on a small exposed rock jutting up from the reef in 1695. Just to reach the site involved engineers and labourers in an eight-hour row from the Barbican. Everything from granite blocks to pickaxes had to be taken out by sea. The

Carrick Roads and Falmouth town, 1678.

work took three years and claimed many lives, including that of the builder Henry Winstanley when a huge storm toppled the finished lighthouse shortly after its completion. This should not be seen as a reflection on the workmanship of the Eddystone light. Across Britain the same storm wrecked over 150 ships and drowned approximately 7,000 seamen.

Successive lighthouses were built – the third by John Smeaton was re-erected on the Hoe and can still be visited – but the Eddystone was never unguarded thereafter. That factor and the vast sheltered anchorage provided by the breakwater made Plymouth a harbour that would continue to thrive whatever the exigencies of war and peace. With the coming of the railway in the mid-nineteenth century transatlantic liners began to stop at Plymouth to disembark passengers whose business was sufficiently urgent to justify taking the train up to London. This was a tradition that was to continue right through into post Second World War years when the liner service began inexorably to decline. Crack expresses on the Great Western Railway, such as the Cornish Riviera, would be scheduled to connect with ships such as the *Queen Mary* and SS *Normandie*.

Marine trade of an altogether humbler variety was to be found in the sheltered creeks and rivers of Falmouth harbour. Here small, locally built, schooners and smacks provided a network of human and commercial communication that persisted into the early years of this century. There was nothing unique about this pattern but it shows in microcosm a style of living with the sea and using the sea that prevailed across the West Country, with the possible exception of North Cornwall where the coastline was inhospitable to a degree.

There was another layer of marine active in the Fal estuary beyond the purely local traffic and that was best summed up in the ringing phrase 'Falmouth for orders'. Once the electric telegraph had linked Cornwall to the great trading houses of London, an inbound ship would duck in behind the sheltering bulk of the Lizard peninsula and then seek instructions for her cargo. A local paper of the 1840s reports of Falmouth Roads 'Two hundred sail of merchantmen, chiefly corn-laden, awaiting orders'. The grain clippers would often refit in Falmouth and within living memory there were old shipwrights

Drying sails in Falmouth harbour.

who had served their apprenticeships aboard the *Cutty Sark* or *Thermopylae*. But the bread-and-butter craft were the 'inside' and 'outside' barges of the Fal. Properly they were more smacks than barges with a fore-and-aft rig manageable by a two-man crew and shallow draft – although not the wide bow and flat bottom common to the inland barge. The outside barges were sound little seaboats of about sixty feet (eighteen metres) overall and seven feet (two metres) draft, with the capacity to carry a load of around thirty tons up to Plymouth in a day – this at a time when a four-horse cart might cover twenty miles (thirty-two kilometres) in a working day. One of the last surviving examples of such boats, the *Shamrock*, can be seen on the River Tamar, at Cotehele Quay between Plymouth and Tavistock.

'Inside barges' were a somewhat different shape. With no seas to contend with they ran to a bigger beam, shorter length overall and a draught of only three feet. They were cheap to construct and even less expensive to run. Often a family-run yard on the banks of a Fal creek would 'knock one up' from the timber left over from the construction of a sea-going schooner. They could go anywhere within the tidal limits of the vast estuary, carrying cargoes that varied from quarried marble to new potatoes. Until the 1950s they could still be found criss-crossing the waters, taking heavy loads to spots that neither the railways nor the commercial carriers found it worthwhile to visit. One major trade was the unloading of guano, or bird manure, from the big merchantmen which had brought it up from South America. The little inside barges could take it from the main anchorage and deliver it virtually to the farmers' front gate.

The growth of Falmouth as a major mail packet port in the eighteenth and nineteenth centuries gave impetus to a community who were already accomplished seamen and boat-builders. All along the shoreline, villages sprang up little commercial syndicates putting together the finance to build and operate schooners and ketches of seventy to 150 tons. Many of the schooners from this area came to specialize in the Azores fruit trade. It required fast ships and good seamen who could get the perishable oranges and lemons which were such luxuries in those innocent days back to England before the rot set in. If the

Clipper weighing anchor in Falmouth Bay.

fruit went up to London, a frequent return cargo was coal which was simply unloaded on to the nearest beach to the village.

Some voyages took small Falmouth schooners as far afield as the Grand Banks of Newfoundland, to trade in the huge volumes of cod being caught there. The 1,800-mile (2890-kilometre) voyage was long and dangerous but it seemed worthwhile when back in the leafy creeks with a big profit to share out in the local pub or meeting house. These were very much village ships. When they set sail they would be victualled from the village resources and their water barrels filled from the tiny 'schooner wells' which can still be found in the rocky walls of most Fal creeks by those who know where to look.

It was a romantic life and by most seafaring standards a relatively comfortable one. Yet the growing sophistication of the shipping business and the dominance of the big steamship lines made the demise of home-built schooners inevitable. Most of the Cornish seamen, although fine, almost intuitive, mariners, chose not to stay at sea with the big shipping lines as the schooner trade died.

The ships were too large, with as many men in the foc'sle as the population of a Penwith village. It did not suit the Celtic preference for family-sized crews. Instead they drifted back to the trade of their forefathers – fishing from the many harbours and coves that stud the peninsula.

Cornish fishing is worth looking at in some detail, since it followed a pattern of pre-industrial methods and techniques right into the present century. Devon fishing was always more large scale and technology based. Remember, it was the Brixham fishermen who introduced the beam trawler to the Yorkshire ports. In Cornwall, the traditions of small locally built boats and two- or three-man crews had been handed down through generations.

The backbone of the Cornish fishing fleet was the lugger. The French navy developed this unusual quadrilateral sail to a high degree in the class of Channel privateers called the *Chasse-Marée*. It was fast, sea-worthy and simple. Most of the fishing boats had three masts, each with a lugsail, although the boats from the far west, around St Ives and Sennen seemed more to favour two. In the nineteenth century a size of between thirty-five feet (10.5 metres) and forty-five feet (13.7 metres) became the norm, although local building variations meant that luggers from one port might all have square transoms, while the boats from twenty miles (thirty-two kilometres) away might be double-enders. Certainly they were fast, a necessary attribute as the coming of steam railways meant that it was a race to get the catch aboard the London train. The speed of the luggers also gave them a not entirely unwelcome degree of suitability for smuggling. So worried did the excise men become in the late eighteenth century and early nineteenth centuries that laws were passed regulating the ratios of beam to draught to length that, ultimately, controlled hull speed. If the customs authorities found a lugger that contravened the rules she would be ritually sawn into three and burned on the beach.

The target for all of these boats was primarily the pilchard. In previous centuries huge shoals of this handy-sized and nutritious cousin of the herring would appear off the headlands and bays of Cornwall. The size of some shoals would defy modern credibility. One shoal netted off West Cornwall and landed mainly in St Ives weighed 1,050 tons and was estimated to have contained in excess of seventeen million fish. The nets that could handle these whole townships of fish were themselves prodigious. The main net would be carried in the lugger, but would be tended by men in the tow boat and the 'lurker' or follower. So many weights, sinkers, floats and adjustment lines did a major seine net have that it would take two or three carts to move it down from the village to the shore. The capital involved was high, so since Tudor times small companies had been formed in each village to own the seining gear in shares. In the 1820s it was estimated that a fully equipped seine might cost as much as £800 – whereas the boat itself was probably worth little more than £120.

August's long hot days would bring the pilchards in off the Cornish coast. Special watchers called 'huers' were posted on the cliff paths and headlands and given the task of watching for the great reddish-purple patch on the water. When a shoal was sighted the cry went up 'Hevva, hevva' and all work would cease in the village while the nets were brought out and the boats made ready for sea.

With villages quite close together along the southern coast of Cornwall and the value of a big shoal being well into the thousands of pounds it was necessary to have a system of arbitrating possession of the pilchards. Each village had a pitch or 'stem', the boundaries being marked by headlands. If the shoal moved from one to the other then the ownership went with it.

Once the vast seine net, the size of several football fields, was enclosed around the pilchards, a steady stream of small boats would ferry the catch ashore a bit at a time. It could take weeks. In the village the women and children 'bulked' the fish, building a wall of solid pilchards up to four feet (over a metre) high, each layer being covered with salt. Later they would be barrelled. The great fear was that the settled harvest weather might break before the fish could all be brought ashore. The pilchards that were not sent to market were kept in store beneath the houses. In villages like Portscatho the details of fish cellars can still be clearly seen.

Pilchards were the best-known Cornish catch, a bonanza to be enjoyed but not counted upon. Mackerel were at least as important and provided a catch spread more evenly through the summer months. The mackerel fishing boats were around ten feet (three metres) longer than the pilchard luggers and known as 'drivers'. From Easter until mid-summer the boats would work the Channel coast, trying always to be within a day's sail of market since mackerel were notoriously bad fish for keeping. When the pilchards came, so too did hake, the big predatory fish cruising around the edge of a shoal. Each seine fisherman would be armed with a rugged hand line – the shank of each hook being as much as six inches (fifteen centimetres) long – for going after hake, which could be sold for as much as three pence each well into the autumn months. Handlining was also practised for mackerel by the smaller boats, its advantage being that it was the cheapest gear available. In Cornwall handlining was always known as 'whiffing' and has enjoyed a considerable revival in recent years, especially during the winter months – when it was once thought impossible to catch mackerel.

Nevertheless, the decline in the Cornish fishing industry has been severe. In the early nineteenth century it was the biggest factor by far in the county's economy. In a town like St Ives, over one-fifth of the 6,000 population would be engaged in fishing or handling the fish and fish oil ashore, boat-building, box-making and barrel-making. As

Unloading pilchards at Porthleven, 1930s.

Meeting the catch at Newlyn, 1880.

a rule of thumb around a fifth to a quarter of the male population in the coast villages were at sea fishing and about the same proportion worked in ancillary crafts ashore.

It would be hard to guess at the proportion of fishermen to people working in the holiday industry nowadays, but the latter would be larger by many multiples. Yet Cornish fishing survives, from the big boats of Newlyn to the small rowing boats hauled up in tiny coves. And it is not uncommon in the early spring to see a farm worker finish his paid labour at the gate and slip down to the harbour to shoot a few early-evening lobster pots.

────── GAZETTEER ──────

THE WEST COUNTRY FROM BEER TO MINEHEAD

The coast of Devon and Cornwall is characterized by small stone harbours lodged in the bays and coves that nestle between the region's many rocky headlands.

BEER was the last port to have 3-masted luggers, well adapted for the beach conditions of steep shingle slopes. The original Washbourne Memorial Fisherman's Capstan is still in place at the top of the hill.

Beer was a smuggling centre until the mid-nineteenth century when Jack Rattenbury, one of Devon's most celebrated smugglers, defied the excise men for nearly 50 years. He retired and published his *Memoirs of a Smuggler* in 1837. The coast around Weston Mouth, west of Beer, is pitted with caves which earlier served the smugglers as hiding places for contraband.

SIDMOUTH's days as a port ended when silt and shingle made it unsuitable for navigation. Small fishing boats still use the beach near the river mouth.

Sidmouth's past sailing fishermen have been

Shelter but no harbour for Beer fishermen.

well recorded, firstly by the marine painter Robert C Leslie, who arrived in 1854 and saw how dangerous the working lives of the beach fishermen were, and recorded this in his work.

Author Stephen Reynolds came to Sidmouth in 1906 and taking lodgings with a fisherman wrote *A Poor Man's House* in 1908, a factual book about the harsh lives of fishermen at that time. He went on to write similar books while himself living and working as a fisherman.

BUDLEIGH SALTERTON is where Millais's famous painting *The Boyhood of Raleigh* was conceived: the sea wall which featured in the picture and Millais's house can still be seen. Raleigh was born at Hayes Barton near Budleigh Salterton.

EXMOUTH's heyday as a port was in the sixteenth century, when it was one of Devon's most important maritime centres and used as a base by Sir Walter Raleigh.

TOPSHAM at the head of the Exe estuary, was a thriving port until the rail link for Exeter to Exmouth was opened in 1861. John Holman and Sons built sailing boats here.

TOPSHAM MUSEUM
25 The Strand.
Situated in Holman House with sail loft which covers history of Topsham as a port, particularly 1680–1720 when the serge trade flourished. Shipbuilding in Topsham: wooden sailing vessels from Napoleonic Wars to 1880s. Ship models, tools, anchors, figureheads, paintings and photos.
Open Feb – Nov, (Mon, Wed & Sat).

EXETER is the chief city of the South West and one of the oldest in Britain. It was an inland port in the time of the Romans and probably long before that.

THE MARITIME MUSEUM
The Quay.
Uses the basin of a ship canal built in 1567 and the oldest pound-lock waterway in the country, to keep many of its exhibits afloat. It has the world's largest collection of boats, 150, many of which can be boarded and explored.

Exhibits include Brunel's canal dredger of 1844, the oldest working steam ship in the world and working vessels, small craft and boats from all over the world, particularly the Pacific.
Open daily except 25 & 26 Dec.

TEIGNMOUTH has a long history as a fishery

Busy Brixham around 1909.

and shipbuilding centre. Its sheltered harbour faces upriver and the quay built in 1830 is still used by small coasters.

Red sandstone cliffs tumble down to the sea in a series of small coves round **BABBACOMBE BAY** and **TOR BAY**. Babbacombe Beach was an important local smuggling centre – with 153 casks of contraband spirit being discovered once in a raid in 1833. Customs officers now tend to find containers of illegal drugs.

TORQUAY, called by Tennyson 'the loveliest sea village in England' has hundreds of yachts and pleasure craft moored in its harbour. Although mainly developed since the mid-nineteenth century, in 1588 Torquay was 'host' to prisoners from the Armada, kept in the 'Spanish Barn', a medieval tithe barn still standing.

BRIXHAM was England's major fishing port for 300 years. It is famous for developing one of the most powerful sailing vessels for its size, the Brixham trawler, which became the prototype for the huge fleets of trawlers established on the east coast. A few can still be seen as yachts. A statue on the quay nearby commemorates the landing of

William of Orange on 5 Nov 1688 to begin his invasion of England.

BRITISH FISHERIES MUSEUM
The Old Market House, The Quay.
Describes 500 years of British deep-sea fishing.
Open daily, Apr – Oct.

BRIXHAM AND HM COASTGUARD NATIONAL MUSEUM
Bolton Cross.
Has local and maritime history including Brixham trawler models, *Mayflower* display, and local wrecks. There is a section illustrating the history of the coastguards.
Open Easter – mid Oct, daily.

DARTMOUTH: The deep water at Dartmouth has been the assembly point of many fleets including those of two crusades in 1147 and 1190. Sir Walter Raleigh sent 9 ships from here to fight the Armada and in 1620, the Pilgrim Fathers' ships *Mayflower* and *Speedwell* put into Dartmouth for repairs. Their visit is commemorated on the cobbled quay at Bayard's Cove which ends by Bearscove Castle, a small fort built as a coastal defence by Henry VIII. Dartmouth is also the home of Britannia Royal Naval College built in 1905.

DARTMOUTH TOWN MUSEUM
The Butterwalk.
Housed in a former merchant's house built in the 1630s, there are many historical maritime exhibits. Ship models illustrating the development of vessels from pre-history to the twentieth century. Fine British eighteenth-century 1:48 scale warship models. Exceptional nineteenth-century Dartmouth lifeboat model.

Up the River Dart at **TOTNES**, St Peter's Quay is still the scene of ships unloading, just as it was in the Middle Ages when exports of tin and wool made Totnes one of the major ports in England.

START BAY: By the late nineteenth century contractors building the new naval docks at Plymouth received permission to dredge sand and gravel from Start Bay. Despite the warnings from local fishermen about undermining the foreshore, the dredging continued and between 1900–1904, 650,000 tons of sand and gravel were dredged, with the predicted consequences. The worst erosion took place in a storm of 1917 when all but one of 30 cottages at Beesands and Hallsands were washed into the sea.

Ships under repair at Devonport, 1845.

START POINT, the sharp headland running almost a mile into the sea on the south side of Start Bay, is one of the most exposed peninsulas on the English coast. The lighthouse established in 1836 on the extremity, is approached by a narrow road cut out of the rock face.
Open daily (except Sun).

SALCOMBE has one of the West Country's finest natural harbours opening on to nearly 2,000 acres (800 hectares) of tidal creeks. It is now a popular sailing centre and has an annual regatta. It was first held in 1857.

OVERBECK HOUSE
Sharpitor, south Salcombe.
Museum of local interest including model Salcombe ships and shipbuilding, paintings and ephemera.
Open Apr – Oct, daily.

ISLAND CRUISING CLUB: Not a museum but looks after preserved ships *Hoshi* (1908), a 2-masted schooner and *Provident* (1924), a ketched-rigged Brixham trawler.

From Soar Mill Cove can be seen Ham stone rocks which claimed the Finnish barque *Herzogen Cecille* in 1936 – one of the last sailing ships to be wrecked on Britain's coast. Likewise, Bolt Tail, a headland first fortified during the Iron Age, has witnessed many shipwrecks. In 1588, during the rout of the Spanish Armada, the *San Pedro el Major* went down near here with the loss of 40 lives. In 1760, 700 men died when the warship *Ramillies* went down.

PLYMOUTH: Plymouth started life as Sutton Harbour, a fishing village which in 1231 became Plymouth. Set on the Sound, it has one of the finest natural harbours in the world. Its record as a naval port goes back as far as the end of the thirteenth century. Devonport on the west of the city was established as a naval base in 1691.

Sir Francis Drake, the greatest of all Elizabethan seafarers, set sail from Plymouth in 1577 for his circumnavigation of the world; on his return 3 years later he became mayor of the city. There is an imposing statue of Drake on Plymouth Hoe.

Sir Walter Raleigh also set sail from Plymouth to Carolina in 1584, as did the Pilgrim Fathers in September 1620 and at a later date, Captain James Cook and Charles Darwin. The place of embarkation of the Pilgrim Fathers is marked by The Mayflower Steps.

PLYMOUTH CITY MUSEUM AND ART GALLERY
Drake Circus.
A good collection of maritime paintings by artists with local connections. Ship models, including French prisoners of war, bone models, some ship equipment.
Open Mon – Sat.

ELIZABETHAN HOUSE
32 New Street.
Elizabethan House as would have been occupied by a sea captain of the time.
Open Mon – Sat.

MERCHANT HOUSE MUSEUM
33 St Andrews St, Plymouth.
Local social history including one room on life of the sailor.
Open Mon – Sat.

HM NAVAL BASE
Devonport, South Yard.
Naval memorabilia, historic and modern.
Visitors must be in groups of 10-25.

BUCKLAND ABBEY, 9 miles (14 km) inland, near Milton Combe was the home of Sir Richard Grenville, the Elizabethan sea captain renowned for his gallant fight against the Spanish fleet in his tiny ship *Revenge*. Later the home of Drake. Among other relics can be seen Drake's Drum which is supposed to sound at times when the nation is in peril. Now a folk and naval museum.
Open daily, Easter – Sept.

EDDYSTONE LIGHTHOUSE lies about 14 miles (22.5 km) SSW of Plymouth and was the scene of so many shipwrecks in Stuart times that a decision was taken to erect a permanent light-house. In 1696 Henry Winstanley, an eccentric, obtained a patent to build on Eddystone Rock. The first structure, in stone and wood, looked like a Chinese pagoda. Yet he had such confidence in his work that he decided to be at the lighthouse during a gale and in November 1703 went out there with a repair gang. On the evening of 26 November, the 'Great Storm' sprang up. When dawn broke nothing remained of men or light-house.

Despite its failure it was Britain's first success-ful attempt to establish a rock lighthouse. It was not until further appalling wrecks around the Eddystone, that a second tower was built of stone clad with timber. This was destroyed by fire in 1755.

Next came John Smeaton's granite lighthouse which had to be dismantled because of fissures in the rock on which it stood. It now stands on Plymouth Hoe as a memorial to Smeaton and his introduction of a new era of lighthouse buildings.

MORWELLHAM, (off A390 between Tavistock and Gunnislake), was once the busiest port west of Exeter and 'the greatest copper port in Queen Victoria's Empire'. Morwellham ceased to func-tion at the beginning of the twentieth century, after 900 years of activity. Now its quays on the River Tamar which once shipped ore from Devon's copper and manganese mines, have been restored and turned into an outdoor museum.

MORWELLHAM OUTDOOR MUSEUM
Tavistock.
Here can be seen items connected with local navigations and the tub boat canals. Recon-structed as in 1868, crafts and port's activities re-enacted.
Open daily.

COTEHELE HOUSE
On the upper reaches of the River Tamar, it is a National Trust property.

SHAMROCK QUAY MUSEUM
Cotehele Quay, St Dominick, Saltash.
Tamar barge *Shamrock* (1899), Plymouth built, in service until 1950s. Available for charter in the summer. Eighteenth century office and warehouse contain displays on regional coastal and river trade and local industries. *Shamrock* is run by the National Maritime Museum in conjunction with the National Trust.
Open Apr – Oct, daily.

POLPERRO: For centuries Polperro's narrow cobbled streets were a haven for smugglers. Fishing was another source of income until the nineteenth century but the village's future was threatened by a great storm in 1824 which destroyed several buildings and wrecked almost all the fleet of 50 boats. The smuggling past of the village is chronicled in Polperro's

MUSEUM OF SMUGGLING
Open daily.

POLRUAN is to the west of the magnificent 450 ft (137 m) high Pencarrow Head from where 80 miles (129 km) of coast from south Cornwall to Bolt Tail in Devon, can be seen. On a rocky outcrop are the ruins of the fifteenth-century blockhouse from which a chain was stretched across to Fowey to block the river mouth protect-ing pirates from the authorities.

Alongside at Truro, 1912.

FOWEY, although small, is a thriving commercial port which since the Middle Ages has supported trade. Now it is expanding to accommodate both the continuing world demand for Cornish china clay and the upsurge in yachting for pleasure. Fowey's daring sailors, known as 'Fowey Gallants' featured in many medieval campaigns and were at the Siege of Calais in 1346.

CHARLESTOWN: This picturesque harbour near St Austell dates from the end of the eighteenth century and was named after the local mine owner, Charles Rashleigh, who financed it. It soon became an important outlet for china clay from St Austell. Behind the dock a building complex houses

THE SHIPWRECK CENTRE has a fine display of old anchors and naval guns, the most important exhibit being the entire wreck of a wooden vessel, *The Grand Turk*. There are artefacts, pictures, photos, charts, anything connected with shipwreck. History of diving and salvage.
Open Easter – Oct, daily.

MEVAGISSEY is an ancient fishing port which was established in the Middle Ages. It was important for pilchards in the eighteenth and nineteenth centuries, Italy being its major customer. In the navy pilchards were called 'Mevagissey Duck'.

MEVAGISSEY MUSEUM, on the east quay, is housed in an old boatyard dating from 1745. It has roof supports made of ships' masts and exhibits of local interest.
Open Easter – Sept, daily.

The beautiful headlands and rocky harbours of the east and west side of St Anthony Head flank the busy shipping estuary of 7 rivers: the Carrick Roads, which extend inland with many attractive creeks leading off it. On a bluff at the foot of the headland on the eastern side of the harbour stands St Anthony Head lighthouse built in 1835. It is open to the public daily.

FALMOUTH has one of the world's finest natural harbours. The ancient port, used by Phoenecian galleys, is still used by shipping from all over the world – its dry dock can handle tankers up to 90,000 tons.

It was the first port of call from the seventeenth century for many ships homeward bound and last stopping place for those sailing west. It was the first place in Britain to learn of Nelson's victory at Trafalgar.

On the main quay is the 'King's Pipe', now

Home waters on the Tamar for the *Shamrock*.

called 'Queens Pipe' – a chimney beneath which tobacco seized from smugglers was burnt by the excise men. The Toen Moor or central square has a memorial to the crews of the fast sailing packets for which Falmouth was famed.

MARITIME MUSEUM
Bells Court (up an alleyway off Market St).
In this building in 1810 the Riot Act was read to mutinous packet men. Illustrates the maritime history of Cornwall with displays on shipbuilding, the ports and trade of Cornwall. Most of the exhibits deal with the 150-year history of the sailing packets with numerous models. The museum has moored at the head of Penryn River the Gorran Haven crabber, *Ellen* (1882); *Softwing* (1910), a Falmouth oyster dredger and *Barnabas*, a 2-masted lugger.
Open daily.

ST DAYS (berthed at Custom House Quay in harbour) open late March to early November. A steam tug unique for having the only Caprotti valve marine steam engine in existence, worked in Falmouth from 1929–1980. On-board display mainly illustrates local ship- and boat-building.

FALMOUTH ART GALLERY
The Moor.
Has among its collection several fine eighteenth- and nineteenth-century maritime paintings and prints.
Open Mon – Fri.

MYLOR BRIDGE, on the west of the Carrick Roads and north of Falmouth, has an inn supposed to be the oldest in Cornwall. Called the Pandora, it was named by the commander of HMS *Pandora*, the ship which went to the Pacific to capture *Bounty* mutineers after they had set their commander Captain William Bligh adrift.

FLUSHING was named by Dutch engineers who were employed to build its quays and sea walls in the seventeenth century. Nearby Trefusis Point was the scene of the loss of 200 lives when the transport ship *Queen* was wrecked in 1814. There is a commemorative plaque to the victims in St Mylor's church along with stones to many other ill-fated seafarers.

PORT NAVAS, south of Falmouth, is a shaded creek on the Helford estuary where millions of oysters are bred, producing nearly a quarter of

Britain's oysters. They are gathered by rowing boat to avoid disturbing or polluting the oyster beds.

GWEEK, at the end of the river, was a busy port from the Middle Ages to the nineteenth century dealing in cargoes of timber, coal, lime, tin and local farm produce.

GWEEK QUAY MARITIME CENTRE
Head of Helford River.
Historic and unusual boats from the Exeter Maritime Museum collection. Falmouth quay punt 1897; lifeboat (1900); dinghy built in Cornwall by French Resistance and used on raid; gondola; hovercraft. Boats and ships used in films (videos of films) including replica of fourteenth-century Hanseatic cog. Artefacts from licensed wreck excavating.
Open spring bank holiday – mid Sept, daily.

The wild seas around the Lizard have claimed more lives than on any other part of coast. Off the north-east coast of the Lizard lie the **MANACLES**, a treacherous group of deadly rocks a mile offshore. St Keverne church, whose octagonal spire has been a landmark for sailors for 300 years, has more than 400 victims of shipwrecks on the Manacles buried in the graveyard.

COVERACK has a fishing harbour. The Paris Hotel on the harbour takes its name from an American ship which ran aground at the turn of the century. Her passengers and crew of 700 people in all were brought safely to shore. A light was considered necessary here from as early as 1570, but much local opposition had to be overcome before the philanthropic Sir'John Killigrew could gain the patent to build one. Objections came from those who often officially derived benefit from the wreckers' activities and also from fear that it might guide enemy vessels and pirates to a safe landing. It was eventually ready by Christmas 1619. Although it was a superb light for those days and shipowners reaped the benefit, they refused to offer anything for its upkeep. Due to diminishing funds the light was extinguished and the tower demolished. It was not until 1752 that another 4-storied house was built. This is open to the public every afternoon. East of the lighthouse, the cliff Pen Olver is the spot from which the Spanish Armada was first sighted in 1588.

MULLION was very important for pilchard fishing; the 5 companies operating the lucrative pilchard fishing from here before the First World War would get a 'huer' or lookout on the cliff-top to watch for the dark patches of pilchard shoals approaching across the sandy sea bottom.

HELSTON, a market town of steep streets 2 miles (3 km) inland from the sea, was an important port in the thirteenth century. Then a bank of sand and shingle, Loe Bar, finally closed the harbour mouth, creating an inland lake.

Many ships have foundered on Loe Bar, including the frigate *Anson* which in 1807 was driven on to the sands and 100 men died within a stone's throw of the shore. Among the crowd who witnessed this tragedy was Henry Trengrouse, who later invented the rocket apparatus for throwing a line to a ship in distress.

HELSTON FOLK MUSEUM
Old Butter Market.
Open daily.

PRUSSIA COVE gets its name from the smuggler John Carter who was known as 'King of Prussia'. An inn called the same was owned by him and used as a cover for smuggling on a grand scale. He installed a battery of guns on the cliffs round his inn, ostensibly to deter French privateers, but probably to frighten off revenue men.

ST MICHAEL'S MOUNT: A granite island rising 300 ft (90 m) from the waters of Mounts Bay, is capped by a fourteenth-century castle. The priory on St Michael's Mount is dedicated to St Michael because he is said to have appeared to a local fisherman in 495. It was a major base for the early tin trade and, because of its close monastic connections with Mont Saint Michel, it was a trading and migration centre from the earliest days of Christianity.

PENZANCE, once a major West Country port, is now best known perhaps for the operetta *The Pirates of Penzance*. Pirates from France and the Barbary Coast constantly used to raid the town until the mid-eighteenth century.

PENZANCE MARITIME MUSEUM
19 Chapel Street.
Houses a substantial collection of items, mainly from wrecks, including finds from the ships of Sir Cloudesley Shovell's squadron which was wrecked in the Scillies in 1707.
Open Mon – Sat.

NEWLYN's oldest pier dates back to the Middle Ages. Famous for giving its name to the Edwardian Newlyn School of painters who were inspired by the scenes of local fishing life, Cornish fishermen, breaking waves, tranquil peaceful harbours, etc.

NEWLYN ORIAN GALLERIES
Newlyn.
Exhibits include paintings by Newlyn School.
Open Mon – Sat.

MOUSEHOLE, sacked by Spanish raiders in 1595, survived to become Cornwall's main fishing port for many years prior to the rise of Newlyn.

PENLEE POINT LIFEBOAT HOUSE is from where the *Solomon Browne* set sail during a ferocious storm in Dec 1981. She and her 8-man crew were lost trying to rescue 8 others from the coaster *Union Star*. The boat's coxswain was awarded a posthumous gold medal.

PORTH GWARRAY's landing is so small that it is hardly visible from the sea at high tide. It is just a tiny slip leading up to a man-made arch cut in the rock. There are several of these holes in the rock faces, made by St Just tin miners so that horses and carts could collect seaweed for the farms. Pilchard fishing was also an important activity for augmenting meagre cash earned by other forms fishing.

At **LAND'S END**, granite cliffs plunge 200 ft (60 m) to the sea, attracting over 1 million visitors a year. There are maritime exhibitions and craft workshops in the last house in England.

LONGSHIPS LIGHTHOUSE rising 120 ft (36 m) from the sea, 1 mile offshore, protects ships from the many rocks in this stretch. The most dangerous is the Carn Brae, the cause of countless vessels being wrecked in sight of home.

A tower was built at Sennen Cove in 1795 and taken block by block to the Longships. Four keepers were appointed whose harsh lives have been the subject of several stories (eg *Watchers on the Longships* by James F Cobb). One of the peculiarities of the Longships station was that on bad nights, the rush of wind through a fissure and past a cavern produced a terrifying noise. One keeper was so terrified that his hair turned white and he went mad, another was kidnapped by wreckers, but the light was kept shining by his young daughter, who though small, reached the lamps by standing on the family bible.

SENNEN COVE, just east of Land's End, belies its name, for it is open to the full fury of the Atlantic, being just a slightly sheltered side of Whitesand Bay.

Before the First World War, 2-masted luggers were used for crabbing from here and also for undertaking salvage. It was not uncommon for ocean-going sailing ships, unable to fix their position when coming from the Atlantic, to run into this inhospitable coast. A 'good wreck' was looked on as a godsend: a Swedish barque wrecked off Sennen in 1913 is still remembered with affection by the older generation because she supplied them with coal and fire bricks for years.

Sometimes in March, huge shoals of up to a thousand stone of mullet appear in Whitesand Bay, which the Sennen Covers regard as their property, often literally fighting off attempts by fishermen from other villages to 'trespass'.

As recently as 1969, there was an aggressive encounter between 30 Sennen men armed with knives and men from Par which had to be dispersed by the Penzance police.

PENDEEN ore deposits stain the sea a rich dark red around the rocky headland from which the Pendeen lighthouse guides shipping past the headland. The beacon was established here in the sixteenth century, tended by a hermit. The antiquary John Leland observed in the 1530s there 'a chapel of St Nicholas and a pharos for a light for ships sailing by night in these quarters'. The beacon disappeared at the Dissolution. The present light was re-established in 1900 and commands a picturesque situation. It is open to the public.

ZENNOR is a windswept village 350 ft (106 m) above the sea. The twelfth-century chapel of St Senara has the famous medieval carving of a mermaid depicted with a mirror in one hand and comb in the other. She is said to have lured Matthew Trewhella, a local man whose singing she admired, down into the sea at nearby Pendour Cove, beneath Zennor Head.

ST IVES, the picturesque haven for artists and craftsmen and women, is one of the few harbours on the north coast. Today it is extremely popular with tourists. St Leonards, a tiny building at the landward end of the pier was once a fisherman's chapel. It stands on the site where St Ia, after whom St Ives is named, is said to have arrived by coracle from Ireland in the sixth century. It is open from Mar – Oct.

ST IVES MUSEUM

Wheal Dream – in harbour area.

Models and mementoes of Hain Steamship Co, established in St Ives by Edward Hain in 1878, bought by P&O in 1917, phased out in 1974. Clockwork from Pendeen lighthouse. Gibson photos of Cornish wrecks.

HAYLE, in the eighteenth century, was the busiest port on Cornwall's north coast exporting copper and tin from the nearby foundry.

ST AGNES HEAD, 629 ft (192 m) above the sea, was one of the beacon sites to warn of the approach of the Armada in 1588 and from where nearly 30 miles (48 km) of coast can be seen on a clear day.

The ruins of Wheal Coates mine where tin and copper were worked in the nineteenth century can be seen here.

TREVAUNANCE COVE: To the east of the headland is another of Cornwall's 'lost ports' which originally served as a harbour for the tin and copper trade mined from St Agnes set on high ground to the south. Cargoes were unloaded by horse-powered windlasses, mounted on the cliffs while ore went thundering down a series of chutes. Incredibly there was also shipbuilding on this open coast – the trading schooners *St Agnes* (1873), *Goonlaze* (1874), *Lady* (1877) and the fastest British schooner ever built, *Trevellas* (1876) were all built here. Now only tumbled blocks of granite are all that remain of the last harbour.

NEWQUAY, Cornwall's biggest resort and Britain's foremost surfing centre, grew up around 'a new quay' built in 1439. As elsewhere in Cornwall, fishing and smuggling became important sources of income, but trading also extended to North America.

Gig races held in the summer are a link back to the days when gigs, powered by teams of oarsmen, raced out to pilot vessels safely into the harbour. The Newquay Rowing Club have a gig house beside the tiny harbour where they keep the 30ft ((9m) *Newquay* (1812), *Dove* (1820) and *Treffry* (1838).

MAWGAN PORTH, in the lovely Vale of Lanherne, had a settlement from as early as AD 50. At the church at St Mawgan 2 miles inland there is a poignant reminder of the harshness of life at sea. A wooden tablet shaped like the stern of a boat commemorates 9 men and 1 boy who froze to death in a lifeboat after their ship sank in 1846 and who were swept ashore as Mawgan Porth.

BEDRUTHAN STEPS: This astonishing beach 300 ft (90 m) below the gorse-covered cliffs is only accessible by a long flight of slippery and very steep steps. A series of stacks or rocks, some as high as 200 ft (60 m) range across the low tide sands and are said to be the stepping stone of the giant Bedruthan.

PADSTOW, on the Camel estuary, is said to have been in existence before the arrival of St Petroc in the sixth century. He is commemorated by the founding by local merchants and shipowners of the Guild of St Petroc. It was certainly a busy port handling cargoes of fish, wine, slate and ores until the mid-nineteenth century when the silting occurred that produced Doom Bar and prevented larger ships from using the harbour.

PORT QUIN is a tiny hamlet whose few cottages, now owned by the National Trust, are the remnants of an earlier fishing community – has been deserted since the nineteenth century.

Local tradition maintains that when all Port Quin's fishing crew were lost in a storm, the women and children left. What is verifiable is that with the closure of nearby Doyden Point mines, many emigrated to Canada.

PORT ISAAC, the next settlement, has retained both its charm, with a jumble of cottages squeezed into a steep coombe, and its importance as a local centre of lobster fishing. The pots can be seen in the harbour pools. The old fish cellars where fish were salted and stored for export are still in existence.

TINTAGEL is the focus of the Arthurian legend which specified that Arthur was born here and that Tintagel is in fact legendary Camelot. Despite lack of evidence, the dramatic coastal scenery, with the ruins of Tintagel Castle clinging to the wild headland, and the many remains of a sixth-century Celtic Xtian settlement, make it a creditable claim. The beach of sand and pebbles below Tintagel Head is reached through Merlin's Cave, the spot where Arthur is said to have met Merlin.

BOSCASTLE: Although its harbour is difficult to enter, it provides one of the very few havens on this inhospitable coastline ('From Padstow Bar to Lundy Light/Is a sailor's grave by day or night').

THE BARBICAN – HISTORIC HEART OF PLYMOUTH

Few European medieval seaports have survived as intact as the Barbican. It has been Plymouth's maritime heart for centuries. Small-boat fishermen still unload catches and moor their boats against worn granite steps used by Drake, Hawkins and the Pilgrim Fathers. Although the shops, pubs and warehouses – many of them hundreds of years old – contribute to the unchanging mercantile atmosphere of the Barbican, no visitor is likely to escape the military impact of the glowering, grey stone walls of the Citadel towering above the compact harbour.

Sutton Harbour, now a yacht marina, and the adjoining Cattewater were Plymouth's main harbours virtually up until the eighteenth century when construction of the modern naval dockyard began. The streets of the ancient and fortified town surrounded these small havens, and it is this whole area that is now known as the Barbican. The first members of the Hawkins family, a seafaring tribe that became a Tudor dynasty in the West Country, held property in the Barbican area as far back as 1480. In 1513 William Hawkins surrendered his role as master of Henry VII's 'great gallye', married a Trelawney heiress and

Entry to the dry dock, Devonport.

settled in Plymouth as a merchant trader.

In 1528 he financed and commanded the *Paule of Plimmouth* on her voyages to trade with Brazil and Africa's fever-ridden Guinea coast. Two more successful voyages followed and by 1537 William Hawkins was established in a fine house on Kinterbury Street, overlooking Sutton Harbour, and was mayor of his adopted city.

Two sons, William and John, were brought up here. Under this roof John Hawkins planned his expedition to the Bay of Mexico (1567) in the company of a promising young Tavistock sea captain, Francis Drake. Queen Elizabeth provided two ships, the Hawkins family three and Drake his own fifty-ton *Judith*. The voyage was not a huge success and the many skirmishes with the Spanish colonists controlling the West Indies provided the motif that was to run through Drake's life.

Over the next ten years the master mariner, now married, conducted smaller voyages to the Spanish Main – often clandestinely – and planned his circumnavigation of the globe. Five ships, led by the *Pelican* (later renamed *Golden Hind*) gathered in Cattewater and sailed on a bitter winter's day in November 1577. Three years later Drake had rounded both Cape Horn and the Cape

of Good Hope, searched in vain for the North West Passage, and was down to just one surviving ship, the *Golden Hind*. He docked in the Barbican, stowed the looted treasure in nearby Plymouth Castle and enquired of the mayor whether Queen Elizabeth was still on the throne?

In the years that followed almost every major expedition of discovery and commercial adventure that left England departed from this harbour. Some were wildly successful, other failed dismally but all benefited the little port while the ships fitted-out and sought backers and crews.

As relations with Spain deteriorated, the existence of the Armada was an open military secret. The enemy ships had spent years victualling and equipping in ports such as Cadiz and la Coruna. Drake was by now admiral of the portion of the English fleet that lay in Sutton and Plymouth Sound and his friend and contemporary John Hawkins, vice-admiral.

Whether or not they were actually playing bowls on Plymouth Hoe, high above the harbour, when the Armada was sighted off the Lizard is uncertain, but it is certainly an enjoyable piece of mythology. Scholars have ascertained that the tide was unfavourable at the hour the news came and Drake would have known that he could comfortably wait for the ebb before setting sail in pursuit of the enemy.

With the Spanish threat destroyed for generations Drake was able to settle back into the role of prosperous merchant prince and court favourite. He owned two houses in the Barbican: one at Thornhill Park and the other on the corner of Looe and Buckwell streets. Although neither survive today, a similar Elizabethan sea captain's house has been preserved.

Over a dozen expeditions to the New World were organized, financed and manned from this little maritime centre over the next decade. It was the Cape Kennedy of its day, technology, knowledge and adventure clustering around the narrow streets. In 1595 Drake and Hawkins assembled twenty-seven ships in Sutton Pool for an invasion of Panama. They both died on the voyage and were buried at sea.

The Barbican maintained its role as a focus for New World colonization a generation later, when the Pilgrim Fathers sailed in the *Mayflower* from the Barbican. The Mayflower Steps were marked at the spot where they embarked although the actual pier was lost long ago. The Pilgrims were fleeing from persecution in Boston, Lincolnshire,

Sir Francis Drake.

but the tablet speaks of how they were 'kindly entertained and courteously used' by Plymouthians while waiting to have their ship repaired by the local shipwrights.

The city's adherence to progressive causes cost it dear in the Civil War, when Royalist forces laid siege to Plymouth for nearly three years. Deaths from hunger and disease soared; the former only being relieved by what was often called 'the miracle of the Barbican'. A shoal of hundreds of thousands of pilchards swam into Sutton Harbour. Buckets, kettles and many other kinds of receptacles were used by the starving inhabitants to catch the strangely complacent fish. Vast quantities were salted and stored to last through the siege.

When the monarchy was restored, Charles II was mindful of Plymouth's role in the war and began the last major piece of building to affect the Barbican. In 1666 construction work began on the Citadel, a fortress designed on French lines to dominate both the Sound and the Barbican below. It took nearly ten years of unremitting labour but when finished it gave complete security to the little harbour that was then the keystone in Britain's growing maritime arch.

The inlet winds round 2 tall cliffs, the inner jetty being rebuilt by Sir Richard Grenville, the Elizabethan seafaring captain of *Revenge*. From the rocks beyond the stone jetty it is possible to see and hear the famous blow hole through which the sea grumbles and spouts at certain stages of the tide.

THE STRANGLES are named to illustrate the treachery of this coastline. In the 1820s more than 20 vessels were wrecked in a single year. St Genny's churchyard is the resting place for many of these victims.

BUDE: At the seaward end of Breakwater Road in Bude, a sea lock marks the entrance to Bude Canal, opened in 1823. It was the longest tub boat canal ever built, carrying sea-sand for fertilization of inland farms, and on the return trips brought oats and slate to trading vessels in Bude harbour.

THE BUDE HISTORICAL AND FOLK EXHIBITION is open down near the canal during the summer. Its exhibits include local shipwreck scenes, for between 1824 and 1874 over 80 ships were wrecked on this stretch of coast. Figureheads, ship models, photos.
Open during the summer.

MORWENSTOW, Cornwall's northern most parish, was the base of wreckers who signalled ships to their doom on the perilous Hartland Point rocks in order to plunder their cargoes. One of the memorials in the churchyard is the figurehead of the Scottish ship *Caledonia* wrecked in 1843 with the loss of over 40 of her crew.

HARTLAND QUAY: Sir Francis Drake, Sir Walter Raleigh and Sir John Hawkins all financed the building of a small harbour here in the sixteenth century. It has not been used for commercial vessels since the end of the nineteenth century when storms wrecked the quay.

HARTLAND QUAY MUSEUM
Devoted to the Hartland coastline, displaying 4 centuries of shipwrecks, the Quay's history and coastal trade and other activities.
Open Whitsun – Sept.

CLOVELLY, a village like a waterfall, is claimed to be like no other village in the country. It descends 400 ft (122 m) to a tiny harbour sheltered by a stone quay, which during the eighteenth and nineteenth centuries protected a large fishing fleet, but now has a few boats for lobster fishing. Home of Charles Kingsley, the nineteenth-century novelist.

APPLEDORE has been a base for fishermen since Anglo-Saxon times and was granted 'free port status' by Elizabeth 1 in gratitude for the part played by Appledore's ships and sailors in the defeat of the Armada.

THE NORTH DEVON MARITIME MUSEUM
Odun Road, Appledore, Nr Bideford.
Has a collection devoted to sailing vessels. At Hinks Yard, local craftsmen have built full-sized replicas of a Roman galley (among others), a Viking longship and the ubiquitous 'Golden Hind.'
Open Easter Sat – end Sept.

Inland at **BIDEFORD** is where Charles Kingsley based his novel *Westward Ho!*. Richard Grenville is commemorated by a plaque in the parish church which records how he died of wounds in 1591 after fighting 15 Spanish galleons off the Azores. The town had many trade links with North America until the nineteenth century.

BARNSTAPLE: Its importance as a port was reduced when the River Taw silted up.

ARLINGTON COURT has a collection which includes sailor-made models, paintings and a model of Sir Francis Chichester's *Gypsy Moth IV*.

To the north-west of Barnstaple at **BRAUNTON** is the BRAUNTON AND DISTRICT MUSEUM in Church Street. It has exhibits on seafaring history of the area. Open Easter – Sept, daily.

LUNDY ISLAND lies in the Bristol Channel about 12 miles (19 km) off the North Devon coast like a huge granite ship moored in the sea. It has a fascinating maritime history serving as a refuge for many lawless seafarers of the past, being at one time a virtual pirate kingdom and smugglers' haven, hence its title 'Tollgate of the Channel'. It is linked with the mainland by steamer from Ilfracombe.

ILFRACOMBE: Between 1777 and 1888, at least 60 sailing ships were built at this North Devon harbour. However, after 1860, Ilfracombe was developed as a holiday resort which has eclipsed the port. On Lantern Hill above the harbour the chapel of St Nicholas still burns a light for sailors: it has probably done so since it was built some 700 years ago.

Heave-ho at Appledore, 1902.

ILFRACOMBE MUSEUM
Wilder Road (opp Runnymeade Gardens).
Has a collection of photographs of local sailing craft and some ship models.
Open all year.

Exmoor's hills reach the Bristol Channel in a sequence of lofty cliffs and headlands which provide very little sheltered harbour except at **LYNMOUTH**, flanked in the west by the granite mass of 'Castle Rock' which drops 800 ft (244 m) to the Bristol Channel.

THE LYN AND EXMOOR MUSEUM
Foreland Point on the western edge of Countisbury Common rises to 991 ft (302 m) above the sea. The lighthouse at Foreland Point, built on the side of a cliff about 200 ft (60 m) above sea level, can be reached via a cliff-top walk along a path from the old inn at Countisbury.
Open to public weekday mornings.

PORLOCK WEIR: A tidal inlet formed by a shingle bar enabled Porlock Weir to become a small port when Porlock was left dry in the Middle Ages. Old thatched buildings lining the crescent of Porlock Bay once provided food and shelter for sailors in days when Porlock Weir's coasters traded across the Bristol Channel taking timber to South Wales and returning with coal.

MINEHEAD: The quay was built in 1616 and in Victorian times schooners for the coastal trade were built here.

BRISTOL AND WALES

Milford Haven and its industry

BRISTOL AND WALES

BRISTOL'S success as a port during Britain's most glorious maritime years was a triumph of intellect and application over natural disadvantages. An inland city, approached by a tortuous river barely navigable under sail and beset by mudbanks, was not the most promising site for merchant shipping in the years before steam power. Sheer commercial drive and initiative made Bristol what she became. The lack of any naval presence confirms that the area had little inherent attraction for mariners.

The first recorded use of the region for shipping is when the Romans began to use the confluence of the rivers Avon and Severn as an anchorage for their galleys. After rounding Land's End in these open craft and then negotiating the dangers of the Bristol Channel, the crews and masters needed to heave-to and pause for breath. At what is now Sea Mills the Romans built a stores depot and called it Abona. The River Severn itself was known to them as Sabrina. Although there was no settlement at Bristol, Abona did have a significance in the transfer of provisions and military stores to Gloucester and Cirencester.

There is no record at all of when Bristol itself was founded. The first concrete evidence of the town's existence is in the form of coins dating from around AD 1010. A city bridge over the Avon was constructed in the eleventh century adjacent to the present Bristol Bridge, built in 1786. There was obviously growth in the following 100 years for a charter from Henry II mentions that trade in wool, wine, hides and corn were reserved to the Bristol burgesses and could only be dealt with inside the boundaries of the port. In 1171 the city supplied six ships for Henry's expedition to Ireland. In fact, Henry granted Dublin to the men of Bristol, although the gift seems to have excited no particular response.

Bristol did have some trade with Ireland and it was in a commodity that was later to blacken the city's name throughout the world – slaves. As early as the reign of William the Conqueror the trade in captive human beings was focussed in Bristol, with the source being Ireland. It was roundly condemned in a letter by Wulfstan, Bishop of Worcester (1062–1095).

Although Bristol ships and crews were involved in slaving, few of the unfortunate cargoes were ever brought to the city. It was what would now be termed an 'offshore industry'. However, the city's trade in more acceptable commodities was developing rapidly and by the mid-thirteenth century the mud berths round Bristol bridge were proving inadequate for the heavy traffic. Contemporary writers mention the queue of waiting ships forever blocking the narrow channel in the centre of the river.

The solution to the congestion was one of the most ambitious public works schemes ever seen in medieval Britain. After years of debate plans were agreed to divert the River Frome to build additional quays at its junction with the Avon. The canalized section of the river was 880 yards (800 metres) long, forty yards (thirty-six metres) wide and eighteen feet (5.5 metres) deep. It was to cost an extraordinary £5,000 and in its day was the equivalent of the Channel Tunnel.

This capacity to pull together and jointly fund projects too big for any one individual was to be the single most important factor in Bristol's growth and success. By the mid-fourteenth century the port and the town springing up around the canal was second only to London in volume and value of trade; in 1373 Edward III conferred a charter upon Bristol that made it semi-autonomous. The mayor and the common council were given exclusive rights to control the port – a focussing of executive power that provided a quick, simple mechanism for future development. Merchant dynasties were beginning to emerge after several centuries of continual growth and the families built fine houses in the Redcliffe area of the city, close to the docks. In 1467 there is the first recorded mention of the Society of Merchant Venturers, an exploration and trading group that would occasionally lead the world in the coming centuries.

The most famous name of this enterprising and wide-ranging band was John Cabot, a Genoese by birth who settled in Bristol after living in Venice for a time. He was accepted readily by his colleagues and competitors and by the mid-1490s was a leading citizen and merchant of Bristol. On 24 June 1497, Cabot became the first European to sight North America. His fifty-ton ship the *Matthew* was seven weeks out from Bristol when she spied the coast between Maine and Newfoundland – not that the names existed then. Cabot returned home with news of the excellent cod-fishing waiting to be developed off the 'newe foundeland'.

John Cabot was lost at sea in 1498 but his endeavours laid the foundation stone of an annual voyage to North America that began in 1501 and continued until 1506. His son Sebastian Cabot explored the east coast of the new continent from Baffin Island to Florida during 1508/9. During the first half of the sixteenth century very little was done to exploit the discovery of this potential El Dorado. Back in Bristol attention was focussed on the run-down and inadequate nature of the port. In 1552 the merchants complained jointly to the king about the situation. The response was the granting of letters patent of incorporation to the Society of Merchant Venturers (SMV).

It made them the most powerful group in the city, since, unlike the mayor and the council, the SMV had a considerable income to devote to their policies and ideas. Shortly after the grant of the charter, the society succeeded in having trade into and out of Bristol closed to foreign interests. The Merchant Venturers had a monopoly on all these cargoes.

Theorists may argue about the long-term wisdom of monopolies but in the short-term they guarantee prosperity. Once more a boom came to Bristol. By the time of Elizabeth I's visit in 1574, the first by a reigning monarch, the population of the city had risen to 6,000. Her Majesty processed down river by royal barge to inspect the shipping and declared herself delighted by the busy prospect before her.

By the early 1600s Bristol was developing a modest pre-eminence in the trade with the fledgling American colonies such as Virginia. Robert Aldworth, a family name that would become famous in the city, established the foundation of the sugar trade with the West Indies. In 1631 a small ship called the *Henrietta Maria*, backed by the Society of Merchant Venturers, set off to pursue the chimera of the North West Passage. She failed, of course, but during the year that *Henrietta Maria* spent ice-bound in Hudson's Bay, the fur trade between northern Canada and Britain was planned and begun.

The early eighteenth century was Bristol's golden age. In 1700 her population was 20,000 prosperous and outward-looking citizens. Rum, sugar, and tobacco were the principal commodities of the port, all from America or the West Indies. Slaving was beginning to boom at this time, as the West Indian plantations demanded labour for the sugar crop. Around fifty ships a year were making the triangular voyage down to West Africa, across to the Caribbean and then home to England. In 1725 ships owned or based in Bristol carried 16,950 slaves across the Atlantic.

The slave ships were small, around ninety tons, and fast. They needed to be, since captive human beings were the ultimate in perishable cargoes, at risk from both pirates and savage on-board epidemics. Up to 300 black Africans would be chained together in the hold for the three-to-four week voyage.

The *Great Western* rides out a storm.

The same type of small, swift ships led the Bristolian mariners into a secondary activity as privateers – ships that go to war against the nation's enemies for the reward of captured ships and prizes, rather than pay from the Crown. The War of Spanish Succession, which began in 1702 and lasted eleven years, saw 120-plus privateers based in Bristol. Half a century later during the next major international conflict, the American War of Independence, over 150 of these mercenary sailors made their home port in Bristol.

Unfortunately for the city, the cramped and congested quay conditions were not keeping pace with the swashbuckling enterprise of her native sons. The mud berths along the banks of the Avon and Frome were becoming intolerably crowded and the factor of drying out twice a day was a drawback to shipowners coming to expect more convenient facilities. In the trade to the western colonies Liverpool began to race ahead of Bristol by the late eighteenth century.

The answer had to be a man-made 'wet dock' where ships could remain afloat at all stages of the tide. There were decades of argument about who should pay for it, but finally work began on this project, still today dominating the heart of the city, in 1804. The scheme involved an entire new ship basin, re-routeing the Avon through a cut, three dams, a canal and two new bridges. The cost was slightly over £600,000 – double the budgeted figure – when the new wonder of the West Country opened in 1809.

It was to be the start of decline for the port rather than a bright new dawn. Shipping dues were raised to meet the cost over-runs and the quays became the most expensive in Britain. London and Liverpool boomed as shipowners voted with their feet.

The slave trade had in been in decline for some decades as humanitarian concerns overtook those of profit and it finally ended with Wilberforce's famous Abolition Bill in 1807. The consequences to the colonies were severe, if not immediate. In 1833 the West Indian sugar trade collapsed totally upon the emancipation of the existing slaves.

If one man could be said to be the saviour of a whole city it was Isambard Kingdom Brunel. He became consulting engineer to the languishing docks while designing the Clifton suspension bridge and made several major harbour improvements at minor cost. It was, however, in his role as engineer to the Great Western Railway that Brunel gave his greatest service to Bristol.

The railway from London ended at Bristol. Brunel simply suggested that they build a steamship to continue it to New York. His ship the *Great Western* was launched in 1837 and made her maiden voyage to Manhattan in April 1838. It took just fourteen days. In her first eighteen months she made seventy crossings and carried 5,774 passengers. Bristol was back in the forefront of transatlantic trade

– and once more transporting people, although in a very different fashion to that of 100 years earlier.

It seems almost a Bristol trait to push success just a little bit too far and the *Great Western* was followed by the *Great Britain*, (see inset). As the city's docks struggled to find trade and pay off their enormous debts, there were mid-nineteenth century plans for, in the vogue word of the time, 'Dock-ization'. This involved the lining of the entire Avon from river mouth to city with quays. It was far too ambitious for a council that had already had its fingers burned and the compromise was Avonmouth docks, opened in 1877.

Bristol began to win back its earlier prosperity, with companies like the Great Western Steamship Line, Dominion Line and Elder Dempster making their base there. Tobacco and bananas became the port's staple commodities, with the great brick

City centre docks, Bristol c1900.

Launch of *New York City*, Albion Dry Dock 1917.

warehouses of the Wills company dominating the south side of the city shore. Connections with tobacco dated back to the 1600s but the first banana was not landed until 1900. However, it quickly grew into a major part of Avonmouth's trade.

Shipbuilding developed in the city largely because of proximity to the excellent oak available in the Forest of Dean. Samuel Pepys, in his duties as a senior official of the Admiralty, visited Bristol to check on naval shipbuilding and 'walked with my wife through the city, in every respect another London'.

Among the yards lining the banks of the Avon, the Albion Dockyard of Charles Hill & Co was pre-eminent. It first built steam tugs in 1813 and then began on small freighters in the 1820s. The yard continued until the mid-1970s and her last ship was the SS *Miranda Guinness*. Like all her predecessors

she carried a small brass plaque on the bridge. It showed a bas-relief of the Clifton suspension bridge and bore the legend 'Ship-shape and Bristol fashion'. Even today, with the city docks a marina and the *Great Britain* a museum piece, those words are still heard and written wherever English is spoken.

Facing the merchant capital across the Bristol Channel was the low, sandy coast of South Wales. It was not, in its essence, a seafaring region. Cardiff had been a strategic military centre since the creation of the huge Norman castle (where Robert, brother of Henry I, was kept prisoner for twenty-six years) and Sweyn's Ea (to give Swansea its original name) was once a Scandinavian settlement. The beachside colony at Llantwit Major, on the Gower peninsula, predates the Romans and St Paul is said to have preached there. Yet this was not an area where men went down to the sea in ships – until the Industrial Revolution.

As steam power began to turn the wheels of

the world so the coal of the South Wales valleys, ideally suited to boiler use, became nearly as valuable as gold. The demand was there but the facilities to export it were not initially promising. In the eighteenth century the small town quay on Cardiff's River Taff could handle small seagoing vessels of seventy to eighty tons. There was a regular ship service to Bristol, ferrying out agricultural produce and bringing home manufactured goods. Smaller Bristol Channel ports such as Bridgwater and Minehead were also serviced on a less regular basis.

However, the sea was never a regular highway and major means of communication as it was for the rural population of, say, Devon and Cornwall. With a tidal range of up to forty feet (twelve metres) and fierce banks and rocks, the Channel was a place to avoid. Up until the nineteenth century one in seven of all British shipwrecks are calculated to have happened there.

The first sign of major change came in 1798 when the Glamorganshire Canal linked the still tiny port of Cardiff with the iron foundries of Merthyr Tydfil. The canal was paid for by the ironmasters of Merthyr and obviously fulfilled an exploding need. It carried 100 tons of iron in 1806 and 85,000 by 1829.

The growth of the coal industry was even more astonishing. Cardiff became the centre of the exporting network not through natural advantages but because local investors (notably the Marquis of Bute) were willing to pour huge sums into creating a modern and efficient dock. The battle between Bute and the ironmasters was savage but eventually the nobleman prevailed since ships simply became larger and the eighteenth century dock gates into the canal complex could not accommodate the bigger vessels. In 1806 there is no record of Cardiff shipping any coal. By 1819 the annual total was 34,000 tons, in 1829 85,000 tons and a decade later the output had grown to 211,000 tons.

It took just eighty years for South Wales to overhaul the North-East, established in the trade for centuries, as Britain's prime exporter of coal. Of course, Cardiff was not the only port involved. Newport and Swansea were always important and the huge port of Barry, now given over to tourism, was a complete creation of the coal industry. As recently as 1880 it had just seventeen houses and a population of around eighty. Cardiff's pre-eminence came from the Coal Exchange and by the turn of the century it could rightly be called 'the coal metropolis of the world'. Whether the coals were shipped from Barry or Swansea, the paperwork went through Cardiff and swelled its economy.

Swansea marked the natural western limit of marine industrialization. Looking east across the bay – which eighteenth-century writer Walter Savage Landor thought finer than Naples – one sees the dockside steel and chemical industries of Port Talbot; yet immediately to the east are the small bays and pretty fishing communities of the Gower peninsula. There are also places like Mumbles, of which the delightful children's rhyme says:

> Mumbles is a funny place
> A church without a steeple
> Houses built of old ships wrecked
> And a very peculiar people.

Fishing, and very local fishing at that, was the backbone of survival on the coast of west Wales. Some types of craft, such as the coracle, were not seen elsewhere in Britain. In the estuaries of major rivers such as the Tywi, seine-netting went on unchanged for generations. One man stood on the shore tending the end of a 200-yard (180-metre) net while two or three others rowed out the remainder in a small dinghy, eventually circling back to shore. Salmon caught this way were so plentiful that, far from being the occasional delicacy which they are today, only 100 years ago they were sold dried and salted in the streets of Carmarthen.

Remoteness was the economic problem. Much of what could be caught, from salmon to lobsters, was valuable in the growing

Coracle users from the River Teifi.

inland cities of England but there was simply no way to get it there across the mountains of inland Wales. A tradition of coastal shipping might have been the answer but it simply did not exist. Writing in the twelfth century Giraldus Cambrensis remarks on the near absence of native shipping in the region. Could it have been a long-term consequence of Viking terrorism? From the ninth century to around AD 1100 the longships had a trading base near Milford Haven and would loot and plunder at will. They sacked St Davids eight times during these years.

Whatever the reasons, west Wales remained a remote and inaccessible region undisturbed by marine trade. For this very reason, probably, Henry Tudor landed at Milford Haven in 1485, an event leading indirectly to the union of England and Wales under his son Henry VIII.

The country's next monarch, Elizabeth, ordered a careful survey of this coastline because of the perceived threat of a Spanish invasion via Ireland. Her surveyors found only four large vessels and 400 seamen. A decade or so later in 1561 a visiting Dutch seaman wrote an account describing west Wales as having 'no trade or merchandise but all full of rocks and dangiers'.

It was a natural breeding ground for pirates. One of the most famous of all time, Black Bart, was born in 1682 at Little Newcastle, a village just inland from the ferry port of Fishguard. Bart is believed to have been the first pirate to hoist the skull and crossbones aboard his vessel. A strict teetotaller and sabbath-keeper, there was never any prostitution or gambling aboard Bart's ship which was run more like a Methodist chapel than a pirate brig. Habitually dressed in crimson shirt and breeches and always accompanied by a band, Black Bart amassed a fortune worth around eighty million pounds at today's rates before being killed by the Royal Navy off Brazil in 1722. His last words were, 'A merry life… and a short one.'

It was not until the early eighteenth century that a pattern of local coastal trade began to grow up in Cardigan Bay. Locally built sloops of around fifty tons crewed by two men and a boy were the earliest regular trading vessels. On this coast of sandy estuaries and drying harbours they were round-bottomed to take the shingle at low water. By the nineteenth century the hull shape had changed little but the sloop rig had evolved to a more manageable ketch, since the long boom made gybing horrifically dangerous and had caused many accidents at sea.

Simultaneously, as skills developed, these small communities became skilled at building and sailing fleets of small three-masted trading schooners that came to be regarded as models of their kind. The prime export trade was slate and emigrant Welshmen – the latter to destinations as far away as America and New Zealand. Even tiny coastal villages such as Llangrannog would set up navigation schools, where the Welsh passion for education would combine with a love of the sea that seemed to have been buried for generations.

Right up until the turn of the century this schooner industry thrived, but as steam ships came to dominate even coastal trade routes, so the villages and small towns like Cardigan and Aberystwyth turned in on themselves again, losing the links with a wider world. For west Wales the ferry services to Ireland from Fishguard and Pembroke Dock are now the principal maritime activity. The latter town is interesting for the way, against all odds, it became for a brief prosperous century a substantial centre for naval ship-building.

Pembroke itself had been a prosperous little town for generations. Henry VII was born in the castle so there always seemed to be a link to the wealth and influence of London and the Crown for Pembroke people. However, Pembroke Dock nearby was an inherently improbable place for a shipyard. There was no timber in the locality, very little skilled labour, and poor communications with London.

The reasons for its existence were always short term. During the Napoleonic Wars the size of the Royal Navy doubled very quickly and every available shipbuilding site was utilized. Distance from all other centres such as Plymouth and Chatham was not regarded as a disadvantage and proximity to oak from the Forest of Dean was a bonus. Pembroke Dock launched its first warship, the fifth-rate *Ariadne* in 1816. It was the beginning of sixty years of innovation and high standards. The yard built the navy's first steam warship, HMS *Tarturus*, in 1834 and its biggest to date, HMS *Lion*, in 1847. The introduction of the iron-clad warship in the 1860s was the beginning of the end for Pembroke Dock. There was no iron nearby and staff did not know how to plate it. However, small ships with iron frames and wooden planking became a speciality. Pembroke Dock built five royal yachts during its brief existence. When the dreadnought class arrived in the early twentieth century it was beyond the technical and physical capacity of Pembroke Dock. The last ship was launched in 1922 and the

yard closed in 1926, effectively killing the town.

One has to travel north to the island of Anglesey, the north-western extremity of Wales, to find the final town of any maritime significance in the principality. Holyhead had been a fort in Roman times but nothing for centuries after. The principal naval garrison from Norman times onwards was Beaumaris, with its huge secure castle.

Holyhead remained little more than a creek until Ireland became a significant and troublesome British possession. In the reign of Elizabeth I conditions in Ireland began to necessitate regular and secure communications. In the 1570s a postal system was set up with a sea-crossing from Holyhead to Dublin as its last link. Most passenger traffic for the province still left from Chester but the closeness of the crossing from Anglesey began to be a factor.

In the early 1600s a letter from the influential nobleman Lord Burleigh refers to one Captain Robert Pepper and his post barque stationed at Holyhead. At a time when a letter from London to Dublin cost sixpence, Captain Pepper was paid a fee by the government of £10 per lunar month. Holyhead had nothing to offer the traveller. Jonathan Swift, author of *Gulliver's Travels* and Dean of Dublin, was often forced to wait there by storms in the rough and dangerous St George's Channel. On one occasion he wrote:

> Oh Neptune, Neptune, must I still
> Be here detained against my will.

And later in 1727, in even worse humour:

> Lo here I sit at Holy Head
> With muddy ale and mouldy bread.

In the 1820s Thomas Telford's great suspension bridge across the Menai Straits was opened and the coach time to London was cut to thirty hours. Around that time improvements began at Holyhead, changing it from a simple natural haven to a system of piers and docks. Change was unwelcome to the British

Holyhead's new harbour, 1840.

Post Office, whose initial reaction to the arrival of steam propulsion was to employ two paddle-steamers to tow the sailing mail packets across in calm weather. However, improvements were inevitable and the completion of the vast breakwater at Holyhead (it took twenty-eight years to build, all told) and the construction of the Britannia railway bridge to the mainland finalized a process that was to give life and purpose to Holyhead. In 1848 the London Night Mail began to run direct through to the ferryport. The journey took ten hours. Today it is five, but little else has changed except that the beer and bread have both improved since Dean Swift lamented his predicament.

———— GAZETTEER ————

BRISTOL AND WALES
FROM BRISTOL TO PENRHYN

BRISTOL

In the seventeenth and eighteenth centuries Bristol was one of the world's greatest ports and is particularly rich in maritime material. It grew up around the river Avon and was based largely on ocean trade.

THE BRISTOL HERITAGE WALK will take you through all the main buildings associated with Bristol's seafaring heyday, such as the huge statue of Neptune at the head of the Floating Harbour's western arm. Just below it is the memorial to Samuel Plimsoll 'the seaman's friend', the Bristol-born MP whose Merchant Shipping Act of 1876 introduced the 'Plimsoll Line' to indicate how much cargo a vessel could take in safety.

The Llandoger Trow Inn in King St is renowned as a meeting place for pirates and smugglers and the model for 'Spyglass Inn' in *Treasure Island*. It was also probably the haunt of Alexander Selkirk on whom Defoe based *Robinson Crusoe*.

BRISTOL MARITIME HERITAGE CENTRE
SS *Great Britain*, Great Western Dock, Gas Ferry Rd (off Cumberland Rd).
See inset.
Open daily all year.

BRISTOL INDUSTRIAL MUSEUM
Princes Wharf, Prince St, Bristol.
Home of *Mayflower* (1861), oldest steam tug still afloat in Britain. Boilers and engine still in working order. Collection of transport items dealing with land, sea and inland navigation. Items connected with the port of Bristol such as models of Severn trows.

NATIONAL LIFEBOAT MUSEUM
Princes Wharf, Wapping Rd, Bristol Tel: (0272) 213389.
Open April – Sept.

THE BRISTOL CITY MUSEUM AND ART GALLERY
Queen's Rd.
Collection of ship models which include eighteenth-century warships built at Bristol, notably HMS *Mars*, a 28-gun frigate of 1778, the privateer *Mars*, HMS *Arethusa*, a 38-gun frigate of 1781 and HMS *Melampus*, a 36-gun frigate of 1785.

PILL is a village on the River Avon approximately half-way between Bristol and Avonmouth and for centuries was the home of pilots who took ships up to Bristol. The Pill pilots jealously guarded their knowledge and rights in pilotage and fought attempts of the city of Bristol to dominate them. The pilots all operated independently and there was great competition among the cutters to put their pilot on to an incoming ship. At Pill the pilot boats were called skiffs.

When sailing pilot cutters were at their height in 1900, new ideas were introduced from yachting but from about 1910 until 1950 cruising yachtsmen were strongly influenced by working boats. Bristol pilot boats were famous for their speed and sea-keeping.

AVONMOUTH: As ships grew larger, they had difficulty in coming up the river to Bristol with the fast flowing tide. A new set of docks was established at Avonmouth 6 miles (9.6 km) downstream from Bristol in 1877. These docks can take ships of up to 70,000 tons and are some of the busiest docks in Britain. During the summer, Avonmouth is a base for cruises by *Waverley*, the world's last seagoing paddle-steamer.

WALES

As the estuary of the Severn narrows towards the road bridge linking Wales with England, the coast sinks below river level, protected from regular flooding only by a long sea wall.

GOLDCLIFF, one of the small villages which hug the low-lying shore of the Severn estuary, has a brass plate in its church, recording that in 1606 the flood waters reached high into the church and 22 people drowned. At several points along the estuary can be seen the large conical baskets used to catch salmon swimming out into the estuary.

CHEPSTOW: Although some miles from the estuary, Chepstow in the Wye valley has strong shipbuilding traditions.

CHEPSTOW MUSEUM
Gwy House, Bridge St, Chepstow.
Deals with local shipbuilding and sea trade and salmon fishing.
Open March – Oct, weekdays.

CARDIFF: Founded by the Romans, Cardiff was once one of the busiest ports in the world. In 1839 with the expansion of the docks by rail links with the pit heads and iron works inland, its fortunes increased. The area to the east of the Taff became known as Tiger Bay, frequented by seamen from all parts of the world.

WELSH INDUSTRIAL AND MARITIME MUSEUM
Bute St.
On the edge of the docks, set in Bute town, formerly one of the most extensive ship owning districts in Britain. Working exhibits tell the story of motive power and its use in ships, mines and power stations. Outside on the edge of the old Bute west dock basin, the museum displays the early Bristol channel tug *Sea Alarm* 1941, a turn of the century sailing cutter *Kindly Light*, RNLB *Watkins Williams*.
Open daily (except Mon).

Just to the north of Cardiff at St Fagans is the WELSH FOLK MUSEUM, an open air museum with a good collection of Welsh boats and nets connected with the inshore and river fisheries.
Open April to Oct, daily; closed Sun from Nov – March.

BARRY: In 1880 this was a village with a population of just 85. Situated 9 miles (14 km) west of Cardiff with a sheltered deep-water approach, the first dock at Barry was opened in

Barry docks, 1906.

1889. It covered 73 acres (30 hectares) and was the largest enclosed dock in the country. In 1890 over 3 million tons of coal were shipped out in 1,700 ships: in 1913 the total was 11 million. Coal is still exported but in relatively tiny quantities and the last coal loading hoists in South Wales can still be seen.

Following the coast round past the steel works and old coal harbours the cliffs reappear.

The new Hashpoint lighthouse built in 1830 on the cliff-top sited next to the disused one can be visited on weekday afternoons. It was built to mark sandbanks off the point following a public outcry after the wreck of the passenger steamer *Frolic* with heavy loss of life.

DUNRAVEN BAY is the area where, according to local legend, ships used to be lured to their doom by a family of seventeenth-century wreckers who fixed lanterns to the horns of cattle grazing on the cliffs. The ships would come close inshore to look for the harbour entrance and run aground on the rocks at the base of the cliffs where the crews were murdered and cargoes looted.

SWANSEA: Before the Industrial Revolution, Swansea was a small harbour and fishing village. By the eighteenth century with the supply of cheap coal and smelting works, the harbour expanded and by the middle of the nineteenth century more than 10,000 ships sailed in and out of the port each year. By end of the 1950s however, the lower Swansea valley had turned into an industrial moonscape.

SWANSEA MARITIME AND INDUSTRIAL
MUSEUM
Museum Square, Maritime Quarter.
This is housed in a huge maritime complex at the mouth of the River Tawe, including a 600-berth marina with sailing and sea-angling schools where boats have access to the channel through rapid-action lock gates, in themselves a visitor attraction. Maritime and industrial displays include the opportunity to step aboard the boats floating alongside the museum. The old Mumbles lifeboat the lightship *Helwick* and the steamship *Canning*, can all be boarded.
Open daily.

MUMBLES has a lighthouse and a lifeboat station and was the terminus of one of Britain's earliest railways; a cross between a seaside tramway and a genuine railway until the mid-1950s.

At **LAUGHARNE** the boat house from which Dylan Thomas looked out 'on the mussel pooled and heron priested shore' and wrote *Under Milk Wood*, has been restored but the whole village still retains its picturesque jumble of fishermen's cottages.

SAUNDERSFOOT was established as a port exporting high-quality anthracite from local pits. The last mine closed in 1939, but now the broad quays and safe anchorage make Sandersfoot one of the finest yachting centres in Wales.

TENBY: Brixham sailing trawlers used this as one of their bases and so did the oyster skiffs from Mumbles.

TENBY MUSEUM AND PICTURE GALLERY
A maritime gallery commemorating Tenby's seafaring past and its achievements as a lifeboat station.
Open daily, Easter – Oct.

At **FRESHWATER WEST** seaweed used to be collected for making laver bread, a South Wales delicacy. One of the huts in which the seaweed was dried can still be seen, the last survivor of more than a dozen built 80 years ago.

SOLVA's seclusion at the head of a winding creek, protected the village from passing pirates and raiders in earlier times. In the nineteenth century 30 vessels worked out of Solva fetching limestone for the village kiln. Today it is a popular sailing and boating centre.

At one time the rocks along this treacherous coast claimed a high toll of shipping so in 1771 a lighthouse was built on the Smalls west of Skomer. It was the scene of a tragedy in 1802 when its keeper Thos Griffiths died during a violent storm. His partner Thomas Howell, lashed Griffiths's body to the gangway until help could arrive so that he could prove Griffiths death had been due to natural causes. Help took 3 months to arrive by which time Howell was mad. Since then the minimum crew of a lighthouse has always been 3 keepers.

PEMBROKE DOCK, built in 1814, is where in one century more than 200 ships were built, including all the Royal Yachts except the earliest (Charles II's *Mary*) and latest (today's *Britannia*).

The biggest 3-decker man-of-war ever built, the *Duke of Wellington* left Pembroke Dock in 1852 to become the flagship of Admiral Napier in the Crimean War. The dockyard closed in 1926 but during the Second World War it was a base for Sunderland flying boats protecting the Atlantic convoys.

Upstream at Haverford West, once a busy port, the town's mayor is still entitled to call himself 'Admiral of the Port of Haverford West'.

MILFORD HAVEN, on the Milford Haven Waterway, is regarded as one of the greatest natural harbours in the world, it meanders for over 24 miles (38.6 km). Nelson called it one of the finest harbours he had ever seen. Over the centuries Viking and Normans, and Flemish immigrants have come here. Shipbuilding, piracy, Quakers, whaling fleets, transatlantic liners, what once was one of Britain's largest fishing fleets and now one of the largest oil ports in Europe – the Haven has seen a huge variety of activity.

At the end of the headland at the south side of the inlet is a nineteenth-century coastal defence fort built in the days when Milford Haven was an important naval centre. On the high cliffs of St Ann's Head stands the oldest lighthouse still in continual use in Wales.

CARREGWASTAD POINT was the scene of the last landing by a foreign army on the soil of mainland Britain in 1797 when a force of 1,400 French soldiers and convicts under an American colonel landed. A plaque at Carregwastad commemorates their surrender to the local Pembroke yeomanry.

Today the only vessel to land at **FISHGUARD** is the Irish cross-channel ferry which plies the shortest sea route between Britain and Ireland twice a day. Lower Fishguard is still recognizably an old fishing village set around wharves and quays (it made an ideal location for the film *Under Milk Wood* and the epic *Moby Dick*).

On the outskirts of Fishguard, **LITTLE NEW-CASTLE** is the birthplace of the notorious pirate Black Bart.

CARDIGAN was once an important port for coastal shipping with 291 ships registered in 1831. Schooners could only reach Cardigan on a spring tide so part of the cargo was often discharged at St Dogmaels, from where there used to be a regular steamer service to Bristol.

SS GREAT BRITAIN – BRUNEL'S REVOLUTION

Nothing epitomizes Bristol's bravura attitude to maritime innovation and risk better than the SS *Great Britain*. When launched in the summer of 1843 she was quite simply the most revolutionary ship afloat anywhere in the world. *Great Britain*'s appearance changed the face of transatlantic shipping, just as the first jumbo jet transformed aviation.

It was her historical importance that justified the herculean efforts made nearly twenty years ago to salvage the *Great Britain* from a beach in the Falkland Islands and return her to Bristol. Since then work has progressed steadily on the complete restoration of a ship that changed the world.

She was the brainchild of Isambard Kingdom Brunel. His first ship, the *Great Western*, was also Bristol-built in 1837. Her speed and reliability on the run to New York quickly eclipsed the swift Yankee sailing packets of 300-500 tons that had dominated the route since the turn of the century.

Brunel's initial plan was to build a sister ship to the *Great Western*. Although full of incremental engineering improvements she would still have a wooden hull and be driven by paddles. As design work proceeded she became larger and larger, in tandem with Brunel's ambition. Furthermore his vision of the possible encompassed both iron construction and screw-propellor propulsion.

Queen Victoria visits the *Great Britain*, 1845.

The latter came about following the visit of the *Archimedes* to Bristol. This experimental little ship was propellor-driven and Brunel chartered her for six months to study the new technology. Convinced of the radical system, Brunel swung the planned installation of *Great Britain*'s steam engine through ninety degrees and announced that she would become the world's first ocean-going, propellor-driven ship.

In other, more technical matters, Brunel's ship was at the cutting edge of contemporary technology. She had longitudinal girders for stiffness, plated above and below to give, effectively, the first double-bottom in a major ship. *Great Britain* had transverse bulkheads which were watertight, another first in safety. And she had the first balanced rudder, so that tons of iron felt to the helmsman like the tiller of an admiral's gig.

Brunel's original propellor was fifteen feet six inches (4.7 metres) in diameter and weighed four tons. Despite being virtually a prototype, contemporary assessments have rated it favourably against the modern propellors used on ships of over 100,000 tons. The steam engine was of four cylinders and raised slightly above 1600 hp on steam with a pressure of five psi.

Although the engine was the primary propulsion system, sail was not ignored entirely. *Great Britain* had six masts and could carry full sail when the wind was favourable, saving consider-

able bunker coal. On deck was a huge engine-room skylight which covered the uppermost section of the vast engine flywheel, with a chaindrive direct down to the propellor shaft which was two feet six inches (75 centimetres) in diameter.

Building the *Great Britain*, in a special dock created for the purpose, took four years. Certainly the Great Western Steamship Company was nervous at the risks inherent in the hi-tech project. But Brunel had been proved right in so many of his earlier gambles – as they had seemed at the time – that the company had little practical option but to grit its corporate teeth and keep ploughing the profits from the Great Western Railway and the *Great Western* herself into Isambard's new ship.

Bristol was *en fête* for the launch. Shops and factories declared a holiday and thousands of ordinary citizens flocked to the quayside to watch the leviathan float gently off her building blocks – she was too big to go down a slipway and the new dock was flooded instead. Prince Albert travelled down from London on the railway to see with his own eyes this historic event.

Fitting out was completed by the New Year of 1845 and the ship's first voyage was to London, where she was greeted as the eighth wonder of the world. Queen Victoria visited the ship, doubtless swayed by her husband's glowing account of the launch. So did thousands of other Londoners; from patriotic cockneys to the great merchants and aristocrats who would soon be booking passage in her.

By mid-summer it was time for *Great Britain* to earn her living. She sailed for Liverpool and on 26 July began her maiden voyage to New York. Despite capacious accommodation for over 300 passengers, the ship carried but 50 people and 600 tons of cargo on her first trip across the Atlantic. She was still seen as an exciting, but risky, innovation. Fifteen days later she was entering the Hudson River, to a riotous welcome from the citizens of Manhattan. *Great Britain*'s average speed was 9.4 knots and she maintained this figure on her return trip.

Some hint of suspicion or reluctance seemed to dog the ship. Although she had much to offer, her vast promenade deck and sumptuous dining saloon were seldom more than one-third full on her early voyages. However, confidence grew and in September 1846 the revolutionary steamship embarked 180 passengers, her record, for a voyage that would end in commercial, if not human, disaster.

On the night of leaving Liverpool her captain, James Hosken, put his ship aground in Dundrum Bay, County Down, through gross navigational errors. The passengers were saved but it was eleven months before one of the most complex and ingenious salvage operations ever mounted could free the ship from the Irish beach.

Great Britain had been under-insured and the cost of saving her was too much for the slender finances of the Great Western Steamship Company. Both the new vessel and her sistership the *Great Western* were put up for sale. It took some time but in 1850 she went to new owners who planned to carry 730 passengers per trip to the booming goldfields of Australia. Technical modifications doubled the steam pressure to 10 psi, a new three-bladed propellor was fitted and the rig was reduced to four auxiliary masts.

In every respect her new incarnation was a success. During twenty years of steady east-a-bout passages from Liverpool to Melbourne, the old lady carried thousands of emigrants to their new home. In 1861 she took out the first-ever England cricket team to tour 'Down Under', having been restored from her 'hostilities only' duties as a troopship in the Crimean War.

By the late 1870s *Great Britain* was becoming obsolete as a passenger ship and became a conveyer of South Wales coal to San Francisco. The strain of going 'the wrong way' round Cape Horn proved too much to bear and in 1886 she limped into Port Stanley, damaged in a South Atlantic storm and never to sail under her own power again.

Almost a century as a supply-hulk and finally just a disregarded wreck followed. Her rescue was largely the work and inspiration of naval architect Ewan Corlett. He tirelessly raised funds and increased national awareness of a treasure, the equal of Concorde or Stephenson's Rocket, that was rotting on a beach in the Falkland Islands.

After a salvage operation that would be the subject of a book in itself the *Great Britain* was towed back to Bristol on a vast semi-submersible pontoon. She entered the Avon on 23 June 1970. Over 100,000 people lined the banks of the river to watch this battered, but historically important ship come home. As she slipped into her original building dock, Prince Philip was aboard, echoing the presence of Victoria's consort 127 years earlier.

Schooners loading slate in Porthmadog.

Upstream from Cardigan on the River Teifi between Cilgerran and Cenarth can be seen coracles used for salmon fishing. Made of intertwined lathes of willow and hazel covered with fabric and pitch, their basic design has scarcely changed since the Iron Age. In 1807 a contemporary observer wrote 'there is scarcely a cottage in the neighbourhood without its coracle hanging by the door'. In 1880 nearly every fresh water river in Wales had coracles fishing in large numbers, but after 1918 the diminishing stocks of salmon caused licensing to be introduced.

CENARTH: Situated on the road between Newcastle Emlyn and Cardigan at Cenarth Falls, is a fishing museum. Started as a private collection of antique fishing tackle, it now has a coracle display which can be visited in the summer.

CARDIGAN WILDLIFE PARK (entrance along old railway track from Cilgerran).
Every August the Cilgerran Coracle Regatta is held here.
Open daily.

NEWQUAY, named for the building of the quay in 1835, provided the only safe harbour along this stretch of coast. A century ago there was a thriving shipbuilding and ship-repairing trade here. On the quayside a noticeboard can be seen showing the list of tolls dating back to the time when there was a busy coastal trade. It cost 6 pence to bring ashore a box of cigars, a shilling for a ton of gunpowder, 2 shillings for a coffin and 5 shillings for a marble tombstone.

ABERYSTWYTH, the principal seaside resort of west Wales, lies at the centre of the long sweep of Cardigan Bay. The small harbour was the home in mid-Victorian times of sailing ships in the deep-sea trade.

CEREDIGION MUSEUM
Coliseum, Terrace Rd.
Houses a mainly folk collection with a section on Aberystwyth seafaring past. Builders' models and sailor-made items. Maritime artefacts. Charts and navigational instruments. Paintings and photos of sail and steam vessels.
Open Mon – Sat.

ABERDOVEY is a picturesque harbour whose prosperous trading past is recalled in the many houses built for sea captains engaged in trade with ports all over the world.
The local yacht club's sail-marking of a black bell is a reminder of the song *The Bells of Aberdovey* which is based on a Welsh legend about

Setting nets, north Wales coast, late nineteenth century.

a city supposed to lie beneath Cardigan Bay – the bells can be heard ringing when trouble threatens. On the pier is a MARITIME MUSEUM housed in old warehouses on the jetty, recalling the days when sloops, brigs and schooners sailed as far as Newfoundland and Labrador.

BARMOUTH was once a thriving slate port with yards on the Mawddach estuary which built small wooden sailing ships. The fishing port still exists and there is an RNLI Maritime Museum on the quay. It has photographs dating back to the 1860s and records of early rescues.

TY GWYN
Barmouth harbour.
In this medieval house can be seen part of the haul from the famous *Bronze Bell* shipwreck off Cardigan Bay, probably the most important ancient shipwreck in Wales.

A hundred years ago the small ports of Gwynedd were crammed with working sailing ships, hundreds of them owned and built locally, engaged in both coastal and oceanic trades. In villages like Moelfre, Newborough, Nefyn and Criccieth, almost every cottage bred generations of seamen.

Porthmadog, Barmouth and Pwellhelli and the slate ports of the Menai Strait all had much in common with similar maritime communities in Scandinavia and North America. Many large wooden sailing ships built in the Canadian Maritimes and the United States were owned and managed in Gwynedd in the last century.

PORTHMADOG: This little harbour town was created in the early nineteenth century with the building of a 1-mile embankment across the Glaslyn estuary to reclaim land. The town's prosperity was founded on the slate trade. There were also 2 wooden shipbuilding yards here which specialized in 3-masted top sail schooners.

GWYNEDD MARITIME MUSEUM
Situated in one of the old wharves the last remaining slate shed houses a display on maritime history of Porthmadog. The exhibition describes the achievements of the Porthmadog shipbuilders and those who sailed in their vessels. The later Porthmadog schooners were outstanding vessels considered to be the ultimate development of the small wooden merchant ship in Britain.
Open Easter Week and May bank holiday – end of Sept.

The Lleyn peninsula thrusts out into the Irish Sea from the mountains of Snowdonia: the seas round here are savage and dangerous with many secluded coves and villages on the north-eastern side.

Castle views from Caernarfon quayside.

Many of these are prehistoric sites and during the Middle Ages pilgrims used them as stopping places on their way to sacred **BARDSEY ISLAND**, a centre of early Christianity. Here the lighthouse, a massive square tower, stands at the island's southerly tip and is open to the public.

Port Dinllaen is a cove sheltered from the south-west by a headland and is the main beach landing for the inland town of **NEFYN**. This was an important herring centre in medieval times as well as a shipbuilding centre. Between the launching of the sloop *Hopewell* in 1760 and the schooner *Venus* in 1880, 185 ships were built here.

NEFYN MUSEUM
Old St Mary's Church, Church St.
Re-creates the atmosphere of the area's maritime tradition by recording, mainly through visual displays, local life and activities from the early nineteenth century to today.
Open July – beginning of Sept.

FORT BELAN is a grim block house built at the entrance to the Menai Strait to keep out Napoleon's navy.

THE WYN COLLECTION
Fort Belan.

Vessels include coracles and 1908 steam launch gun punt. Belan dockyard. Belan maritime exhibits include marine equipment from steam yachts; ship models including HMS *Pike* 1813, nautical instruments, ordnance.

This area sees the Menai Strait Regatta July 29 – August 12: 2 weeks of competitive sailing for 17 classes of yachts. On the mainland side of the Menai Strait **PORT DINORWIC** was built as the outlet for the export trade from the Great Dinorwic slate quarries in Snowdonia. The port's history goes back to the eighth century when Viking raiders used this part of the strait as a secure anchorage.

CAERNARFON has been settled since Roman times. Edward I built the vast castle to keep the Welsh under the crown. It took 37 years to build and was completed in 1283. Naval and civil vessels could sail right up to the quay beneath the castle walls.

SEIONT MARITIME MUSEUM
Victoria Dock, Caernarfon.
1938 steam dredger and ferry *Nantlys* (1920) on view. It is a rare survivor from the days of coalfield steamships and can be boarded. The whitewashed museum next to it houses a collection showing the development and drawings of the

area's maritime history.
Open Easter – end Sept.

The town of **MENAI BRIDGE** on the strait was a major port in the nineteenth century with tall ships in full sail passing under the high arches of the suspension bridge on their return from California via Cape Horn. At the waters edge at **LLANFAIRPWLLGWYNGYLL** there is a statue of Nelson inscribed with the message 'England expects', from the Battle of Trafalgar.

Towards **HOLYHEAD ISLAND** the **ANGLE-SEY** coastline rises in cliffs over 200 ft (60 m) in the south-west.

SOUTH STACK is a rock island about 100 ft (30 m) in height, separated from the cliff face by a wide chasm through which the sea surges with great force. The lighthouse, built in 1909, is situated on the rock's plateau-like top and spectators can look down on it from the cliff-top. To reach the rock, Trinity House workmen cut 400 steps in the cliff face to take them to rock level and slung a rope bridge across the chasm and a hemp cable along which supplies were sent. This was replaced by an iron suspension bridge in 1828.

The most memorable day in the history of the lighthouse was 25 October 1859, when one of the worst gales of the century occurred and over 200 ships were either driven ashore or lost at sea with 800 passengers and crew. Among them was the *Royal Charter*. The lighthouse is open to the public most afternoons.

HOLYHEAD is Anglesey's largest town with pre-Roman connections. Its harbour was built 100 years ago with a massive breakwater 2 miles (3.2 km) long which shelters 700 acres (280 hectares) of water from the furious north-westerly storms. It now sees a brisk trade in container traffic and passenger carriage to and from Dun Laoghaire. Holyhead is the third largest passenger port in Britain.

HOLYHEAD MARITIME MUSEUM
St Elbod's Church, Rhos-y-Gear Ave.
The museum covers the maritime history of west Anglesey with emphasis on the ancient port of Holyhead. Exhibits include photographs, plans, ship models, figureheads, marine tools and other maritime artefacts recording the history of Holyhead and the exploits of its ships and seamen, the lifeboat and coastguard service and ship wrecks. Information on Trinity House lighthouses, marine craftsmen and the whaling industry.
Open during the summer.

THE SKERRIES is a low tract of land part of which is submerged to become an extensive shoal 7 miles (11 km) north-east of Holyhead and in the path of shipping Mersey bound from the south.

Many seafarers have been shipwrecked off the north coast of Anglesey, including St Patrick. Before the RNLI was founded, there was a lifeboat at **CEMLYN** manned by the local vicar. Today a lighthouse guides ships around the cliffs and is open to the public. The first proposal to build a lighthouse here came in 1658 but it was not until 1714 that William Trench was successful in gaining a patent giving him the right to build one and exact dues. However the venture was marked by tragedy and disappointment; his son died when the first shipload of materials was wrecked. On being built and the fire kindled, traders evaded payment of dues and Trench died in 1729, a broken man.

MOELFRE: This picturesque village straggles along the edge of the rocky headland and is famous for its lifeboat heroes who have saved almost 1,000 lives in 150 years. Chief among these heroes was Dick Evans, coxswain of the Moelfre lifeboat and one of the most decorated coxswains in the RNLI. Its most famous rescues occurred a century apart to the very day. One was the wreck of the *Royal Charter* lost with 452 lives and gold treasure in 1859. There is a memorial to the victims in **LLANALLGO** church and another on the cliffs where the rescuers strove in vain. 100 years later, 8 crew members of the 650-ton coaster *Hindlea* were rescued by the Moelfre lifeboat.

PENRHYN: The industrial locomotive museum at Penrhyn castle on the Menai Strait has builders' models and pictures of the steam coasters which loaded slate at Port Penrhyn and Port Dinorwic. The quarries were nearer to these man-made ports than to Porthmadog so slate was shipped out more cheaply.

THE NORTH-WEST

**Last view of Liverpool,
leaving the Mersey**

THE NORTH-WEST

IN the earliest years of recorded British history the premier port and shipping centre of north-western Britain was undoubtedly Chester. The Roman city stood at the head of the Dee estuary and controlled the export of salt from the Cheshire mines across the vast empire. The galleys that rowed up the river were modest enough in draught and the Dee had not lapsed into the process of silting that makes the river virtually unnavigable today. As elsewhere around the coast, once the Dark Ages following the collapse of the Roman empire were over and seaborne trade resumed, bigger ships came into use and river harbours which had once thrived became too small to cope. The scene was set for the rise of Liverpool.

The earliest known document relating to Liverpool, then just a village at the mouth of the River Mersey, was a deed from the reign of Richard I, whereby the Crown gave Henry Fitzwarin of Cheshire the town of Liverpool. The tidal pool where the Mersey met the Irish Sea was already a key point in the salt export trade, although Chester was still far from an eclipsed rival at this time.

King John decided to reclaim Liverpool for the Crown. It was the stepping stone to his desire for a conquered Ireland. Realizing, ultimately, that supple and prosperous friends make the best allies he granted Liverpool the status of a free borough in 1207. Growth was steady and impressive from this point on. Edward II was a visitor in 1323 and the name Liverpool begins to recur in various state documents. Almost every mention relates to its activities as a port. The principal trade was in corn, tallow, iron and wine.

By the 1500s Liverpool was known to every mariner on the west coast of Britain and had become the dominant centre for the growing trade with Ireland. The significance of the harbour to the town of Liverpool can be gauged by an incident in 1561 when a major storm destroyed the jetty which protected the pool and ship haven. The borough decided that to assist the urgent construction of a new quay, every house within the town boundaries would have to supply a labourer free of charge to work on the harbour project. The rebuilding was an almost immediate success for by 1586 the harbour dues from Liverpool were more than those of Chester, Conway and Beaumaris combined.

Another indication of the importance of shipping within the town can be seen from an exchange during Cromwell's governance of Britain. Parliament proposed a tax to support the New Model Army based on the yearly value of every man's estate – an early form of rates. To this suggestion Liverpool borough replied with a disdainful counterblast that its better sort of inhabitants had their estates in shipping 'which is a daily hazard and adventure' while the remainder of the citizenry were too poor to pay anything. In 1715 Liverpool opened the first commercial wet dock in the country, of about four acres extent. Subsequent docks along the Mersey waterfront followed almost every decade.

Not every specialization – or lack of it – can be explained in commercial terms. Despite its position Liverpool appeared to take no significant early role in the trade with the New World to the west. No Raleigh or Drake, nor *Mayflower* sailed from the Mersey. Indeed some notable early Puritan emigrants to America sailed from Bristol. It was in the mid-seventeenth century that the beginnings of a significant trade in tobacco, imported from the plantations of Virginia, emerged. A record survives of thirty tons of tobacco being imported in 1648 – with £3.00 duty paid. One of the sights of the waterfront was a huge 'pipe', actually more like a pottery kiln,

Mersey pilot schooner bringing the fleet in safely.

where all damaged tobacco had to be burned. Salt continued to be important and the main Salthouse Dock bears testimony to that important cargo.

The eighteenth century was a period of massive growth for Liverpool, a time when the growing municipal power of a strong and independent borough began to be integrated with the trading success of the port. All manner of factors affecting shipping began to be controlled, or at least regulated, by the council and aldermen. Safety and ship management were areas of concern, particularly as larger numbers of big ships began to moor mid-stream in a highly tidal river. An ordinance of 1702 required that all ships below Water Street were to moor with three cables – and three anchors.

A pilot service began in 1756 and the first council-operated lighthouse lit its lamp a decade earlier. On the waterfront the dockworkers were already becoming highly-organized. Although this was still over a century before the rise of trade unionism a 'Master of Attendants', one Thomas Steers, was appointed in 1717 at a salary of £50 a year

(a considerable sum in real terms) to keep order among the hard-working, hard-drinking Liverpool men who loaded and unloaded the ships.

One feature that is hard to grasp, particularly given its importance today, was the rapidly expanding eighteenth-century canal system. In a pre-railway era moving heavy goods was still enormously difficult and water transport was the main solution. With access to three navigable rivers – the Mersey, Dee and Weaver – Liverpool was already attuned to inland waterways and as the great eighteenth-century canals began to be constructed it seemed almost a gravitational pull that led them to connect (via a river or directly) with Liverpool and adjacent transhipment centres such as Runcorn. By 1796 the system was so developed that a timetable listing available freight services could list forty-two scheduled canal boat sailings per day from Liverpool to Manchester.

The prosperity that Liverpool was enjoying as the early 1800s came into view was based to a considerable extent on the slave trade. As the city's links with North American lines of commerce such as cotton and tobacco – both dependent on slave labour – had developed,

Emigrants wait to embark at Liverpool.

so it was natural for the shipowners and masters to see the commercial advantages of taking captive black men rather than ballast westbound across the North Atlantic. In the waterfront shops and chandleries along the Mersey, establishments selling leg-chains and neck-irons were as common as those purveying ship's biscuits.

Bristol may have suffered the historical infamy of being the heart of the slave trade but such reputations are random and often unfair. In 1807, the last year before abolition, 185 Liverpool ships carried over 50,000 slaves from West Africa to captivity in North America. One year later the entire trade was gone, struck out by the legislator's pen. Viewed from the Mersey the humanitarian position was fine but what would replace the lost trade? The inward cargoes of timber from the northern colonies, and cotton and tobacco from the south, continued as before, but Liverpool ships could scarcely make profitable voyages with an empty west-bound leg.

Once again Liverpool turned to exporting

people. When emigration commenced in earnest after the end of the Napoleonic Wars, the city quickly established a hold on two-thirds of Europe's entire emigration volume. Bremen and Le Havre also played a role but somehow Liverpool seized the Continent's imagination as the bridgehead to the limitless possibilities of the New World. The Pier Head became a kind of launch-pad for millions of daring hopes and aspirations. Countless families huddled there, staring across the brown Mersey, trying to imagine a country that was more remote to them than the moon – at least one could see the moon.

The physical surroundings matched up to the grandeur of the emigrants' hopes. The Victorian docks of Liverpool were solid, massive structures of granite and marble, towered over by such commercial cathedrals as the Liver Building. The Albert Dock was a kind of maritime Blenheim. The emigrants might be destined for the rickety timber piles of jetties in the East River but at least they were leaving in style. By the mid-nineteenth century Liverpool was the second largest city in Britain and very nearly as big as New

SS *Adriatic* leaves Liverpool, 1889.

York. Fine classical buildings such as the St George's Hall were built with the profits from the emigrant trade. In 1845, for example, the port of Liverpool handled over 20,000 vessels: their arrivals and departures recorded with due prominence in the city's ten daily and weekly newspapers.

Yet away from the neo-classical buildings and the showy grandeur of the merchants' houses, Liverpool was a bizarre mixture of poor, desperate people and sailors on a spree. Prostitutes looking for seamen customers mingled with the agents and runners of the emigration bureaux. Just to buy a ticket for passage on a ship was a risky business, leave aside the voyage itself. Shipping companies generally declined to deal directly with the public, preferring to sell blocks of tickets wholesale to agents. These passage brokers were the touts of their day. Waterloo Road and Goree Piazza were the epicentre of the business, with dozens of agents lining each street. One experienced but cynical policeman commented that the desperate emigrants were defrauded from the day they left their homes. Once in Liverpool most had nowhere near enough money to stay and fight a dishonest agent through the courts. They survived in squalid boarding houses, many reduced to living in cellars like rats waiting for their ships.

These ships were generally of 800–1,000 tons, safe for the voyage but hardly commodious. Compared to the much smaller 'feeder' ships that brought travellers to Liverpool from all over Europe, particularly Ireland, they were palatial. These leaky, cramped little brigs and converted trading schooners were in reality the most dangerous part of the voyage for many emigrants. The standard trip to New York from the Mersey took around six weeks and in the mid-nineteenth century a steerage ticket could be had for £3.10s. With bad weather and head winds the trip could easily stretch to 100 days or more. With a ship crammed with hungry, bored and wretched children and bored, frightened parents it could be a nightmare.

The American ships were bigger and more comfortable, lines such as Black Ball and

Dinner aboard an America-bound emigrant ship, 1844.

Swallowtail being regarded as providing an almost comfortable crossing. Yet even so it was commonplace for dozens of children to die of seasickness or dysentry on a trip. Occasionally a serious disease such as cholera would sweep through an emigrant ship, with predictable results. There was a farcical medical examination arranged by the Liverpool authorities before an emigrant could board a ship. Sometimes over 1,000 people would pass through a single doctor's surgery in a day. The pay of £1.00 per 100 did not attract the most scrupulous practitioners. One doctor was overheard to boast, through a haze of claret, that he had examined 650 patients before luncheon.

Before the ship left the dock each passenger had to step forward and show his or her ticket at a quarter-deck roll-call. The mates would search the ship from stem to stern for the frequent stowaways, often adventurous youngsters from Merseyside orphanages who had heard rousing dormitory tales of life across the Atlantic. There are endlessly varied first-hand accounts of the scenes as emigrant ships left. Some reporters said that

when the vessel, particularly those carrying Irish emigrants, cast off her lines there was vast shouting and cheering, exultation to be rid of the workhouse and poverty without hope. Other accounts speak of wailing and keening from the decks as the passengers realized the dangers before them and the scant chance of ever seeing home again.

On one memorable occasion the *Illustrated London News*, the picture magazine that was the television documentary of its day, devoted a whole issue to Liverpool's emigration trade. One, now famous, anonymous poem summed up the anguish of those who were to leave:

> Farewell England. Blessing on thee
> Stern and niggard as thou art.
> Harshly, mother, thou has used me,
> And my bread thou hast refused me.
>
> But 'tis agony to part.

Conditions aboard the ships improved as the century wore on. Until 1855 passengers had been responsible for their own victualling and many of the poorest simply did not have enough food to bring with them for a voyage of uncertain duration. Officers sometimes

Fun on Morecambe Bay, 1914.

recorded how painful it was to see a mother waste away as she gave all the available food to her youngsters. More unscrupulous crew members sold the starving passengers food at prices that would have been a scandal in a city under siege. If one escaped the ravages of hunger, fire, shipwreck and typhus were fairly frequent alternatives. For the 200,000 or more hopefuls leaving Liverpool each year, it was far better to arrive than travel hopefully. Those commentators, particularly the 'yellow press' or 'muckrakers' in New York, who claimed that the slave trade out of Liverpool lived on by another name were not far wrong.

In modern times the coastline north from Merseyside to the Scottish border has been predominantly a tourist shore: from the lovable excesses of Blackpool to the scenic calm of the Lake District meeting the ocean. There are exceptions, of course, ranging from the deep-water fishing industry at Fleetwood to the speciality submarine construction yard at Barrow-in-Furness. Yet on the whole, leisure pursuits outweigh commerce. It was not always so.

Coal and iron ore were the heavy, ship-crushing exports from the region just below the Scots border. Iron ore from the Furness peninsula had been exported from Barrow since the early part of the eighteenth century. Small sloops and the distinctive local 'dolly flats' were the primary means of trade but as the coming of the railways and the industrialization of Britain proceeded, so demand for the highest grade iron ore in the country began to soar. In 1844 just over 50,000 tons left the port but in the next twenty years that increased to over half-a-million tons. Whitehaven and Barrow began to specialize in heavily built but fast schooners that could take the jagged cargo.

As the big schooners were built for the iron, so the traditional and highly specialized Morecambe Bay prawners found a niche in the sheltered village of Arnside. In the nineteenth century a thirty-two-foot (9.8 metre) prawner would take four men six weeks to build and cost around £70. The Victorian custom of having shrimps for tea provided a steady and lucrative market for the fishermen. In Morecambe at the turn of the century there were still over 100 boats, considerably down from a generation earlier.

These prawners were adapted to form one of the earliest attractions at Blackpool. The seaside town had been built in the late nineteenth century solely to cater for day visitors from industrial Lancashire. A bathe in the sea, grey and cold even then, and a trip round the bay were part of the fun. The open day-boats that provided the latter were developed from the prawners – not least on grounds of stability and safety. A boat that had proved its ability to withstand the steep, savage seas of Morecambe Bay and take the rough, trembling sands was thought sound enough for the shrieking mill-hands on their annual holiday.

The 1840s were a time of great upheaval for the north-western ports, a period of regional realignment. Liverpool was too grand and strategically important to be affected. In 1845 the railway reached Barrow and the port became virtually an overspill for Liverpool, being second only to the latter in volume. Whitehaven suffered by default, particularly as the town's unshakeable devotion to sailing schooners was against history.

Fleetwood was founded in 1840 in a concerted effort to take trade away from Liverpool. The citizens of north Lancashire had observed the greed and corruption of the port just as the burghers of Manchester had done and resolved to try a remedy of their own. Sir Peter Hesketh-Fleetwood laid out the streets of the new town with a plough, somewhat pre-dating the twentieth-century movement that produced Letchworth and Welwyn Garden City. The lighthouse was erected and working by 1841 but the ships had to lie exposed in the River Wyre anchorage for thirty years before the enclosed docks were complete. Eventually the town became a renowned fishing centre, the greatest on the west coast, but its ambitions as a cargo port were never fulfilled.

At Barrow the shipbuilding company was registered by interests representing the Dukes of Devonshire in 1871. This was no organic transition from craft shipbuilding of the Middle Ages but a deliberate technological approach. Ships were to be built solely of iron. Petrol and oil tankers became an early speciality of the Naval Construction and Armaments Company, as the yard later became, although many of them were sailing vessels. It was not until the comparatively late date of 1933 that Barrow launched her last sailing ship, the four-masted barque *Almirante Saldahna*, a training ship for the Brazilian navy.

In the intervening years, however, the town had become part of the arsenal of democracy. Dreadnoughts and heavyweight naval ships of every description moved from her ways. The town itself expanded enormously, but always dependent on just one industry. Gradually specializing in submarines, the Barrow-in-Furness yard now produces Britain's nuclear submarines. Just as this obscure isolated town once produced the ships that cowed the Kaiser's navy, so it now launches vast nuclear missile-carrying submarines whose movements are tracked daily in the Kremlin.

— GAZETTEER —

THE NORTH-WEST FROM LEASOWE TO MARYPORT

The Wirral peninsula, between the estuaries of the Dee and the Mersey, is a green oasis separating the docks of Liverpool and Birkenhead from the heavy industry of north-east Wales.

LEASOWE, overlooking Liverpool Bay, has a lighthouse tower that stands on flat ground behind a rampart of dunes and a sea wall. This was a soft and treacherous area of shifting sand which was unable to support a tall enough tower. But in 1760, a ship loaded with cotton was stranded on the sands and its cargo left to rot on what was then

The leaving of Liverpool, 1900.

the beach. The tough cotton bales served to bind the sand and vegetation into a base solid enough to support a lighthouse.

At **BIRKENHEAD** the once bustling docks' traffic has declined.

WILLIAMSON ART GALLERY AND MUSEUM
Slatey Rd.
Displays of maritime and local history, notably builders' models from Cammell Laird and Co, especially the *Alabama* and the *Mauretania*.

EASTHAM FERRY, the first ferry between Eastham and Liverpool, was Job's Ferry, run by a brotherhood of local monks. Regular ferry boats plied between here and Liverpool carrying passengers and freight from Chester and Shrewsbury, from the early 1800s until 1929.

ELLESMERE PORT came into being as the port where the original Ellesmere Canal reached the Mersey and eventually the sea. Later it became the hub of the whole Shropshire Union Canal system. Magnificent warehouses built for the Port by Thomas Telford now house

THE ELLESMERE PORT MUSEUM
Dockyard Rd, Ellesmere Port, Cheshire (access from junction of M53).

Here over 50 of the brightly painted canal boats from the earliest type of canal craft to the Mersey flat boat *Mossdale* (1870s) can be seen and boarded. Others include narrow boats and flats, box boats, day boats, motors, tugs, ice-breakers, starvationers and joshers. There are 7 large indoor exhibitions tracing the history of canals, their craft and people. There is a restored boat-builder's workshop, a blacksmith's forge and exhibitions on canal life. Visitors can take a trip on a horse-drawn narrow boat.
Open daily, Apr – Oct.

WARRINGTON MUSEUM AND ART GALLERY
Bold St, Warrington, Cheshire.
Backstaff, octant, quadrants, nineteenth-century sextant, mariners' compasses, including one c1730, Chinese mariner's compass. Memorabilia of Bank Quay Iron Co shipbuilders, longboat remains eleventh and twelfth century. Scale model of tug boat *Cadishead*.
Open Mon – Fri.

LIVERPOOL is still one of Britain's busiest ports, shipping more cargo by value than at any time in its history. However the shift of the main dock system downriver to new centres such as the Seaforth container port complex means that many of the older docks are now quieter and so more of the rich maritime history of the city can be appreciated.

THE RISE AND FALL OF THE MANCHESTER SHIP CANAL

To the bankers and politicians, not to mention the newspaper readers, of Victorian England, Liverpool and Manchester were the inseparable twins of Northern prosperity. One city was the port and mercantile centre, the other was the heart of the nation's manufacturing and technological sciences. One of the earliest commercial railways linked the two metropolises, and down it passed vast quantities – in opposite directions – of both raw and finished cotton. It seemed a happy synergy but it was not.

In the mid-nineteenth century Manchester's trade, both cotton and general manufactured goods, was seen as being hindered by Liverpool's exceptionally large town and harbour dues. Plans began to be discussed in Manchester to link the city with the Irish Sea by making the River Irwell navigable. Several reports were produced but the technical problems seemed insuperable.

Flooding the Manchester Ship Canal.

By the 1870s Manchester was entering a period of severe financial decline and transport difficulties were blamed for her fall from eminence. The Manchester Ship Canal was conceived as the answer to those problems and a parliamentary bill was passed once five million pounds had been raised for construction costs. In a precursor of contemporary share issues and privatizations, great efforts were made to get a wide spread of public ownership of the stock. Although it was difficult at first, there were eventually 39,000 investors, the largest spread of any public company at that time.

When opened by Queen Victoria in 1894 the Manchester Ship Canal had taken six years to build, not the planned four. It also cost fifteen million pounds, three times the original estimate. It was thirty-five and a half miles (fifty-seven kilometres) long and over fifty-four million cubic yards (forty-one million cubic metres) of spoil were moved in excavation, half as much as for the

much longer Suez Canal. It linked the Salford area of Manchester with Eastham on the Mersey estuary. At a stroke it created a new inland port and shipping centre whose unavowed aim was to surpass Liverpool.

Contemporary writers described it as 'the greatest non-martial triumph Britain will ever achieve' and certainly to see huge ships of nearly 10,000 tons gliding serenely through the Lancashire coalfields was a sight that drew admirers from all over the world. Manchester racecourse was purchased by the canal company and its land used to create the vast No 9 Dock. Around it Trafford Park was begun as the world's first and largest industrial estate. Ships, barges, and an internal railway brought raw materials to the factory gate from anywhere in the world.

Ironically, cotton manufacturers never did come to Trafford Park. By this time it was already an industry in decline and one that preferred to cling to the dark satanic mills of Rochdale and Oldham. It was younger, more scientific industries, often offshoots of American companies, that came to the new estate.

In the decade from 1894 Manchester rose from a baseline of zero to become the fourth biggest port in Britain: a league position that she lost only briefly during the Depression of the 1930s. The achievement was not made without a struggle against both the burghers of Liverpool and the railway companies – who refused to connect the Manchester docks to the outside rail system until over six years past the canal's opening day.

Yet as the 'cut' was dredged to allow bigger ships access to Manchester, the canal came to rank with Suez and Panama as one of the wonders of the world. Films and slide-shows were popular on the subject of its construction, comparing the pre-mechanical labour of thousands of 'navvies' to the toil of the Egyptians who built the Pyramids. As recently as the 1930s steamer trips along the length of the canal, billed as 'educational and entertaining' were a popular day out for people from all over the North of England.

By the end of the Second World War the canal's decline could be glimpsed. Ships were becoming bigger every year and Manchester's pre-eminence as a manufacturer of machine tools and other large-scale machinery was shrinking. Without the geographical necessity that sustains Suez and Panama the Manchester Ship Canal lingers on, kept alive by a diet of small coasters and more used by fishermen than mariners.

MERSEYSIDE MARITIME MUSEUM
'D' Block Albert Dock, Pier Head.
Located on the waterfront at the heart of Liverpool's historic cockle lands, this multi-acre site includes a good collection of over 30 historic vessels such as the schooner *De Wadden* (1917), the Weaver packet *Wincham* (1946), the pilot boat *Edmund Gardner* and the Mersey flat *Oakdale* built in 1953. It also houses relics washed ashore from the terrible *Royal Charter* wreck at Moelfre in 1859. There is an original builder's scale model of the *Titanic*, a Liverpool ship. Particular emphasis is on nineteenth- and twentieth-century merchant shipping and port operations, cargo handling, pilotage, etc. Seafaring life is displayed in a range of historic buildings, which show demonstrations of old maritime crafts, the story of the millions of Europeans who set sail from Liverpool between 1830 and 1930 for North America and Australia. Marine paintings include the work of nineteenth-century Liverpool artists Robert Salmon, Miles and Samuel Walters, Joseph Heard.

Mersey Dock and Harbour Co offices on Pier Head have some ship models in the main hall. There are frequent cruises up and down the Mersey, and Pier Head is a good point from which to watch coasters, passenger boats, tankers and

New lives and new worries for these emigrants.

container ships making their way to the Manchester Ship Canal.

In the alley Hackins Hey, an inn called Ye Hole in Ye Wall was renowned in sailing ship days and was the scene of many battles between merchant seamen and the Royal Navy's press-gangs.

LIVERPOOL MUSEUM
William Brown St.
Among the main collection is the gallery on the history of Liverpool including the social, industrial and commercial background of the port.
Open daily.

SOUTHPORT: Although there was a pool out on the sands, Southport was never a port. The name was given so that people knew that it was by the sea and would go there. However, fishermen also settled there and sold shrimps to visitors. 70 prawners were owned in Southport and Merseyside in 1904.

THE BOTANIC GARDENS MUSEUM
Botanic Rd, Churchtown.
Interesting displays of local history and, in particular, shrimping. Longboat, lifeboat and fishing boat models.
Open May – Sept, (Tues – Sat).

ST ANNES: There is a memorial in Alpine Gardens to the worst lifeboat disaster in British history. In 1886 the St Anne's lifeboat answered a distress call from the German barque *Mexico*. In trying to reach the ship, the lifeboat and her 13-man crew were lost together with all but 2 of the 16-man crew of the Southport lifeboat which turned out for the emergency. The tragedy led to an improvement in lifeboat design.

BLACKPOOL: During the 'wakes' weeks thousands flocked to Blackpool and a trip on a sailing boat was part of the attractions. William Stoba, a master shipwright at Fleetwood, designed the sailing pleasure boats which worked off the central beach from 1890. He was a progressive designer and one of the few British designers to incorporate successfully centre-boards into working sailing boats.

FLEETWOOD: The port established in 1836 became famous for its deep-water trawlers which fished the Icelandic Arctic waters, before the 'cod wars' with Iceland. In 1976 there were 70 fishing vessels at Fleetwood. As well as deep-water trawlers Fleetwood had a fleet of inshore sailing boats known locally as half deckers.

FLEETWOOD MUSEUM
Dock St, Fleetwood.
Museum of the fishing industry with displays covering Lancashire fishing industry on the ground floor and basement. Re-creation of trawler bridge. Deep-sea and inshore fisheries covered. Plans for display of local inshore boats, including Morecambe Bay prawner *Judy*.
Open Easter to Oct, daily.

SUNDERLAND POINT, a lonely hamlet halfway between Fleetwood and Morecambe, is a microcosm of ancient fishing methods. In 1979 a high tide washed away part of the saltings in the River Lune just above Sunderland Point, revealing an old fish trap. A wattle fence across a sand bank was made to drive the fish into a pocket, the fish were collected at low water. This was a widely used method in medieval times. Other old methods using whammel nets are still in use, but with the opening of a custom house at Lancaster, Sunderland Point lost its trade and the hamlet became known as 'Cape Famine'. The 3-floored warehouses have been converted to houses but the quay remains where ships once brought in rum, timber, and it is reputed, the first shipment of cotton to arrive in Britin.

ISLE OF MAN, 32 miles (51 km) long by 13 miles (21 km) wide at its widest point, has cliffs with narrow glens plunging down to the sea on its east, west and south sides.

RAMSEY marks the transition between this low-lying north coast and the eastern cliffs. The harbour formed where the Sulby river reaches the sea is packed with yachts and pleasure craft.

DOUGLAS, the island's capital, was the home of Sir William Hillary, who having witnessed many shipwrecks and himself rescued over 300 people, published *An Appeal to the British Nation* in 1824. This resulted in the founding of the RNLI.

The southern and western coasts have small fishing harbours in the glens cut into the rock by fast-flowing streams. Man was colonized by the Vikings in the ninth and tenth centuries and the Norse type of boat remained standard until the late eighteenth century.

THE MANX NAUTICAL MUSEUM
Bridge St, Castletown.
Ships and models recall the time when much of the island's life depended on sea-borne trade. Preserved in its original boathouse, is the schooner-rigged armed yacht *Peggy* built in 1791 and

Morecambe Bay mussel boats unloading, 1910.

last in a line of clippers made in the Isle of Man in the seventeenth and eighteenth centuries.

There is also personalia of the Quale family (her owners) and a sailmaker's loft, ship models, nautical gear and early photographs of Manx maritime trade and fishing. Manufacture of ship's biscuits. Part of the original building is constructed as a cabin room of the Nelson period. Open May – Sept, (Mon – Sat).

GLASSON: The Lancaster Canal meets the sea at Glasson docks, which,unlike many other harbours along this coast, is still busy both as a boating centre and as a principal area for small trading vessels. The harbour was built in 1783 and its docks were among the earliest in England to have lock gates which could keep the water level

constant as the tide outside rose and fell. The original West Indies trade through Lancaster died early in the nineteenth century.

LANCASTER: In the middle of the eighteenth century Lancaster was a busy port trading with the West Indies. At one point it had a greater registered tonnage than Liverpool. Its history goes back to the Romans who built a fort on the hill overlooking a bend in the River Lune. The Normans founded a castle here, from which today there is a marvellous view of the coast as far as the mounts of the Isle of Man.

St George's Quay is the centre of the old river port, with tall gabled, eighteenth-century warehouses and the Old Custom House with its Ionic columns and tree-lined quay being reminders of Lancaster's prosperous trading past. The ancient inn Carpenter's Arms and Skerton Bridge, were the haunt of press-gangs. Lancaster still has a cockle and mussel feast in May.

MARITIME MUSEUM
Old Custom House, St George's Quay.

Sets out the history of Lancaster's contact with the sea over 2,000 years in galleries using reconstructions, displays, audio-visual programmes, sound effects recordings of personal reminiscences and even smells. It starts off in the restored Custom House (1762–4) and extends into the adjoining eighteenth-century warehouse where visitors can see how commodities such as sugar, cotton and tobacco were handled and stored in this port.

Outside, the former fishermen's lifeboat *Sir William Priestly* is one of a number of full-sized vessels to see around the museum.
Open daily.

ARNSIDE is a pretty little fishing village and was once an important port. A custom house was built here in about 1845 and ore was shipped in from Barrow for the Leighton furnace.

The old customs warehouse is now the Arnside Sailing Club. The village has become a nationally known name in the traditional boat world because the Morecambe Bay prawners originated here.

ULVERSTON: From 1861 to 1878 John and William White built 12 wooden ships here including the well-known schooner *Millom Castle* and ending with the *Ellen Harrison*. Shifting sand banks silted up the harbour and so the 2-mile (3.2 km) long Ulverston Canal was built in 1795 to link the town with the sea. It prospered as a port and shipbuilding centre but was sealed off at its seaward end in the 1940s.

On Hoad Hill, 435 ft (132 m) high and north-east of the town, is a monument in the form of a replica of the Eddystone lighthouse commemorating Sir John Barrow, geographer, explorer and secretary to the Admiralty who was born in Ulverston in 1764.

BARROW-IN-FURNESS grew up around Furness Abbey established in 1127 by Cistercian monks who had their own fleet of ships which used to trade in iron ore. In the eighteenth century the first local furnaces were built and by 1870 Barrow's steel works were the biggest in the world. Shipbuilding came to surpass iron in importance.

FURNESS MUSEUM
Ramsden Square.

Housed in the same building as the County Record Office and Local History Library. Illustrates all aspects of the Furness area and has the Vickers collection of ships' models. Two fine maker's models are *Amphitrite*, the armoured cruiser, and the battleship *Erin*.
Open Mon – Sat.

MILLOM: Iron ore was shipped over to a jetty built on the open Duddon estuary at Millom. It is a very exposed place and strongly built schooners were specially designed at Ulverston and Barrow to trade here.

The last wooden schooner to be built at Millom, and in the United Kingdom, was the *Emily Barratt* in 1913. She had the pointed stern which was typical of schooners from Lancashire and the north-west coast of England. When the mines and steel smelting works closed, Millom became a depressed area. Today virtually all trace of the port of Millom has gone.

WINDERMERE
WINDERMERE STEAMBOAT MUSEUM
Rayrigg Rd, Windermere.

Once an old sand wharf it is now the magnificent lakeside setting for a unique collection of working steamboats and other historic craft, many still afloat. The collection includes *Dolly* one of the oldest mechanically powered boats in the world and the *Esperance*, built on the Clyde in 1869: the oldest vessel in Lloyd's Yacht Register, and famous as Flint's house-boat in the Ransome classic *Swallows and Amazons*.

There are many other vintage craft. Main displays trace the development of sailing on the lake from pre-Roman to medieval times. Visitors can ride on steam launch *Osprey*.
Open Easter – Oct, daily.

WHITEHAVEN: In 1566 Whitehaven consisted of six fishermen's cottages and possessed a single 9-ton vessel, the *Bee*.

Early in the seventeenth century it was developed as a port for shipbuilding and exporting Cumbrian coal to Ireland and developing the tobacco trade from Virginia and Maryland.

By 1730 it was one of the major ports in Britain. John Paul Jones, the Scots born American naval commander who had served as an apprentice seaman there, mounted an attack on it in 1778, during the American War of Independence. He failed in his attempt to set fire to the merchant fleet. The coal and iron trade which founded the town's prosperity have dwindled.

WHITEHAVEN MUSEUM AND ART GALLERY
Civic Hall, Lowther St.
Local history including maritime.
Open Mon – Fri.

MARYPORT: The Romans built a fort here to prevent seaborne raiders from the north outflanking the defences of Hadrian's Wall. Maryport, however, owes its name to Mary the wife of the local landowner Humphrey Senhouse who built the docks and harbour in the eighteenth century to serve the local coal trade.

Later Senhouse dock was used for loading ships with cargoes of iron rails made in Cumbria for railways all over the world. It is now only a refuge for sailing yachts and small fishing craft.

Fletcher Christian, first officer of HMS *Bounty* and leader of the mutiny against Captain Bligh, was born in Maryport in 1764. Having turned Bligh adrift Christian and the mutineers landed on Pitcairn Island. Christian St in Maryport is named after him.

MARITIME MUSEUM
1 Shipping Brow, Senhouse St.
Has exhibits of local maritime history. Deals with post Napoleonic War shipbuilding (last ship launched in 1914); fishing; sailmaking. Of note is Thomas Henry Ismay and the White Star Line; Maryport lifeboat (1865), local pilotage; ship models; half-blocks and marine paintings.
Open Mon – Sat.

Preserved ships in the harbour include: *Chipchase* (1953), a harbour tug; *Vic 96* (1945), a steam lighter; *Harecraig 11* (1951), a steam tug; *Scharhorn* (1908), a steam yacht; *Emily Barratt* (1912), a trading schooner and the only English example still afloat.

CLYDESIDE AND THE LOWLANDS

Clydebank shipbuilding

CLYDESIDE AND THE LOWLANDS

'BUILT on the Clyde.' The words once had a a ring and stature in the world of shipping that is hard for a modern generation to fathom. It was the equivalent of a gown from Paris or a claret from Bordeaux. The broad, fjord-like estuary, with Glasgow at its head, was for a century the most creative and focussed single-industry region in Britain. At the peak of its powers and influence more ships were built on the Clyde than in any other single location in the world. During the six years of the Second World War, probably the crescendo and last act of the Clyde's supremacy, her yards built nearly 2,000 ships, and repaired over 23,000. An incredible daily total of thirteen new or refurbished vessels ran down the slipways into the river.

John Brown's yard.

Names like Fairfields, John Brown, and Barclay Curle were known and revered wherever in the world a seaman went. Little riverside towns such as Paisley, Geenock and Clydebank were as familiar in the shipyards of Hoboken or Rotterdam as they were in the Lowlands of Scotland. So great was the scale of the regional operation that the Belfast firm of Harland and Wolff could have a Clyde offshoot with seven berths capable of building 80,000 tons per year and be regarded by Glaswegians as just the 'branch office' for Belfast. Yet Glasgow itself had origins and an early history which were far from maritime.

Most estimates say it was around AD 560 when St Mungo founded a community on the site of modern-day Glasgow. The name meant 'happy family' but the town counted for little. It was twenty miles (thirty-two kilometres) up the shallow and winding River

Dumbarton shipyards, 1855.

Clyde from the sea and other ports on the estuary had greater natural advantages; towns such as Renfrew and Rutherglen which were sufficiently important to be made royal burghs centuries before Glasgow, which had to wait until 1611. Dumbarton, further downstream, had been the earliest capital of the kingdom of Strathclyde.

The one simple reason for Glasgow's emergence as a regional centre was the nature of the river at this point. Here sandy, manageable fords had provided a regular crossing point since ancient Celtic times. In 1345 Bishop Rae caused a fine eight-arch stone bridge to be built across the Clyde, reinforcing the community's role as a natural communications hub in the region. An indication of the growth in the town is that in 1451 the university was founded and soon prospered, acquiring a distinguished reputa-

tion which spread out across Europe.

However, the city's shipping needs came in through Port Glasgow or Dumbarton, and were transhipped by packhorse or cart along the riverbank. Dumbarton was, in fact, offered the chance in 1668 to become the official entry port for Glasgow, but the town's magistrates turned down the opportunity because they feared 'the influx of mariners should raise the price of butter and eggs to the townsmen'.

Henry Graham's eighteenth-century work, the *Social Life of Scotland*, gives the first accurate – and downbeat – description of Glasgow's maritime role in the period immediately prior to Union with England, '... the trade was mean and the commerce was insignificant, for the citizens owned no more than 15 vessels whose aggregate tonnage was 1,182 tons, the biggest of 160 tons burthen'.

The nearest that any seagoing vessel could

get to the Broomielaw, in the heart of Glasgow, at this time was fourteen miles (22.5 kilometres) downstream, making the city a poor competitor as a port to such west coast rivals as Bristol and Liverpool. The ports and harbours on the east coast of Scotland were thriving at this period, for they had direct access to the Low Countries and Scandinavia, whose citizens were eager to trade. Prior to the Act of Union, Scots vessels were prohibited from trading with the American colonies or the Caribbean settlements, their natural trading partners to the west. The Royal Navy enforced the law rigidly, often sinking Scots ships that attempted to break the embargo.

While the gerrymandered passage of the Act of Union brought violent rioting to the streets of Glasgow and Edinburgh, not everyone was downhearted. A handful of Strathclyde traders realized that the barriers to transatlantic trade were over. They chartered a schooner out of the Cumbrian port of Whitehaven and sent her off to Virginia in search of opportunities. The ship returned with a cargo of rum and tobacco, and the foundations of a good Glasgow trade. English merchants based in Bristol and Liverpool lobbied Parliament against their new upstart rivals and generally made life as difficult as possible for the Scots. It was irritating but ineffective. By the 1750s Glasgow had a burgeoning commercial relationship with the colonies of the eastern seaboard of North America.

It was two decades later that several factors simultaneously came into play that launched the city on a path of immense industrial and maritime growth. The first serious efforts to dredge the Clyde had been made as early as the 1560s but they were largely ineffectual. However, by 1775 the channel had been deepened and straightened sufficiently for it to be worth building quays and warehouses at the Broomielaw. Finally, in 1780, the Customs and Excise designated Glasgow as a Port of Entry. Across the Atlantic the War of Independence had put a virtual stop on the export of tobacco although, showing that every cloud has a silver lining, the war brought forth an enormous demand for the boot and shoe industry where Glasgow was also strong.

External factors apart, these were the decades when Britain changed from a military and agricultural force to becoming the first industrial nation. Glasgow was in the forefront. Just outside the city lay extraordinarily large deposits of coal and iron ore. The iron industry grew exponentially in Lanarkshire and Ayrshire, adjacent to the city. Industries took the place of trading. Printing came to Glasgow in 1770, Tennant Bros brewery in 1780, and in 1789 the Clyde Iron Works. Glasgow's own Chamber of Commerce was inaugurated in 1783, the first such organization of its kind in Britain.

In parallel to its physical resources Glasgow proved it had the innovatory brainpower that enables change and progress to occur. Steam kettles and flashes of brilliance notwithstanding, James Watt was probably more a technologist than an inventor. He was already the mathematical instrument-maker to the University of Glasgow in 1764 when he was simultaneously repairing a scale model of the Newcomen pumping engine. Watt was convinced of the value of steam as a motive force; his genius was to consider the value of condensing the steam outside the cylinder. In making his calculations he was handicapped by the lack of data on steam and conducted complex experiments to improve understanding of how it behaved. In the long run this priceless research data may have been of more value than the machines Watt built.

In 1765, in partnership with Matthew Boulton of Birmingham, he constructed the first steam engine with a separate condenser. Other major innovations were the change from reciprocating motion to a rotating shaft via a crank, and the creation of a centrifugal governor to regulate engine speed. Watt made Glasgow a focal point for the interchange of technological knowledge during the early years of the industrial revolution.

At Bowling Harbour on the north bank of the Clyde is the western terminus of the now-derelict Forth & Clyde Canal. Opened in 1790, after twenty-two years of construction, its thirty-five miles (fifty-six kilometres) of loops and locks linked Edinburgh and Glasgow along the line of Antonine's Wall. Nearby is the memorial to Henry Bell, more than Watt the father of British steam navigation.

It was Bell's steamer *Comet* that was the first viable steamship in British waters. A year or two earlier the *Charlotte Dundas* had made a few successful towing trials on the eastern reaches of the Forth & Clyde Canal but the *Comet* was modelled far more on the SS *Clermont*, already steaming successfully on the Hudson River in New York.

Bell, born in 1767, had trained in a Bo'ness shipyard and with a London engineering firm, but by 1807 he had settled in Helensburgh and kept himself busy with the unusual combination of studying mechanics and running a hotel. His first ship, the *Comet*, was reliable and fast (at 6.7 knots she outperformed her Hudson rival) but most importantly she was accessible to the public and changed their thinking. She was no scientific abstraction but a real means of transport for which you could buy a ticket. With a crew of eight, including a piper, and a skipper who was a Helensburgh schoolmaster, the *Comet* was an immediate success with the public, if not the professional Clyde sailors. They prophesied doom and praised the Lord that they were propelled by 'the Almighty's ain wind and nae by the deevil's sunfire and brimstone'.

Within a year of *Comet*'s 1812 debut on the Clyde, Bell had another steamer, the *Elizabeth*, plying the route between Glasgow, Greenock and Helensburgh. So fast was the rate of innovation at this point in history that by 1814 nine steamers were competing for custom on the lower Clyde. Bell expanded to London, running a fleet of five steamers down the Thames to Margate. *Comet* may have been crude, with the configuration of a one-cylinder steam engine per paddle making her difficult to manoeuvre and steer, but the point about her is that she carried a scheduled service thirteen years before the opening of the first public railway. Glasgow's genius always consisted of alloying technology with commercial need.

Within a very few years the Clyde boasted a fleet of pleasure steamers and ferries that was without a match anywhere in the world. They fitted into an environment that was accustomed to using the gentle climate and calm sheltered waters of the Clyde for recreation. At the close of the eighteenth century the newly rich merchant classes of Glasgow would hire a 'fly', a light sailing gig, to convey themselves and their families down to the islands and lochs of the lower Clyde for family holidays. With the coming of steam the process became immeasurably easier and more exciting. Steamers were reaching Gourock in about four hours for a fare of four shillings. The islands of Bute and Cambrae were opened up by speculative builders creating summer villas for the middle-classes, and staid Dunoon became a summer resort to rival Monte Carlo.

Wealthy owners often chose to skipper their 'paddlers' themselves; rather in the way that pioneer motor-cars were too exciting to be left to chauffeurs. Naturally there was a desire to push design forward and go faster. By the 1850s the process had come down to a clash between speed and comfort. Alexander Smith, considered the 'hottest' designer of his day, built long, low greyhounds with minimal deckhouses and enormously powerful engines.

A natural extension of both design rivalry and competitiveness between owner/skippers was the practice of 'steamer racing'. The authorities frowned upon such frivolity, claiming that it led to careless navigation and accidents when newly developed machinery was pushed beyond its limits. The most famous race of all took place on 27 May 1861, between the *Ruby* and the *Rothesay Castle*, two steamers owned by different and rival

Clyde paddle-steamers at Broomielaw quay.

companies. Huge crowds lined the banks as the two boats prepared to leave Glasgow at 4.00 pm. The newspapers gave enormous coverage to the contest and bookmakers were doing a brisk trade among the highly partisan onlookers. Many were connected with ship-building and each would have a highly biased opinion of the merits of any ship.

It was a hard-fought race down the Clyde with the two vessels seldom more than hailing distance apart. After two and a half hours of steaming the *Rothesay Castle* arrived at Gourock just two minutes thirty seconds ahead of her rival. On the following Monday both skippers were fined a guinea for danger-ous navigation. It was a small deterrent. Races continued on an informal and *ad hoc* basis until the early twentieth century.

A more leisurely steamer ride down the Clyde from Broomielaw would give the mid-nineteenth century passenger a chance to observe what a powerful metropolis the city had become. Shipyards lined both banks of the river once out of the affluent western suburbs. Clydeside began her route into shipbuilding via fitting steam engines in wooden hulls; but with the proximity of the Lanarkshire iron industry there was no shor-tage of workers skilled in the new material and so iron ships became Glasgow's special-ity. Between 1859 and 1889 the tonnage of iron ships produced increased tenfold.

The riverscape was not for the country-cottage aesthete. A nineteenth-century poet who took a trip downriver gives a tingling description of the scene:

The steamer left the black and oozy wharves
And floated down between dank ranks of masts
We heard the swarming streets, the noisy mills
Saw sooty foundries full of glare and gloom
Great-bellied tipped by tongues of flame
Quiver in heat, we slowly passed
Loud building yards, where every slip contained
A mighty vessel with 1000 men
Battering its iron sides

It might have been an inferno, but one of the advantages that Glasgow possessed ahead of other industrial cities such as Manchester and Birmingham was, for the price of a steamer ticket, the oppressed shipyard or factory worker could sail downriver to Arcadia.

To the right the deck passenger would see Dumbarton, bearing a distinct resemblance to Gibraltar with its great fortified rock. The Romans occupied it as a natural fortress, the Vikings attacked it repeatedly and King Arthur is supposed to have adventured there. What is certain is that the six-year-old Mary Queen of Scots sailed from Dumbarton Rock to France, to escape the clutches of Scottish nobles who wanted the child monarch for their own power struggles. Much later, during her military struggle for the country, she was making for Dumbarton and safety when her army was defeated at the Battle of Langside.

On the north bank the Clyde curves round to open into the Firth, virtually an inland sea. At Cardross the shore stretches round into the Gareloch. Cardross was the place where Robert the Bruce died in 1329. He was very fond of the Clyde and had little ships built at Dumbarton so that he could potter about the sheltered waters. He could well have been an even earlier royal yachtsman than Charles II at Harwich.

Gareloch means a short loch and, indeed, it is only six miles (9.6 kilometres) long. Nevertheless it has a potential vastly out of proportion to mere length, for this is the home base of Britain's ballistic missile submarine fleet; currently armed with Polaris and soon to be replaced with Trident. The association with underwater boats began in the First World War with the testing of new submarines in the deep, sheltered waters and the tradition has continued to this day.

Adjoining the entrance to Gareloch is Holyloch, where the United States navy has based its own submarines since the days of the Second World War. At the mouth of Holyloch is the altogether more peaceful spot of Hunter's Quay where the Royal Clyde

Yacht Club has its headquarters. In the zenith of Glasgow's economic fortunes, towards the end of the nineteenth century, yachting was becoming popular in every leisured society and Glasgow was no exception. Clyde Week during early July was at that time an international sailing festival to rival Cowes Week. No more, unfortunately, although the sailing remains as good as that in the Solent. Clyde-built yachts from this era, particularly from the yard of William Fife, soon had as good a reputation as the big iron steamships built upriver.

Across the Clyde lies Greenock, birthplace of James Watt and, less revered but equally famous, the pirate Captain Kidd. Scotts of Greenock is the oldest purpose-built shipyard in the world, the slipways having been first used in 1771. Southwards down into Ayrshire the land becomes flatter and the principal maritime use of the foreshore has been to create the world's finest stretch of golf links. Not for nothing is this known as 'the golf coast'.

Glasgow embraces her docks in the heart of the city with characteristic vigour and rough energy. The more refined, at least in its own estimation, capital of Edinburgh has its quays and wharfage at Leith. The linear distance is a mere mile and a half but psychologically a great deal more. Edinburgh has never seen itself as a maritime city, merely enjoying the proximate sea as a delicious blue/green backdrop to art, conversation and politics.

Leith has long been a sea port worthy of attack. In the fourteenth and fifteenth centuries the English forces burned both the houses and the ships in the harbour repeatedly. Eventually in the sixteenth century Leith was fortified to a degree that its strategic importance warranted. Mary Queen of Scots arrived here from her French exile in 1561.

Later in Scotland's marine history Leith achieved a dour prominence as the departure point for the ill-fated Darien expedition which sailed in 1698 with five frigates, 1,500 men and much of Scotland's monetary wealth pledged to it.

This was Scotland's answer to the East India Company, but shut off by English manoeuvring from trading with Africa, India and America the shareholders were reduced to establishing a colony on the Isthmus of Darien, which separates North and South America. Separating as it does the Pacific from the Caribbean it was seen as a future focus of world trade, and hence Scottish expansion.

The five ships sailed on 18 July. Huge crowds from Edinburgh came to wave them adieu. The voyage went well and took a swift three months. Once ashore matters deteriorated. There was not enough food aboard the ships and the English intrigued with Spain to prevent other colonists in the region supplying the Scots adventurers.

Dying of starvation and under military attack from Spain, the founding colonists left Darien after a year. For the next decade a series of relief expeditions and reinforcement groups were either lost at sea or cut to pieces by the Spaniards. All of the £400,000 capital was lost to the Edinburgh subscribers who had invested in the project and the sole enduring consequence of the scheme to found Caledonia (the name of the colony) in Central America was an increased hostility to all things English and particularly the venal East India Company.

Leith's original single quay has grown into a locked-dock complex covering a vast area of foreshore. Perhaps the most telling description of Leith as it must have seemed in the last few hundred years is from David Balfour in the Robert Louis Stevenson novel *Kidnapped*: 'In the granite mansions of "Whisky Row" up above the town the merchants stood at their windows with a dram and watched their ships come and go.'

From the ports of the Firth of Forth round to the English border at Berwick is a low, sandy coast given over to modest seaside resorts and small villages with a little inshore fishing. It is said that those Scots who are to leave their home by sea should leave from this exit rather than the Clyde – there being so little to tug at their already overloaded heart-strings.

GAZETTEER

CLYDESIDE AND THE LOWLANDS FROM ANNAN TO FERNIEHILL

The Solway Firth is the western boundary between England and Scotland. It is noted for its 30 ft (9 m) tidal range and miles of sand-banks. The many narrow inlets along the shore, where smugglers once landed contraband wines and tobacco, now provide sheltered anchorages for yachtsmen and fishermen and despite the nuclear power station at Annan and a scattering of oil and chemical concerns, the Solway Firth is probably Britain's least polluted large estuary.

ANNAN: On the shore, commercial fishing is done by haaf-nets (originating from the Norwegian word for 'heave'). In 1850s and 60s Benjamin Nicholson built clipper ships for the China trade here. His best-known clipper was the *Annandale*, built in 1854 with timber from the Annandale estate. Local shrimpers built by Wilson at Annan were in the style of the Morecambe Bay prawners.

GLENCAPLE, on the east bank of the tidal channel of the Nith, was once a satellite harbour for the port of Dumfries, handling emigrant ships and coastal vessels.

DUMFRIES, now inland, was once a small port at the head of the River Nith. Silting was always a problem on the Solway Firth, so at Kingholm Quay, further downstream, water was trapped in a pool above the dock and released at low water so the silt was washed from the berths.

DUMFRIES MUSEUM
The Observatory.

Good collection of photographs of the schooners which traded from the Solway Firth.
Open Apr – Sept.

KIRKBEAN is famous as the birthplace of John Paul Jones, who became an American naval hero in 1778 when he sailed into the harbour at Whitehaven, captured a small fort and attempted to burn 3 British ships. A baptismal font in the church presented in 1945 by officers and men of the US navy, honours Jones who was baptised there, as the American navy's 'First Commander'. Jones is commemorated again further round the coast, north of **SOUTHERNESS** where his cottage birthplace stands. A disused lighthouse is situatead forlornly on the headland facing across the Solway Firth to Cumbria: it was built in 1748 to guide schooners sailing out of Dumfries bound for the American colonies.

AUCHENCAIRN BAY, a village inland from Balcary Point, is an old smuggling centre. Balcary House, now a hotel, was specifically built in the eighteenth century by one of the most successful smuggling concerns as a headquarters and secret store for contraband.

PORT MARY, which fronts Dundrevinan Abbey, is the spot from which Mary Queen of Scots fatefully sailed across the Solway Firth in an open boat seeking refuge in England, a voyage which resulted in her 19-year imprisonment and eventual execution.

KIRCUDBRIGHT, one of Scotland's most ancient towns, is situated on the River Dee near the head of Kircudbright Bay whose shores were the haunt of Dirk Hatteraick and his smugglers in Sir Walter Scott's romance *Guy Mannering*. It was also one of the places selected for the landing of the Spanish Armada and for the French invasions in aid of the Stewart dynasty.

STEWARTRY MUSEUM
Has local material and displays on John Paul Jones, a founder of the American navy who was born here.
Open Easter – Oct, (Mon – Sat).

CREETOWN, set on the marshy estuary of the River Cree, was a thriving nineteenth-century port whose main export was granite. The harbour is now only used by private craft.

AUCHENMAIG BAY: A private house to the west of Auchenmaig Bay retains the name of Sinniness Barracks, built in the 1820s for a company of 50 revenue men installed to stamp out the prolific Solway smuggling trade.

MULL OF GALLOWAY: This wild peninsula, whose rugged headland forms Scotland's southernmost point, is the legendary site of the 2 last Picts, a father and son. The father, rather than betray the secret of the Pictish drink known as 'heather ale' to the Scots, allowed his son to be thrown off the cliffs here. He then hurled himself over.

PORTPATRICK, on the extreme west end of the Rhins Peninsula, is the small stone-walled exposed harbour from where sailing packets once crossed to Northern Ireland. The distance to Donaghadee is only 22 miles (35 km) but sailing packets often took 24 hours to make the crossing, and the ferries faced a constant battle against winter gales. In 1822, to speed up communications, the Post Office introduced steam packets. Portpatrick lost its importance as a port when Stranraer, 6 miles (9.6 km) away, became the ferry terminal.

CORSEWALL POINT: This rocky headland is a good vantage point for ship spotters. There are fine views of the Kintyre Peninsula, Arran, the Firth of Clyde, Aisla Craig and even Ireland. The 86-ft (138-m) high lighthouse, usually open in the afternoon, was built by the father of the nineteenth-century novelist Robert Louis Stevenson.

STRANRAER is a ferry port for Ireland. The North West Castle, now a hotel, was built in the shape of a ship by Sir John Ross, the nineteenth-century Arctic explorer.

WIGTOWN DISTRICT MUSEUM
London Road, Stranraer.
Local history with material relating to Sir John Ross.
Open all year, Mon – Fri.

CAIRNRYAN: Since the war, many famous ships have ended their days at the shipbreaker's quay here including the aircraft carriers *Eagle* and *Ark Royal* scrapped in 1979–80.

BALLANTRAE: Throughout the eighteenth century Ballantrae was the headquarters of a highly organized smuggling ring.

AILSA CRAIG: 10 miles (16 km) to the east of Girvan this granite island 1,114 ft (340 m) high and 2 miles (3.2 km) in circumference, is the core of an ancient volcano. Most of the islands are rimmed by spectacular cliffs. Since the closure of the granite quarries the island has become the main breeding ground for 10,000 pairs of gannets. (In the past, tenants of the island used to pay their rents in gannet feathers.)

GIRVAN, an attractive harbour with an active fishing fleet, is now the main building centre for the Strathclyde fishing industry. The wooden inshore fishing boats built on the west coast are usually recognizable by their raised foredecks.

MAIDENS, named after the treacherous offshore rocks, Maidens was once a lively fishing and fish-curing centre. Burns's *Tam O' Shanter* was based on the real Douglas Graham, occasional smuggler and tenant of Shanter Farm above the village.

AYR stands on the banks of the Ayr at its point of entry to the Firth of Clyde. It was once Scotland's principal west coast holiday resort.

IRVINE, once the main port of Glasgow until the River Clyde was deepened in the eighteenth century, it is now a resort. There used to be a schooner trade from the quay near the tidal yacht moorings and trading schooners were built here in the 1870s.

SCOTTISH MARITIME MUSEUM
Laird Forge, Gottries Road.
Ships' artefacts and machinery of maritime importance. Local and maritime history. Active boat-building, welding, rigging and other restoration work in workshops. Vessels include the last surviving Kirkintilloch puffer, *Spartan*; the plank-on-edge racing cutter, *Vagrant* (1884) built by William Fife; lifeboats *St Cybi* and *TGB*; yachts; the old 3-masted lugger *Lady Guildford* (1818).
The SMM now has an offshoot at Dumbarton, in the form of The Denny Tank. Built in 1882 and 328 ft (100m) long by 8 ft (2.5m) deep, the tank is the oldest surviving experimental tank in the world. Thousands of hulls and propellors were tested here, and the written records and results all survive.
The museum has also re-created a typical shipworker's flat in a late Victorian tenement building. It is equipped and furnished just as a working-class family would have lived in 1910. Open April-Oct, daily.

SALTCOATS is a busy seaside resort. It originated as a harbour between 1684 and 1700 for the coal trade between the Clyde area and Ireland, which declined in the early nineteenth century. The harbour wall has been heightened and provides a vantage point for viewing fossilized trees visible at low tide.

Two miles west of West Kilbride and Seamill is **FARLAND HEAD** where tradition says that one of the vessels of the Spanish Armada was wrecked: a cannon said to be from the wreck stands on the green by Portencross Castle.

MILLPORT, on Big Cumrae near Keppel Pier, was established in 1897 and maintained by Glasgow University. It has a marine biology station and museum which graphically illustrates the topography of the Clyde and its sea life. It was here that scientists worked out a method of extracting agar – the medium on which bacterial cultures are grown in medical research – from seaweed. Live sea creatures, from tiny crabs to giant eels, can be seen in the aquarium.
Open during the summer.

FAIRLIE, has an old-established boatyard. William Fife of Fairlie was among the leading yacht yards from the mid-nineteenth century to 1939. Fife yachts were noted for being particularly well built, although this sometimes made them rather heavy for racing. In the 1890s, Sir Thomas Lipton built his famous racing yachts *Shamrock* and *Shamrock II* here.

LARGS stands on the banks of 2 streams, the Gogo and the Noddle, and is a popular resort. Sheltered by the Cumbraes, Largs has some of the best sailing in Britain with regattas held almost weekly from the end of May to the middle of September. A local monument, 'The Pencil', commemorates the Battle of Largs 1263, when a Viking fleet was driven ashore here and bloodily defeated by the Scots, thus ending Viking domination. Every September, Norwegians visit Largs to attend celebrations such as the re-enactment of the battle, burning of a longship, etc.

WEMYSS BAY has a magnificent outlook across the Firth and is the starting point of steamers for Rothesay, being one of the main passenger ports on the Clyde. The famous paddle-steamers are gone, except for the *Waverley*, but their heyday is recorded in the Edwardian station and pier where the old steamers' crests are displayed next to old photographs.

CLOCH POINT lighthouse to the north is a landmark on the Clyde built in 1797.

GOUROCK on Lyle Hill. Between Gourock and Greenock there is a monument in the combined forms of an anchor and Cross of Lorraine commemorating the Free French sailors who died in the Battle of the Atlantic during the Second World War. In 1920 Clyde pilots were transferred from Greenock to Gourock and a new pilot house was built on the pier.

GREENOCK: Three centuries ago Greenock was a small fishing village, but because ships had difficulty in getting up to Glasgow, it prospered as a trading centre. Its motto was 'Let herring swim that trade maintain', indicating the importance of the herring trade to France and the Baltic.

In the nineteenth century the channel up to Glasgow was made deeper but Greenock still remained a centre for industry, especially sugar refining. Abraham Lyle of Greenock was one of the Victorian merchants dealing in sugar and he, like many other local businessmen, built up a fleet of sailing ships which were built in Greenock yards. In the 1850s and 60s the most sought-after contracts were for clipper ships in the China tea trade. Robert Steel and Co, whose firm went out of business in 1883, built among others, the famous *Sir Lancelot* of 1865, which sailed from Foochow against the south-west monsoon to the Lizard in 85 days.

A few elegant buildings dating from this era, such as the early nineteenth-century custom house, still remain and can be glimpsed between the towering cranes and derricks. The Old Kirk on Seafield Esplanade contains an interesting sailor's loft. The Clyde roadstead off Greenock, known as Tail of the Bank, was one of the most important assembly points for Atlantic convoys during the Second World War.

THE McCLEAN MUSEUM
9 Union St, West End.
Shipping exhibitions and a number of relics of James Watt. Among the ship models are SS *Comet* (1812); PS *Iona* (1863); PS *Mona's Isle* (1882); half-model PS *Windsor Castle*, the first steamer made of iron; SS *Clan Ross*; MV *Clan Sutherland*; and nineteenth-century Chinese ivory ship mod-

els. The picture collection includes works by Bone, Boudin, Clark, Daniel, Downie and Salmon.
Open Mon – Sat.

HELENSBOROUGH, on the northern bank of the Firth and opposite Greenock, has an obelisk on the front commemorating Henry Bell, designer of the *Comet*, Europe's first commercially successful steamship.

PORT GLASGOW: The town was built by seventeenth-century Glaswegian merchants to overcome the disadvantages of the shallow river. Boats could not then come up to the city so a new port was founded where there was deep water and although its original purpose was lapsed, Port Glasgow is still of considerable importance on Clydeside. At least 50 different shipbuilders have operated on this stretch of the Clyde. Henry Bell's famous steamer the *Comet* was built by John Wood at Port Glasgow in 1812 and there is a memorial tablet and a replica of the *Comet* in front of the Municipal Hall. A local ropeworks made the ropes for both the *Comet* and the first *Queen Elizabeth* and the most important industry in the town is still shipbuilding.

DUMBARTON, on the north bank of the Clyde, and north-east of Port Glasgow, was sited above the lowest fordable point of the Clyde and was once an important shipbuilding centre. Many of the early yards were small and one of these was Scott and Linton which built a few vessels in the 1860s and went out of business while building the famous clipper *Cutty Sark*. It was finally launched from here in 1869.

CLYDEBANK virtually joins up with Dumbarton and, like it, had dozens of small yards, with John Brown and Co probably being the best known because of the liners built by the firm.

PAISLEY MUSEUM AND ART GALLERY
High St, Paisley.
Has a good collection of archive material relating to Fleming and Ferguson with shipyard models from local firms.
Open Mon – Sat.

GLASGOW: The city's commitment to transatlantic trade since the eighteenth century encouraged the development of a vast shipbuilding industry along the towns of the Clyde. The river had to be 'trained' or deepened in the nineteenth

Steam 'puffer' at Paisley, 1902.

century by the Clyde Navigation Trust, to produce upriver ports. Glasgow's harbour, lacking tidal variations, was practically unique among major ports in not having much orthodox warehousing, concentrating rather on rapid-transit working with a considerable traffic.

MV *CARRICK* (formerly *City of Adelaide*) 1864
Lying in the River Clyde by Victoria Bridge in Glasgow centre this sailing ship with painted gun-ports, is now used by the naval reserve. As the clipper *City of Adelaide*, she once made a record passage of 65 days from England to Australia. Not open to the public but visible from the shore.

GLASGOW MUSEUM OF TRANSPORT
Kelvin Hall, 1 Bun House Rd.
Deals with history of transport with good maritime section. It has a large map showing where most of the shipbuilding yards were situated on the Clyde and has a wide display of large models. Open daily.

PS *WAVERLEY*
Waverley Excursion Ltd, Anderston Quay.
Owned by the Paddle-Steamer Preservation Socie-

ty, and operated by the Waverley Steam Navigation Co. It is one of the last sea-going paddle-steamers in the world. It was built for Clyde service in 1946 by A & J Inglis, Pointhouse, Glasgow. It has a triple expansion steam engine, double-ended boiler, originally coal fired but converted to oil in 1957, traditional fan-vented paddle box. It sails from resorts around England and Wales and cruises on the Clyde.

BOWLING: The entrance to the Forth and Clyde Canal, which used to connect the Clyde with Grangemouth 38 miles (61 km) away on the Firth of Forth, is situated here. The canal closely follows the line of the Antonine Wall, a defensive Roman rampart, and was potentially one of the most useful canals in Britain, since it could save small sea-going vessels some 400 miles (644 km). Because it is 156 ft (48 m) above sea level, it had 39 locks, but it was unpopular because of the number of road bridges which had to be opened for sea-going craft. It was closed in 1962, blocked and partly filled in and is now used only by yachts. The yard of Scott and Sons at Bowling built about 40 Clyde puffers.

KIRKINTILLOCH is situated inland, half-way along the Forth and Clyde Canal, where many

Paddle-steamer *Waverley* off Arrochar, 1947.

puffers were built by yards such as J Hay and Sons and P Macgregor and Sons. The official name for these steamers was 'Cargo Lighters' but in their general trading runs in the Clyde and the Hebrides were called puffers. They had to be launched sideways into the canal. The only puffers now seen on the west coast are the *Auld Reekie* (1943) and the *VIC 32* (1943).

GRANGEMOUTH, the destination of the Forth and Clyde Canal, now has major oil refineries with oil pipelines linked to the Forties oil field.

GRANGEMOUTH MUSEUM
Victoria Library, Bo'ness Rd.
Central Scotland Canals. Exhibits relating to *Charlotte Dundas*, the world's first practical steamship.
Open all year, Mon – Sat.

BORROWSTOUNNESS or **BO'NESS**: This was the main port of the upper Firth of Forth in the early nineteenth century. It was well known as a whaling centre, and one of the hills is still called Tidings Hill from which wives and women would watch for a first glimpse of the whaling ships returning from Greenland. James Watt built his first full-scale steam pumping engine in a cottage near Kinneil House.

BLACKNESS CASTLE, down the Firth from Bo'ness, was built by the Scots to protect the once important port of Blackness. They had been refused permission by the English to do this and in response to the suggestion that they should build a ship instead, built the castle in the shape of a ship. At certain angles it still conveys the look of a medieval warship today.

QUEENSFERRY is situated on the south shore of the Firth of Forth near the Forth rail and road bridges. As this is a narrow point in the Forth, a ferry used to cross here for at least 800 years. Indeed the town's name derived from the frequent use by Queen Margaret of Scotland of the ferry when travelling between Edinburgh and Dunfermline. Since the suspension bridge opened in 1964 the ferry's role has been diminished and the pier and its environs are now a base for inshore rescue and a dinghy harbour.

EDINBURGH
GRANTON: The large harbour at Granton is the western end of the dock area serving Edinburgh.

THE BUILDING OF A QUEEN

Early in the twentieth century the transatlantic passenger trade was the most prestigious and profitable route in the entire world. Since the 1830s, when Samuel Cunard successfully tendered to convey the British government's mail across the Atlantic, the Cunard Steamship Company had led the field in a highly competitive environment. Cunard had built its first paddle-wheel steamship, the *Britannia*, on the Clyde and she was so reliable and successful that the foundations were laid for Cunard's century of glory.

Yet by the 1920s, the steamship line was struggling. Many of its crack vessels, headed by the *Lusitania* (another Clyde-built liner), had been sunk in the 1914–18 war. In the aftermath of that conflict French, Italian and American lines had begun to jostle Cunard for supremacy and the company did not enjoy the competition. In 1926 Cunard took a momentous decision: the line would run weekly sailings between New York and Southampton using only two ships instead of the previous three.

To achieve this schedule the two liners would have to be faster than any existing ship, capable of averaging better than 28.5 knots over a 3,000-mile (4820-kilometre) crossing. To house such propulsion machinery the ships themselves would have to be larger than any ship then afloat. But the technology, in the form of steam turbine engines (pioneered by Cunard) and oil-fired boilers, was available and the company took the risk.

First blueprints called for a ship 1,020 feet (310 metres) long and weighing 81,237 tons, twice the size of the ill-fated *Titanic* – a vessel that came into discussion whenever marine innovation was mentioned. Once the design was settled other problems arose. There was no dry dock big enough to take the ship, no slipway big enough to launch her and the quay facilities at both New York and Southampton would need to be massively enlarged. Gradually agreements were reached to enlarge these facilities, and all the while Cunard's naval architects moved on with tank-testing and engine design to produce the ultimate ship.

Finally, in December 1930, the first rivet was hammered home in the longest keel ever laid down in a shipyard. For Cunard there was no real choice about where to build their new flagship. John Brown's yard at Clydebank had been the benchmark for world shipbuilding for nearly a century. Tradesmen from other Clyde yards would often be in their thirties befffore they considered themselves sufficiently skilled to meet the demands of working at Brown's yard. The hull's designation was job number 534, and she had no other name until her christening and launch four years later.

Already job 534 was becoming one of the wonders of the world. Tourists and technical observers from other countries began to drift towards Clydeside for a glimpse of the behemoth towering above the sheds at Brown's yard. One year later came disaster. Cunard was on the verge of bankruptcy as the Great Depression hit transatlantic trade. The company was saved but there were no funds for job number 534 and work stopped.

Across Britain, not just on Clydebank, workers whose jobs depended on components and fittings for the new ship were laid off. It was just one ship, but a very tangible symbol of the Depression itself. One contemporary American newspaperman wrote: '...the great vessel – no longer reverberating to the rhythm of the hammers – lay silent, a symbol of the cold hand of economic stress which lay on the hearts of the people.' For two years the giant hull rusted in the Clyde rains, a monument to the nation's economic paralysis. Impassioned debates were held in Parliament over whether the government should assist in the completion of job 534; the Keynesian arguments were only in their infancy. Finally it was the potential usefulness of the *Queen Mary* as a war-time troopship that swung the balance and Westminster voted funds to complete the ship. Sadly, the government would soon be shown to have acted with great foresight.

A requirement of the decision was that Cunard merge with their deadly rivals, White Star Line. Cunard White Star Line was duly formed and on 3 April 1934, work resumed at John Brown's. The workers were led back into the shipyard by a pipeband and a mood of cautious optimism swept back across Britain.

Six months later job 534 was ready for launch. Her name was a secret guarded so closely that the popular newspapers had enjoyed a field-day running competitions to guess the new ship's name. The day was chilly, with a steady drizzle,

Queen Mary launches the *Queen Mary*.

but nothing could dampen the spirits of the estimated 200,000 spectators who packed yard, riverbanks and launches to watch the Queen, accompanied by King George V, launch the ship.

A roar that could be heard in Dumbarton went up as the wife of the monarch smashed a bottle of Australian white wine on the huge sheer bow and named the ship *Queen Mary*. No better name could have been chosen, for the Queen herself was one of the warmest and most popular consorts to have occupied the throne in generations. It assured the ship a special place in the hearts of millions.

After the Queen had fired small electric triggers, nothing happened to the hull for twenty-four seconds, then, almost imperceptibly it began to move, sliding down the ways and taking 2,300 tons of drag chains with it. A two-foot (sixty-centimetre) high displacement wave soaked onlookers on the other bank of the Clyde. She was quickly brought alongside at the fitting-out berth for twenty months of work. On 24 March 1936, the *Queen Mary* proceeded down river under her own power. Despite the river being specially widened and dozens of attendant tugs she still ran aground twice. However, she was quickly freed

and after another month of sea trials she was ready for her maiden voyage from Southampton.

It was a media event to end them all. Hundreds of reporters were aboard for the voyage, the BBC had installed radio microphones throughout the ship and during the voyage to New York broadcasters from all over the world transmitted reports to five continents. Fog spoiled the *Queen Mary*'s chances of taking the Blue Riband, the trophy for the fastest Atlantic crossing, from the French liner *Normandie*. However on voyage number six the 'Queen' averaged 30.63 knots from Ambrose Light off New York to the Bishop Rock, an extraordinary feat for a ship of over 80,000 tons gross.

Her success put much of the fight back into Clydeside, re-establishing Glasgow as the centre of the world's most important technology – maritime transport. As war came the *Queen Mary* moved so many American troops to Europe, with speed and safety, that she became virtually the equivalent of another country fighting for the Allies. Unlike any other ship from her era she survives as a museum piece in Long Beach, southern California, operated by the Disney company. After Disneyland she is the second most-visited attraction in the western United States – still a much-loved crowd-puller after more than fifty years.

The fine harbour was started in 1835 and completed in 1845. By 1900 Granton, with Leith, had become bases for steam trawlers working out in the North Sea. At Granton, the central jetty had local sheds and an ice factory to serve the trawlers. In 1928 there were 62 steam trawlers based here, and there is still commercial traffic.

NEWHAVEN is now part of the docking area which extends along the Forth coast north of Edinburgh. Newhaven was established in about 1488 when James III started a shipbuilding yard and ropewalk here. Flemish fishermen are reputed to have settled here to supply Edinburgh with fresh fish. James IV built his warship *Great Michael* here in 1511.

Because of the Flemish influence in the town, Newhaven retained a strong local character, with fishwives wearing the distinctive dress of a white handkerchief tied round the head, a navy blue bodice and skirt gathered up to show a striped blue and white petticoat. During the nineteenth century the women from this area – the Herring Lassies – participated in the herring boom by following the fleet round the coast from Stornoway to Southwold in the season preparing the fish for curing.

ROYAL MUSEUM OF SCOTLAND
Chambers St, Edinburgh.
Many ship models including a significant collection of Pacific Island vessels. Builders' models include Turkish steam frigate *Osman Ghazy* 1864, HMS *Terrible* 1895, HMS *Hermes* 1898, *Empress of Scotland* 1930, whalers *Eclipse* 1867 and *Southern Gem* 1937. There are engineering inventors' and builders' models. Navigational and scientific instruments, including Moorish astrolabe of AD 1026. Marine chronometers.
Open Mon – Sat.

LEITH: By the end of the century Leith was second only to Glasgow in the tonnage of shipping entering the port from abroad.

The docks are the largest complex on the east coast of Scotland. On the west side of the river mouth the Victoria Dock was built in 1852, the Albert Dock in 1869, the Edinburgh Dock 1881 and the Imperial Dock in 1901. The port was improved in 1968 by the opening of a new deep-water entrance lock and still does considerable trade with the Low Countries and Europe.

At the mouth of the Water of Leith are the Old Ship Inn, now a hotel, and the remains of the New Ship, both once famous shipping inns accommodating passenger traffic *en route* to and from London. The Leith Smacks could cover the 460 miles (740 km) to London in 50 hours with a fair wind.

MUSSELBURGH was a bustling seaport in Roman times and with Fisherrow on the opposite side of the River Esk, was an important fishing centre. The Fife boats used to land their catch here and the fishwives of Fisherrow carried the fish into Edinburgh to sell them. These women were noted for their strength, traditionally demonstrated on Shrove Tuesday by a football match between married and unmarried women from the port. Musselburgh also still retains the tradition once common along this coast of the 'Fisherman's Walk' when all the fishing families dressed in their traditional costumes and processed round the town at the end of the herring season.

In 1820, James Patterson made the first successful machine for manufacturing fishing nets, although the tradition of making nets by hand persisted among longshore fishermen until the 1950s.

PRESTONPANS: Its name derives from the saltpans established here by monks in the twelfth century. The seawater was left in pans to evaporate and the salt was then swept up from the bottom. Prestonpans held a monopoly in supplying salt to the east of Scotland until the Act of Union in 1707 allowed cheaper salt to be brought from English mines.

The harbour is at Morrison Haven about a mile to the west of the town. In late Victorian times, a fleet of oyster dredgers sailed from here. A 33-ft (10-m) sailing boat ran a regular service carrying sacks of oysters to Newcastle, often covering the distance in a record time of 13 hours.

COCKENZIE AND PORT SETON: Cockenzie is a little Forth fishing village which still retains its marine flavour. Port Seton, to which it is now attached, was originally a coal-shipping harbour established in 1833. In the 1870s local fishermen paid ninepence a week into a fund to improve the harbour. In 1980 Port Seton celebrated the 100th anniversary of the opening of this second development.

NORTH BERWICK is a small harbour with a narrow entrance. Only a few boats fish from here, but a conical volcanic hill 613 ft (187 m) high called North Berwick Law, is a striking feature of this spot. It is a landmark throughout the Firth, and is topped by a ruined lookout tower, built in 1803 during the threat of Napoleonic invasion. There is also an archway formed from the jawbone of a whale.

BASS ROCK lies 1¼ miles (2 km) offshore, is 1 mile (1.6 km) in circumference and rises in many places perpendicular from the sea for 300 ft (90 m). It features in an exciting episode in Stevenson's *Catriona* and during the summer there are boat trips from North Berwick harbour some 3 miles (4.8 km) away.

TANTALLON CASTLE, built in the fourteenth century and considered then to be almost impregnable, occupies a striking position on a rocky promontory overlooking the North Sea. 'Tantallon's dizzy steep Hung o'er the margin of the deep'. Scott (*Marmion*). The ruins are open to the public.

DUNBAR was once the main fishing centre on the east coast of Scotland. Before the railways, sloops regularly sailed to London with cargoes of lobster and crab, while white fish were taken by road to Musselburgh and sold round Edinburgh by the fishwives. Cromwell allocated money for the building of the first harbour at the east end of the town, and this was replaced by the Victorian harbour to the north-west, near the castle.

COVE in many ways resembles a Cornish fishing village. The tiny village is separated from its harbour, which is reached only by a steep track carved out of the rocks. The notorious smugglers of Cove used the caves as storehouses and it is still used today by lobster and crab fishermen.

EYEMOUTH is a small but prosperous fishing port whose name derives from the fact that the harbour is at the mouth of the Eye Water Burn. Benedictine monks fished from here in the thir-

teenth century and fishing prospered enough for Smeaton to build the stone north pier in 1768. The harbour is one of the largest and most sheltered in eastern Scotland. Further pier building left the harbour quays protected but there is a very narrow entrance. The harbour was deepened and improved in the 1960s and white fish are the important local catch. The first decked boat at Eyemouth, and probably on the east coast of Scotland, was launched in 1856, but they were still often no protection in very bad weather. The town's fleet suffered a terrible disaster in October 1881, when a gale suddenly blew up destroying 23 boats and drowning 129 men.

A colourful local tradition known as the Herring Queen Festival is held in July. The flag-bedecked fishing fleet escorts the newly elected Herring Queen from St Abb's to Eyemouth.

EYEMOUTH MUSEUM
Auld Kirk, Market Place.
The museum houses a 15-ft (4.5-m) tapestry made to commemorate the centenary of the fishing disaster of 1881. It also shows the history of east-coast fishing in general and of the lives of the fisher lasses who seasonally followed the fleet or 'Travelled the Herring'. Other features include a reconstruction of a nineteenth-century fisherman's kitchen, the wheelhouse and a prow of a modern fishing boat. It is also the beginning of the Tourist Board's Fishing Trail that runs up the east coast to Inverness.
Open Apr – Oct.

BURNMOUTH harbour was built in 1830 at the bottom of a very steep cliff. It dries out at low tide and even at high water there are rocks to be avoided in the entrance channel. Like Eyemouth, it was hit by the disaster of 1881 in which a total of 188 fishermen lost their lives.

Inland at **FERNIEHILL** (2 miles (3.2 km) NE of Kelso) is the James Thomson obelisk – he is best known for writing the words of *Rule Britannia*.

ULSTER

**Port na Spaniagh, the
Armada's graveyard**

ULSTER

FROM almost every corner of the city of Belfast the skyline is dominated by two leviathan gantry cranes. Nicknamed Samson and Goliath and painted bright yellow, the cranes stand in the legendary shipyard of Harland and Wolff. Probably no other city in Britain has been so dominated by a single industrial employer as Belfast with this shipyard. Yet, in its early twentieth-century prime, Harland and Wolff was a company with an economic and technological strength on a par with that of many small countries. It gave Belfast its identity. The yard has now withered, although not yet died, and the effect of the city's recent history

needs no recounting in these pages.

Ships have been built commercially on Belfast Lough for over 300 years. In a survey of 1660 there was no tonnage of over fifty tons – but it had all been locally constructed. The maritime trade was always important to the city, as evidenced by the establishment of a Ballast Board to oversee and direct the dredging of the River Lagan, leading into the heart of Belfast. In the early decades of the nineteenth century, as the industrialization of the vast linen industry began in Ulster, Belfast became the most important coal importing port in the province, indeed in the whole of Ireland. Coal was heavily taxed and transport costs were high, but once a regular steamship service to Liverpool started in the

Harland & Wolff shipyard, 1924.

1820s a great expansion in the industrialization of Liverpool was possible. Curiously, these regular steamers to north-west England both opened and shut doors for Ulster. International trade into the docks diminished, since it was easier to send goods to Liverpool and tranship them. However, cheaper coal and imported raw materials gave Belfast industry a huge boost.

Of Ulster's other ports – Derry, Coleraine, Larne and Newry – only Derry could begin to compete with Belfast as the pattern of nineteenth-century trade emerged. And that was because of a speciality trade in the business of emigration. Newry, faced with decline, constructed a ship canal, but by the time of completion in 1850 the average ship had become too large to navigate the cut. Similarly, Coleraine was hampered navigationally by a tricky sand bar at the mouth of the River Bann. Larne was made by the opening in 1867 of the Larne/Stranraer packet service, then and still the shortest crossing of the St George's Channel – a factor much emphasized by the holiday entrepreneurs of the time. This ferry link replaced a haphazard and unreliable service from Donaghadee to Portpatrick which had ended in 1849 and had not been replaced.

By the decade beginning in 1820 Belfast was becoming a prime shipbuilding centre, certainly within Ireland. Three yards based along the Lagan turned out scores of wooden schooners and barques until the launch of the first iron vessel in 1838. This ship, *Countess of Caledon*, was a lake steamer built by the Coates Lagan Foundry (iron ships at this time were more the province of boilermakers than shipwrights) began service on Loch Neagh and was a great success. The boom in industrial shipbuilding that came afterwards was not so much an organic growth from previous craft, as a complete new activity.

In 1840 work was put in hand to dredge and straighten the shallow and difficult Lagan. Construction took nine years but it enormously extended the available wharfage, as well as creating three artificial islands

which would be the heart of shipbuilding in the years to come. When Victoria came to the throne, the port was, effectively, the heart and lungs of Belfast.

In 1853 Robert Hickson moved his iron shipbuilding company to one of the new islands. He built ships for both Liverpool and Ulster owners but the yard failed to thrive as it should. After five years came what would nowadays be called a management buyout, when Edward Harland, manager at the yard, assumed ownership. Harland's assistant was Gustav Wolff, a Jew from Hamburg, who possessed a priceless asset in the form of his uncle G C Schwabe, a Liverpool merchant of wealth and immense connections.

Schwabe's links with the Bibby Line provided the crucial first orders for Harland and Wolff. They were three 1,500-ton, iron-hulled, barque-rigged, single-screw steamers named *Venetian*, *Sicilian* and *Syrian*. Finished hulls were towed to the Clyde for engines to be fitted, since the Belfast yard did not develop its own propulsion division until 1880. The yard's designs quickly became regarded as innovative but inherently seaworthy (not always synonymous terms). Harland's stretched the length to beam ratio for iron ships as high as 11:1, whereas the previous industry standard had been closer to 7:1. These long thin ships were kept seaworthy by the inclusion of a flat bottom and a wide bilge section. It was not a design revolution but a significant incremental change, placing Harland and Wolff at the forefront of world shipping.

As Liverpool expanded and prospered as the nation's principal western shipping centre, and the hub of a vast maritime empire, so Harland's became principal supplier to the Mersey shipping firms. Always in these situations the figure of G C Schwabe was present; making introductions and mediating. It was said, anecdotally, that it was at Schwabe's home over a game of billiards that T H Ismay, principal of the newly formed White Star Line, was persuaded to order ships from the radical young Belfast firm.

Venetia, built by Harland & Wolff in 1859.

Their first ship for White Star, the *Oceanic*, was a breakthrough on the Atlantic trade. The 3,800 ton ship was the first pure passenger liner, making no concessions to freight and moving the sumptuous first-class accommodation to the midships section away from the stern. With her fourteen-knot crossings, in 1871 *Oceanic* set standards which rival lines such as Cunard had to chase and better to keep their share of the booming Atlantic market.

White Star ordered over sixty steamships totalling 750,000 tons from the Belfast yard between 1870 and 1914. The relationships between the two became enormously close, indeed there were numerous cross-shareholdings. At the outbreak of war in 1914 Harland and Wolff were employing 14,000 men, many of them skilled tradesmen induced to move from mainland Britain, and had a uniquely integrated yard covering ninety-five acres (thirty-eight hectares).

It was during this period that the yard built *Britannic*, *Olympic* and *Titanic* for White Star.

At 45,000 tons they were, at the time, the largest liners yet built. The loss of the unsinkable *Titanic* on her maiden voyage dealt Harland & Wolff a body blow which should not be over estimated.

The post-war troubles of partition were still over the horizon but the economic focus had shifted away from Belfast and the city would never again reach nineteenth-century levels of shipping or shipbuilding. An extra capacity in warship-building might have prolonged the inevitable for several decades but Belfast had never focussed on the destroyers and cruisers beloved of Jarrow and Barrow.

Of Ulster's ports, only Londonderry remotely kept pace with Belfast's expansion and prosperity. It was a very different form of trade, based upon hundreds of Canadian-built wooden schooners, that crowded into the Foyle and shipped Irishmen by the thousand to the New World.

Derry was one of the most westerly ports in Europe and ships embarking from there to Canada invariably had a quicker and easier passage than those leaving from the English

SS *Britannic at Liverpool.*

Channel ports. This was important to the owners since the duration of the voyage had a direct effect on profits, and also on the emigrants – particularly in the early years when they had to provide their own food for the voyage.

At the beginning of the nineteenth century the emigrants were primarily relatively affluent Ulster-Scots families, the people of energy and commerce whose independence of thought and action had repeatedly brought them into conflict with the stifling complacency of the Anglo-Irish ascendancy.

As the famine years dawned and ground on, the Derry passenger lists consisted much more of destitute families being plucked from starvation by a fortunate relative or friend who had made the decision to emigrate and was already in New York or New Brunswick.

Until the 1830s the ships were generally of no more than 300 tons. These softwood ships were built of fir and pine on the Atlantic coast of Canada and represented a considerable discount in cost against the increasingly scarce hardwood used in British yards. They had a short working life of only twenty-five years or so but were sound within that period. Often after being built in New Brunswick – those from St John had the finest reputation – they were filled with timber blocks as cargo and ballast, before being sailed across the Atlantic to be auctioned in Londonderry. Later in the nineteenth century the schooners gave way to barques of 500 tons or more. These were purpose built for the emigrant trade and had a much better reputation than the squalid vessels often run by Liverpool and Glasgow owners.

It would be fairly accurate to surmise that Irish shipowners were prepared to look after their people better than the British, who regarded the emigrants as little removed from the recently ended slave trade.

Yet with the coming of iron ships, steamers and the magnetic growth of Belfast, Londonderry could no longer hold its own in the shipping world.

One Barry McCorkell sold the last schooner based on the Foyle in 1895 and a short, intense and colourful trade was over.

—————— GAZETTEER ——————

ULSTER FROM
LONDONDERRY TO WARRENPOINT

LONDONDERRY commands the Foyle estuary and for most of its history has been an important seaport and naval base. In the Second World War some 20,000 American sailors were stationed here and the Allies largest convoy escorts across the Atlantic were centred on the port. A marble memorial in the Cathedral of St Columb commemorates Captain Browning who was killed as his ship *Mountjoy* broke the boom across the river and relieved the starving city during the famous siege of Derry in 1689.

The main thoroughfare of Derry is the exceptionally steep Shipquay Street. Narrow little streets run off it down to the quay where hundreds of thousands of Irish emigrants sailed to the New World. The coastal strip between Londonderry and the north of the Roe, north-eastwards of Loch Foyle, has a polder appearance. Reclaimed from the sea in the nineteenth century for flax growing, these fertile polders are below sea level and are drained by pumping stations.

At **BRIOGHTER** near the coastal marshes surrounding the estuary of the Roe, precious Celtic gold jewellery depicting among other things a masted boat, has been found.

MUSSENDEN TEMPLE, further east on the headland and perched on the cliff edge, contains a Lucretian inscription on the frieze around its dome: 'It is agreeable to watch, from land, someone else involved in a great struggle while winds whip up the waves out at sea'.

COLERAINE, built at the head of the navigable reach of the Bann, is a harbour town and owed its prosperity to the linen trade.

DUNLUCE CASTLE teeters on the edge of an isolated crag. Defenders could come and go through the large sea-cave that slopes up into the castle precincts. It was repaired with proceeds from the wreck of the *Girona* which sank off the Giant's Causeway in 1588.
Castle is open every day except Monday.

From here on is 60 miles (96.5 km) of exceptional coastal scenery. The north Antrim coast became an instant tourist attraction after a description of the remarkable basaltic formation known as the **GIANT'S CAUSEWAY**, was published in 1693 by the Royal Society, since then it has ranked among the natural wonders of the world.

A 5-mile (8-km) circular walk along the coast takes you past majestic rock formations and Port na Spaniagh's Lacada Point where gold treasure from the wrecked Armada galleass *Girona* was recovered by divers in 1968. About 20 Armada vessels were wrecked off Ireland's coasts.

CAUSEWAY VISITOR CENTRE
Displays on Causeway's flora, fauna, geology and social history.
Open daily.

WHITEPARK BAY is a quiet, sandy contrast to the Giant's Causeway. From the top there are views over Rathlin Island and beyond to the Mull of Kintyre and Islay. 2½ miles (4 km) east of the Bay is the Carrick-a-rede rope bridge which spans a 60-ft (18-m) wide chasm, 80 ft (24 m) above the sea in the fishing season, giving salmon fishermen access to their fisheries.

Half a mile outside **BALLYCASTLE** at Bonamargy is a ruined friary. Sailors lost at sea in 2 world wars and washed up on this treacherous coast are buried in a plot with a large cross here. Near Ballycastle harbour, a memorial recalls the experimental wireless link which Marconi and his assistant George Kemp established in 1898 between Ballycastle and Rathlin Island. Signals were transmitted over a distance of 6 miles (9.6 km) between a mast erected near the island's east lighthouse and a house on top of the cliff at Ballycastle.

RATHLIN ISLAND lies 6 miles (9.6 km) north of Ballycastle and only 12 miles (19.3 km) from the Mull of Kintyre. Shaped like a boomerang, most of its coastline is cliff, much of it 200 ft (60 m) high. There are numerous caves with magnificent interiors, most of which can only be entered by boat. The most famous is Bruce's Cave almost underneath the East Lighthouse. Here in 1306,

Robert the Bruce hid after his defeat by the English at Perth. Here he saw the spider and with renewed determination went back to fight victoriously at the Battle of Bannockburn.

There are 3 lighthouses: near the South Lighthouse, at Rue Point, is Smugglers House with hollow walls in which contraband was stored. Slough-Na-More, 'the swallow of the sea', is a whirlpool south of Rue Point which is violently rough when two tides flowing in opposite directions meet and form pyramid waves. The first recorded shipping disaster in Rathlin Sound was in AD 440 when Brecain and his fleet of 50 curraghs were lost in a great tide rip. Boat trips from Ballycastle every Mon, Wed and Fri.

Between **RED BAY**, so-called because of the iron ore mined there in the nineteenth century and **WATERFOT** village, are several interesting caves. The biggest is Nanny's Cave which is 40 ft (12 m) long and was inhabited by Ann Murray who was aged 100 when she died in 1847. She was well known to the revenue men for selling poteen.

Carrickfergus harbour, 1897.

CARNLOUGH: The quarries above Carnlough are worked out now but the recent improvement to the harbour has resulted in an increase in fishing activity, lobsters, crab and flatfish being the main catch. It is a popular yachting harbour.

GLENARM exports limestone and powdered chalk from the harbour.

The coast now passes by the range of mountains whose western peak **SLEMISH** is supposed to be where, as a boy, St Patrick worked as a slave, having been kidnapped from Dunbarton by one of King Niall's pirate parties.

CARRICKFERGUS, 7 miles (11 km) south-west of Whitehead in the south of **ISLAND MAGEE**, was once more important than Belfast. It was established by the Normans who guarded the approach to Belfast Lough with a huge castle.

A plaque at the end of the pier below the castle walls marks where William of Orange landed on his way to the Battle of the Boyne. In 1778, John Paul Jones sailed past the castle and carried off HMS *Drake* in what turned out to be America's first naval victory.

The Armada Legacy

British schoolchildren are often brought up to believe that the destruction of the Spanish Armada was the consequence of two major factors: the derring-do of Drake and Frobisher, coupled with the continental cowardice of the landlubberly Spaniards. In fact, the passage up the English Channel of King Philip's fleet and their failure to link up with the invasion army in Calais was not much more than a routine military misadventure. What turned the defeat into a terrible human tragedy was the deteriorating weather as the Armada attempted to sail north around Scotland and then Ireland before returning southwards to Spain.

At least fourteen major ships are known to have been wrecked on the Irish coast, with others simply lost without trace. Plymouth Hoe may have its legend of Sir Francis Drake's game of bowls but the Ulster Museum in Belfast is the greatest single repository of Armada history. Artefacts recovered from the sea-bed, from huge bronze cannon to delicate personal keepsakes, spell out the story of a doomed fleet which had little to choose between death on the rocky, hostile coast and butchery by the English garrisons if they made their way ashore. A fortunate few, most notably Don Francisco de Cuellar, were fortunate enough to be given shelter by Irish warlords and assisted to return to Spain by a route through Scotland – then still an independent kingdom – and thence to the Low Countries.

The first Ulster wreck to be found, identified and comprehensively excavated was the galleass

Treasure from the *Girona*.

Girona. This adaptation of the Mediterranean oar-propelled galley was nearly 200 feet (sixty metres) long, with 120 crew, 300 slaves at the oars and around 170 soldiers. However, by the time *Girona* found herself in difficulties off the Antrim coast she was carrying close to 1,300 survivors from other Armada vessels. Her loss was the biggest single blow to the Duke of Medina Sidonia's fleet.

There was no accurate account of her resting place, but the cluster of names such as Spaniard Rock, Spaniard Cave and Port na Spaniagh gave a significant clue. In 1967 trained divers found cannon from the ship and began a detailed search that took two seasons. Because of the shallow water and rough, boulder-strewn sea-bed, not a rib or timber of the Girona survived. But an enormous range of metal objects, particularly gold rings, pendants and chains were recovered – providing a significant boost to expert knowledge of Renaissance jewellery. The entire find is now on display at the Ulster Museum

The next significant ship to be found off the rocky north coast was *La Trinidad Valencera*, at 1,100 tons the third largest vessel to sail with the Armada. She was not a naval fighting ship but a transport vessel commandeered from the Venetians. However, with forty guns and nearly 300 soldiers embarked aboard *La Trinidad*, these categories should not be considered too rigid.

La Trinidad ran on to the reef in Kinnagoe Bay on 12 September 1588. There she sat for two days pounded by the heavy surf and gale force winds, before slipping off into deeper water and breaking

Lacana Point, where the *Girona* met her doom.

up. Many of her crew escaped ashore but after accepting an offer of safe conduct and laying down their arms they were murdered by local inhabitants hoping for a pat on the back from London.

Divers from the Londonderry Sub-Aqua Club discovered the wreck by chance while on a training dive in February 1971. Gun barrels were the first items to be brought ashore, but thereafter the excavation became a long, painstaking and professionally organized affair. A great deal of rigging and the odd fragment of planking survived, since here was much deeper water than that surrounding the *Girona*, and a great deal of new information was found. For instance it was discovered that the ship had been held together with metal rivets rather than the wooden pins or trenails customary in the period. A great deal of other army impedimenta, including a tent complete with pegs and storm lanterns was recovered. The existence of a stores' manifest, filed when *La Trinidad* left Spain, enabled the finds to be checked off and identified with great precision.

Much of the equipment is of far wider interest than simply to aficionadoes of Renaissance naval architecture. Claw-hammers of the type a carpenter would use are listed on the manifest and were found on the sea-bed. A boatswain's whistle, almost unchanged from the pattern used in modern navies, was found with the *Girona*.

It was during the era of the Armada, the late sixteenth century, that the use of charts to aid navigation at sea had first become standard practice. While none survives from the wreck sites, half a dozen pairs of quite sophisticated and serviceable dividers have been brought up from the *Girona* and *La Trinidad* – evidence that the fleet was well equipped with charts. Remnants of astrolabes, used for determining latitude and the precursors of sextants, were found aboard the *Girona*. Further evidence that Spanish navigation techniques were quite sophisticated can be seen in Medina Sidonia's sailing instructions:

The course that is to be followed first is to the north-north-east, up to the latitude of 61.5 degrees; you will take great care lest you fall upon the Island of Ireland, for fear of the harm that may befall you on that coast.

His captains followed the first part of their orders well enough but they had neither the knowledge nor the good fortune to avoid the horrors of a foreign shipwreck.

Fitting out at Harland & Wolff.

BELFAST grew from an insignificant town by the river ford into a prosperous port in the nineteenth century famed for its shipyards. To create a port a navigable channel was cut into the River Lagan. The mud from the channel created an island on the east named Queen's Island, later to become Harland and Wolff.

The port of Belfast lies at the head of Belfast Lough about 11 miles (19 km) from the open sea. In addition to being the largest port of Ireland, it is famous as one of the world's great shipbuilding centres. A revival of shipbuilding in 1833 on the site of Queen's Island was controlled by Edward Harland, a Yorkshire man, who recruited the marine draughtsman Wolff from Hamburg. Among the liners constructed here was the *Titanic* in 1912. The port contains 4 dry docks, including the huge Belfast Dry Dock – 1,099 ft (335 m) long, with 8 miles (13 km) of quays and 1,235 acres (500 hectares) of water.

CUSTOM HOUSE is on the north side of Queen's Square, overlooking Donegall Quay. This was the point of embarkation for the Liverpool Ferry.

HARBOUR OFFICE
Corporation Square.
Belfast's seafaring history. Open weekdays 9.30 am – 4.30 pm.

SINCLAIR SEAMEN'S CHURCH
Corporation Square.
Interior is like a maritime museum. The pulpit is a ship's prow, the organ has port and starboard lights.

Belfast, Queen's Bridge, 1897.

HMS *CAROLINE*
Milewater Basin.
First World War light cruiser (1914) – not open to the public but visible.

ULSTER MUSEUM
Botanic Gardens.
Maritime section mainly material from Spanish Armada, all extant material from 3 wrecks: *Santa Maria de la Rosa*, *La Trinidad Valencera*, *Girona*, wrecked on Lacada Point, Co Antrim. Items include 50 lb (22 kg) siege guns. Also marine painting displays on shipbuilding and display on 'the living sea'.
Open everyday.

In front of the City Hall in Donegal Square is a statue of Sir Edward Harland and a marble figure commemorating the loss of the *Titanic*.

HOLYWOOD on the eastern outskirts of Belfast has the

ULSTER FOLK AND TRANSPORT MUSEUM
Cultra Manor.
Which among many transport exhibits, has an exhibition on traditions of seafaring and ship-building industry in Belfast. Collection of over 30 vessels includes the steel, 3-masted topsail schooner *Result* (1892), an ex-RNLI lifeboat *Sir Samuel Kelly* and a range of vernacular Irish boats. There is an extension to this museum at Whitham Rd, Belfast.

BANGOR is situated on the northern point of the Ards, which stretches 23 miles (37 km) south to Ballyquintin Point, varying in width from 3 to 5 miles (4.8 to 8 km). It is popular for boating and yachting with 4 yacht clubs.

DONAGHADEE is the nearest Irish Port to Great Britain: it is 12 miles (19.3 km) to Portpatrick. The lighthouse at the end of the harbour was built by Sir John Rennie and David Logan. From the sixteenth to the nineteenth century Donaghadee was a major port offering the only safe refuge from treacherous reefs on this coast. The harbour was greatly enlarged in 1820 for the mail packet service, but this was later switched to the Stranraer–Larne route in 1849. Local fishermen kept an unofficial ferry going for a while, rowing to Scotland (on a calm day) for £5.

Donaghadee harbour, 1897.

PORTAVOGIE, in the south-eastern corner of the Ards, has one of Northern Ireland's 3 main fishing fleets. It has a modern harbour, boat-building yards and a fish auction on the quay most evenings.

PORTAFERRY on the eastern side of the entrance to **STRANGFORD LOUGH** connects it to the open sea.

AQUARIUM: This marine biology station is open to the public all year, Tues – Sun.

STRANGFORD'S Cistercian monks used to sail the Irish Sea to England in the twelfth century taking corn, fish and salt to English abbeys in Cumberland and Lancashire. They would sail home in 60-oar galleys, heavily laden with Cumberland stone and iron ore.

The area south of Strangford, from the fishing village of **DUNDRUM** on the strait between the Lough and the sea, and around Dundrum Bay, is associated with St Patrick.

ARDGLASS was once the busiest seaport in Ulster. It has a deep double harbour and the town is still noted for its herring as well as codling, pollack and coalfish.

ST JOHN'S POINT has a lighthouse.

The coast from **NEWCASTLE** south of Dundrum Bay, south to the hamlet of **GREENCAS-TLE** was notorious for smuggling in the eighteenth century and still has many old Customs look-out points.

Wines, spirits, tobacco, tea, silk and soap were brought across from the Isle of Man in small boats and carried along the Brandy Pad – an old smugglers' trail to Hilltown in the western foothills of the Mountains of Mourne.

ROSTREVOR and **WARRENPOINT** on Lough Carlingford are small resorts 3 miles (4.8 km) apart on the Lough's northern shore. Rostrevor has such a mild climate that palm trees and mimosa flourish along the shore. Warrenpoint handles container traffic and substantial coal, timber, paper and grain tonnage with regular services to Rotterdam.

INDEX

Acknowledgements

With the exception of the following all the illustrations are the copyright of the National Maritime Museum.

The Hulton-Deutsch Collection 168
The Mary Rose Trust Ltd 9
Simon McBride 14/15, 34/5, 54/5, 74/5, 92/3, 114/15, 138/9, 158/9, 174/5, 192/3
Pitkin Pictorials Ltd 86
Ulster Museum 200 (above, below)
Valentines/Dr Dennis Chapman 146

Continued from front endpaper

Anglesey

Aberyst

Swansea

THE WEST COUNTI

Plymouth

Falmouth

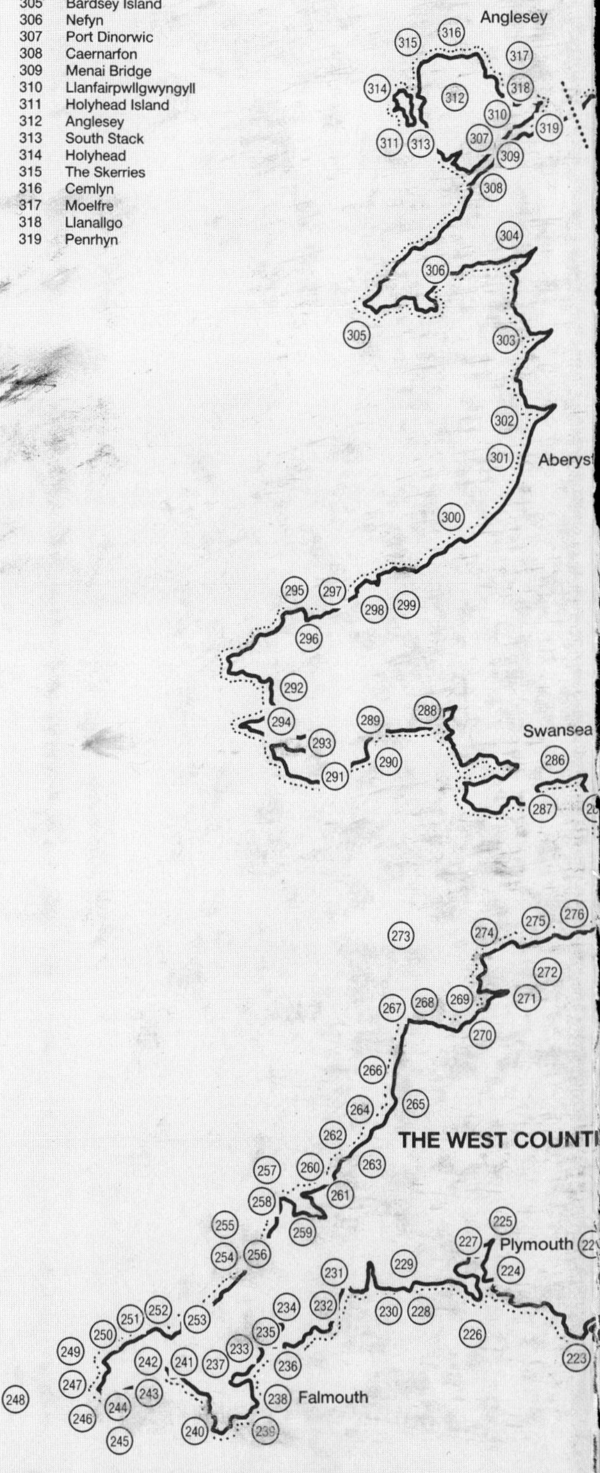